Rickey
&
Robinson

Brooks D. Simpson
Advisory Editor

Rickey
&
Robinson

The Preacher, the Player, and America's Game

John C. Chalberg

Harlan Davidson, Inc.
Wheeling, Illinois 60090-6000

Library of Congress Cataloging in Publication Data
Chalberg, John C.
    Rickey & Robinson : the preacher, the player, and America's
game / John C. Chalberg.
        p. cm.
    Includes bibliographical references (p. 229) and index.
    ISBN 0-88295-952-2 (alk. paper)
    1. Branch Rickey, 1881–1965. 2. Baseball team owners—
United States—Biography. 3. Robinson, Jackie, 1919–1972.
4. Afro-American baseball players— United States—20th
century. I. Title: Rickey and Robinson. II. Title.
GV865.A1 C39   20000
796.357'64'0974723—dc21   99-053688

Cover photo: Jackie Robinson and Branch Rickey, courtesy of
The Sporting News
Cover design: DePinto Graphic Design

Manufactured in the United States of America
02 01 00 99 VP 1 2 3 4

Contents

Preface and Acknowledgments

Permit me to begin with an observation and an admission. Under the best of circumstances, objectivity in historical writing is an elusive, if admirable, goal. These are not the best of circumstances. You see, I was once a Dodger fan. More accurately, I was once a *Brooklyn* Dodger fan. My earliest memory of life as such has me lying next to an imposing piece of living-room furniture (the family console radio) listening to a Dodger-Yankee World Series game. The year must have been 1952 or 1953, but I know for certain that it wasn't 1955. *That* Dodger-Yankee World Series I remember distinctly, and not just because my family had acquired a television set by then.

School day or no, I was home for the deciding seventh game of the memorable Fall Classic. But TV set or no, I couldn't bear to watch much of it, convinced as I was of the inevitability of yet another Dodger defeat at the hands of the hated Yankees. Instead, much to my surprise (not to mention that of the Dodgers and especially that of the Yankees) "next year" finally arrived courtesy of a 2-0 Dodger victory.

Not long after that the Dodgers left Brooklyn and the Washington Senators landed in Minnesota. The transfer of my baseball loyalties was not instant, but by 1965 it was pretty much complete. That, of course, was the year of the only Twins-Dodgers World Series. This time Game Seven was a thoroughly different experience for this novice Twins fan. For one thing, I watched the entire game. For another, my team lost.

Baseball loyalties can be as difficult to fathom as they are to abandon. How was it that a kid from Minnesota became a Brooklyn Dodger fan in the first place? I suppose it might have had something to do with a bred-in-the-bone Minnesota populism, with its accompanying distrust of Yankee imperialism and its automatic identification with underdogs in general and "bums" in particular. But I'd also like to think that it might have had something to do with Jackie Robinson.

Robinson, of course, was a marvelous baseball player. But he was much more than that. If Ernest Hemingway didn't have Jackie Robinson in mind when he defined courage, he should have. After all, Robinson embodied grace under pressure—and not just during that wonderful yet horribly difficult summer of 1947.

The Jackie Robinson story is less an old story than an enduring one. Of course, it is a baseball story. How could it not be? But in the end it is a story that reveals less about America's game than it does about America itself. As Robinson liked to put it, "baseball was only a part of my life."

The Branch Rickey story is less a forgettable story than a forgotten one. But it, too, is less about baseball than it is about the United States over the course of much of the twentieth century.

Alone, each story is a good one. Combined—and they can hardly be separated—the Rickey-Robinson story becomes compelling, even mythical. For those readers not particularly interested in baseball, I trust that this book might help them to consider the game in a new light, or at least appreciate its place in American history. At the same time, those who do not have to be persuaded that baseball truly is America's game will hardly be disappointed by the pages that follow, because baseball necessarily lies at the heart of this work

Branch Rickey often wondered how he, a man trained in the law, could devote himself to a "boys game." However, that's exactly what he did. At no point during his professional life was he anything more—or less—that a baseball man. And even if Jackie Robinson was always determined to carve out a useful life away from the diamond, he was above all else one of the greatest baseball players of all time.

While it is hardly a stretch for me to declare that Branch Rickey and Jackie Robinson are two men whom I admire greatly, hagiography is far from my purpose in this dual biography. Historical objectivity may be elusive, but it should always be the goal. Rickey and Robinson were not saints. The former could be too slow to act and the latter too quick to anger. There were also times when Rickey seemed too driven by the dollar sign and occasions when Robinson seemed too much the political trimmer. Nonetheless, theirs is a wonderful and wonderfully American story, one that reveals a great deal about twentieth-century America and one that deserves the attention of Americans of all generations.

I wish to thank my wife Janet for this unassisted triple play: she listened (when that was called for); she left me alone (when that was asked for): and she read and edited (when that was essential). Thanks also to my late father, John E. Chalberg, who nurtured my love of baseball and introduced me to golf (when it became painfully obvious to both of us that I had no chance of ever hitting a moving ball). And thanks as well to my recently deceased mother, Mildred O'Brien Chalberg, who was always a major league reader and a booster of her first born for as long as I can remember.

I must also mention Gordon Ross, once of Regis College, for being the model college history teacher that I still harbor hopes of one day becoming. Thanks also to Andrew Davidson (of Harlan Davidson, Inc.) and Brooks Simpson (of Arizona State University) for believing in this project. Thanks to friends and colleagues Ray Anschel, Jack Herzog, and Dale Strom for reading chapters along the way and the whole manuscript when I (twice) thought that I had finished.

Finally, thanks to Kristin and Sarah for being great daughters, good sports, and genuine baseball fans. This book is dedicated to sons Michael, Stephen, and Matthew, each a ballplayer and each still young enough to harbor dreams of baseball glory that their father had to bench so very long ago.

J. C. C.
Bloomington, Minnesota

Warm-ups

August 1945 was a month of seismic shocks. On August 6 an atomic bomb obliterated Hiroshima. Three days later Nagasaki was hit with the same terrible weapon. Hiroshima and Nagasaki . . . the names of those two Japanese cities immediately became part of the permanent vocabulary of people everywhere, for what happened on those two devastating August days guaranteed a rapid end to the second great war of the twentieth century. It also provided a very unsettling start to what would soon prove to be a postwar filled with shocks and aftershocks all its own.

A few weeks later a bombshell of a different sort reached an advanced state of readiness in an American city far removed from the carnage of war. On August 28, 1945, a scout for the Brooklyn Dodgers baseball team escorted an intriguing, if not exactly youthful, prospect into the intriguing, if not exactly welcoming, office of a veteran baseball man who had already revolutionized the sport at least once. Jackie Robinson meet Branch Rickey.

What actually happened in that cluttered room over the course of the next few hours has long since passed into American folklore. By definition, folklore exists in a realm at least one step removed from the historical record. But what is beyond dispute is that this meeting set in motion changes in major league baseball and in the nation, changes that would echo long after the postwar became the Cold War. At least one of the participants suspected as much at the moment, if only because he alone knew exactly what he had in mind to do.

It might have begun with a handshake, but in all probability it didn't. Most likely, the host simply motioned for his guest to sit down. Common politeness aside, this gesture implied that their meeting would not be a short one—or at least indicated that the visitor had better be seated before hearing what he was about to hear. Certainly the rest of the country would need to be so situated when it finally learned of the results of this encounter. Two months would pass before those results were made public. This delay made the announcement no less jarring to much of white America, and no less shocking in its own way for many black Americans as well. Branch Rickey could have predicted as much. In fact, he had suspected, even feared, as much for a very long time. But never once did he come close to changing his course or his mind. If anything, his suspicions and fears gave him all the more reason to proceed—so long as he could be sure that he had the right man to carry out his plan. And that was the point of this historic meeting.

Though Rickey knew that the first steps would be the most treacherous, he knew much more than that: he knew that he was doing the right thing. It was right for the younger man who faced him; and it was right for their country, their sport, and for what would soon be *their* team (although not necessarily in that order).

"We first endure," Branch Rickey liked to say. "Then we pity. Finally we embrace." The aphorism was not his—it was actually penned by an Englishman named Alexander Pope and can be found in his "Essay on Man"—but Rickey had long since embraced it as his own.

There would be no embrace between Rickey and Robinson during or after their marathon meeting. But well before—and forever after—their initial encounter each man embraced an ideal. At the heart of that ideal was a color blind America, an America of genuine equality of opportunity, an America in which character counted for everything and achievement was possible for everyone.

But on this warm day in late August ideals could wait. First things first. The Brooklyn Dodger executive knew that his prospect could play baseball. For weeks, Dodger scout Clyde Sukeforth had been trailing Robinson and sending detailed reports back to Brooklyn. But why was he scouting a black ballplayer? If Sukeforth had reason to wonder, his boss had a reasonable answer. The official word was that Rickey was organizing a new team (the Brooklyn Brown Dodgers) to compete in a new negro league (to be called the United States League). The announced idea was to provide competition for the existing Negro Leagues. The unannounced idea was to add to the Dodgers' profit margin by plugging more home dates onto the team's Ebbets Field calendar. Other major league teams rented their ball parks to Negro League teams. Why not the Dodgers as well? Baseball, after all, *was* a business, and no one understood that better than Branch Rickey.

In truth, "Mr. Rickey" (as he was called by virtually everyone, at least by virtually everyone in his presence) had something else in mind when he concocted the Brown Dodgers story. Branch Rickey generally had more than a few things on his mind at the same time, not to mention multiple motives. In this case, a desire to make money and win baseball games (not necessarily in that order) provided most of the motivation he needed. When it came to his sport both goals *always* topped his list of things to accomplish. But in preparing for this meeting he had something else on his mind as well.

As of 1945, the sixty-three-year-old Rickey had already made his share of money. Moreover, his teams, whether the Cardinals of St. Louis or the Dodgers of Brooklyn, had generally won more than their share of games. Some might call that luck. Mr. Rickey would not. "Luck," Branch Rickey liked to say, was nothing more than "the residue of design."

Whether Clyde Sukeforth knew it or not, there was a design to this scouting mission. And certainly there was a mission behind Branch Rickey's design. The proposed Brooklyn Brown Dodgers were a small piece of Rickey's design, but they were never part of his mission. In fact, this paper "team" was nothing more than a ruse. In all likelihood Sukeforth didn't know that. Neither did the ballplayer he had been assigned to scout more thoroughly than any other.

Though twenty-six, Jackie Robinson was only in his rookie season in Negro League baseball. But he was far from a novice at the game. He had played college ball, semi-pro ball, and during World War II he had also played army ball. Following his discharge from the military, Robinson was not ready to put baseball entirely behind him. Hence his decision to play for the Kansas City Monarchs during the 1945 campaign. By August of that year, he had not only established himself as the Monarchs' regular shortstop, but he was clearly a rising star in the Negro Leagues.

Throughout that 1945 season, Branch Rickey was keeping close tabs on a number of Negro League players, but he had more than one good reason to keep an especially close watch on Robinson's progress. Everything he had read and heard about both Robinson the man and Robinson the player impressed him, everything, that is, except a measure of concern over the shortstop's arm. Was it strong enough for the major leagues? There was total agreement within the Dodger organization that Robinson could run, hit, and field. But what about his right arm? Could he get the ball to first base from deep in the hole at shortstop, and could he get it there with "something on it?" To get the definitive answer to that question Rickey instructed Sukeforth to approach Robinson before a game at Chicago's Comiskey Park and ask him to throw the ball from the hole—and to throw it often and to throw it hard.

Robinson declined. Not only was he currently "riding the bench," but he wasn't throwing at all. It seems that he had fallen on his right shoulder a few days earlier. The injury was not thought to be serious, but he did expect to be out of the lineup for at least another week. Another scout might have packed his bags and returned to Brooklyn on the spot. But Clyde Sukeforth was not just another scout. He was Branch Rickey's most reliable and most resourceful agent. As it turned out, Clyde Sukeforth wasn't the only one who packed his bags, and he didn't ride the train back east alone. With Robinson temporarily on the shelf, Sukeforth saw the opportune time for that face-to-face meeting that Mr. Rickey had mentioned to him on more than one occasion. Sukeforth knew that Robinson was at the top of his boss's list of candidates for those Brown Dodgers.

When Sukeforth and Robinson arrived in Brooklyn, "Mr. Rickey" was ready for them. In truth, the Dodger executive had been planning toward this day for a good while: certainly ever since he had taken over the Dodgers after the 1942 season, and possibly as long ago as 1903, when a much younger Branch Rickey was coaching his college baseball team. But for all of his plotting and designing the Dodger president could never have imagined that he would have quite this compelling a prospect on his hands, suspect arm or no. To add to the drama, Jackie Robinson was also a very intriguing human being. Rickey was certainly going to relish the next few hours. At least Clyde Sukeforth suspected as much. After all, Rickey's marching orders to his scout had been clear: if Robinson would not come to him, he would come to Robinson.

Thanks to Sukeforth's initiative, Rickey could remain ensconced in his office at 215 Montague Street in the New York borough of Brooklyn. And what an office it was that a wary Jackie Robinson entered on the morning of August 28. The place had even acquired a nickname, courtesy of Rickey's friends and enemies among baseball reporters. And to friend and enemy alike, it was the "cave of the winds," within which visitors could expect to be subjected to extended rhetorical gusts. The most prominent feature within this dark, paneled room (aside from its terminally "windy" occupant) was a large, illuminated goldfish tank. It entertained Rickey when he was alone and served to distract visitors from whatever business was at hand when he wasn't. Just as distracting was the clutter strewn across Rickey's oversized mahogany desk, a mess that belied the clarity of its creator's mind.

Weighing down at least some of the debris were two well-thumbed volumes, specifically a massive dictionary and a copy of *Bartlett's Quotations*. Behind the desk was a well-worn swivel chair that had as many moves as its regular occupant had ideas. Behind all of that were pictures of the two non-baseball men Rickey admired beyond all others (Winston Churchill and Abraham Lincoln), and a few of his baseball protégés (including Dodger manager Leo Durocher). Somewhere among this select gallery were these framed words:

He that will not reason is a bigot.

He that cannot reason is a fool.

He that dares not reason is a slave.

Off to the side stood an imposing globe. Stretched across an entire side wall was a massive blackboard containing the names of every player at every level in the Dodger organization. Might it have begun to dawn on Robinson that his name would one day appear on that blackboard?

For the moment, all was silent. Behind his bushy eyebrows and trademark bow tie, the host simply stared at his guest. Robinson had no choice but to stare right back. Still maintaining his silence, Rickey reached for a cigar before settling deeper into his chair. Only then did he signal to Robinson and Sukeforth that it was time to take their seats. Then came words, mostly from Rickey's mouth, mostly in the form of questions, and mostly in sudden torrents.

"Do you have a girl?" Rickey asked.

Robinson hesitated before answering. In the first place, he wasn't all that confident of his status with the girl that he did indeed have. Secondly, he didn't quite know what Rickey wanted to hear. When Robinson finally did respond he offered only an equivocal "I'm not sure." His interrogator seemed perplexed. Robinson nervously tried to explain that, yes, he did have a girl, but that he wasn't certain that he could count on her. At this point Rickey's confusion seemed to give way to disappointment. So Robinson tried again. What he meant to say was that he saw no reason why anybody should count on him, what with all the traveling ballplayers had to do. Hearing that, Rickey was mildly encouraged. At least he was encouraged enough to press on. So pressed, Robinson finally said what Rickey wanted to hear: if he had a choice in the matter he'd marry the girl in question. Hearing that, Rickey was openly ecstatic.

Branch Rickey was never one to keep his advice to himself. If Jackie Robinson had found the right girl, he should marry her—and sooner rather than later, because he would need all the help he could get in the months and years to come. This bit of counsel led the Dodger boss directly to the question that placed him one step away from revealing his entire hand.

"Do you know why you were brought here?" he asked.

Robinson started to shake his head. All he knew was that Clyde Sukeforth had asked him to come. Maybe to play for the Brown Dodgers, came the cautious reply.

"No," Rickey interjected. "That isn't it. You were brought here to play for the Brooklyn organization." And not for the Brown Dodgers, he quickly added. Robinson's first stop would be the International League and the Dodgers' top farm team, the Montreal Royals. This was minor league baseball at its highest level. If he performed well there, he would be brought up to the parent Brooklyn Dodgers to begin a career as a major league player.

Robinson was speechless. The increasingly garrulous Rickey was not. Before Robinson could even ask why, Rickey told him: "I want to win a pennant and we need ballplayers!" he roared. Suddenly reflective, Rickey went into full swivel as he took his new prospect on a historical tour of his recent search for black ballplayers. A final turn once again brought him face to face with Robinson. And one more question brought Robinson up short: "Do you think you can do it?"

Robinson could still say nothing. As Sukeforth remembered it, "Jack waited, and waited, and waited before answering."

"Yes, if . . . if I got the chance," he finally stammered.

Jackie Robinson may have thought that this response would signal the end of the interrogation. Instead, he quickly discovered that Branch Rickey was just warming up.

"I don't know how you play, but my scouts do," he hedged. It was true that prior to this meeting Rickey had never seen Jackie Robinson on or off a baseball diamond, but he surely knew that his prospect was a superb baseball player. Under normal circumstances, Branch Rickey would have done his own scouting of a player of Robinson's potential. As a young ballplayer, Rickey had been far enough above average himself to make it to the major leagues, at least for a few years. And as a baseball executive, he had acquired a deserved reputation as a keen judge of baseball talent. What's more, even at his age he still enjoyed being on the road watching ball games. Major league or minor league, it didn't matter. It was baseball, and baseball was at the heart of most everything that Branch Rickey loved in this world.

But these were not normal circumstances. As such, they required something other than the full truth. Or perhaps Rickey genuinely believed that he could grasp a player's potential only after he had personally seen him in action. Still, in this case he had no real choice but to operate on the basis of secondhand information. After all, had *the* Branch Rickey been seen at Negro League games, the whispers alone would have been enough to scotch his plan before he could so much as begin to hatch it. Besides, Clyde Sukeforth was his best scout. With a nod in Sukeforth's direction, Rickey confirmed as much for Robinson with this bit of praise: "If he says you're a good ballplayer, I'll take his word for it."

Now it was Rickey's turn to scout his prospect. "I know you're a good ballplayer," Rickey went on. "What I don't know is whether you have the guts."

His manhood on the line, Robinson readied an angry reply when Rickey cut him off—and set him straight—all at once: "I'm looking for a ballplayer with guts enough *not* to fight back." With that he whacked his desk and began to pace about the room. Returning to Robinson, he pointed a finger at him and exclaimed, "You've got to do this job with base hits and stolen bases and fielding ground balls, Jackie. Nothing else!"

Before a stunned Robinson could respond to this latest surprise, Rickey stripped off his sport coat and assumed the first of a series of roles, each one more offensive than the last. On his own makeshift stage, Rickey played the part of a white hotel clerk refusing to give Robinson a room. Then he posed as a haughty waiter denying him service before ordering him to leave the restaurant. Next he was a rival player cursing everything from his race to his family. Still not through, he took on the demeanor of a racist sportswriter. Closing in on Robinson, Rickey then pretended to jostle him in imaginary hotel lobbies and railroad stations. Finally, he was a vindictive base runner coming out of a spikes-up slide shouting, "How do you like that, nigger boy?"

To clinch his point and ease the tension, Rickey added, "What I am saying to you, Jackie, is that you will have to be more than a good ballplayer." After another interval of silence Robinson finally spoke: "Mr. Rickey, I think I can play ball, and I promise you that I will do the second part of the job, although I can't be an obsequious, cringing fellow."

"Obsequious," "cringing" . . . if Branch Rickey had harbored any remaining doubts, they were dispelled when he heard those words. Obviously, this young man could find his way around more than just a baseball diamond. And just as obviously, Rickey was now thoroughly convinced that sitting before him was the right man to break baseball's invisible, but nonetheless impenetrable, color line.

Rickey suddenly grew reflective. With an unlit cigar locked in his mouth, he leaned heavily back in his chair, all the while still staring directly at Robinson. In measured, but fatherly words, he warned Robinson of the "tremendous load" he was about to bear. From somewhere on his desk he fished out a book, Giovanni Papini's *The Life of Christ*. "Ever hear of it?" Rickey asked.

"No" Robinson replied.

Rickey then began to read aloud:

There are three answers that men can make to violence: revenge, flight, turning the other cheek. The first is the barbarous principle of retaliation. . . . Flight is no better than retaliation. . . . Turning the other cheek means not receiving the second blow. It means cutting the chains of the inevitable wrongs at the first link. Your adversary is ready for anything but this . . . Every man has an obscure respect for courage in others, especially if it is moral courage, the rarest and most difficult sort of bravery. . . . To answer blows with blows, evil deeds with evil deeds, is to meet the attacker on his own ground, to proclaim oneself as low as he is. . . . Only he who has conquered himself can conquer his enemies.

As he finished, Rickey set the book back adrift in the sea of papers on his desk. Turning directly to Robinson, he asked, "Can you do it?" Could he promise to turn the other cheek—and not just for a week or two, but for at least three years? "Three years—can you do it?"

Rickey knew that Robinson was a devout Christian and an intense competitor. When it came to Christianity, Rickey could not imagine anyone being too devout. But when it came to competition, he understood that one could easily be too intense. Hence Rickey's decision to risk this question: "What will you do when they call you a black son of a bitch?"

At this point the only noise in the "cave of the winds" came from a lone electric fan whirring away in the corner, this single concession to what had become a hot August afternoon doing little to cool off a perspiring, agitated Rickey. Now on his feet, Rickey prowled purposefully around the edge of his desk. As he approached Robinson, he curled his gnarled right hand into a fist. Without warning, the older man unloaded a swing in the general direction of the younger man's head. It missed, but the accompanying words did not.

"What do you do?" Rickey shouted while still hovering over his target.

Before the startled Robinson could summon an answer, Rickey let him know exactly what he could *not* do. Above all, "you cannot strike back," he lectured. On the baseball diamond Robinson might be filled with righteous anger. He might have stored up any number of reasons to unleash a few right hand jabs of his own. Each might even have been intended to reach its target. And each of his reasons—and his jabs—might have been justifiably summoned and delivered. But he had to resist everything his mind and heart told him to do. No matter what, he must not fight, Rickey counseled. If he did, everything that the designing Dodger president had plotted would come to nothing. The experiment would fail. The color line would be restored. And what then? Jackie Robinson might go down in history as the first black man to play major league baseball in the modern era. But his career would be brief, and no member of his race would follow him any time soon.

"So what do you do?"

"Mr. Rickey," the younger man finally replied, "I've got two cheeks. Is that it?"

It was. The interrogation was finally over. Now it was time to do a little business. And business, especially baseball business, was never very far down the list of Mr. Rickey's things to do.

Did Robinson have a contract with the Monarchs?

"No, sir," was the reply.

"Do you have any agreements—written or oral—concerning how long you will play for them?"

"No, sir, none at all. I just work pay day to pay day."

Was he under any obligation of any kind to the Monarchs?

"None whatever," Robinson shot back.

That was all an exhausted Rickey wanted to hear. He may have had sweat dripping off his brow. He may have been still trying to catch his breath. But he was not too tired to ask Robinson to put in writing what he had just said. Robinson complied. Rickey then set before Robinson an agreement that would bind him to play baseball for the Dodger organization—that would be the Brooklyn Dodgers, not the Brooklyn Brown Dodgers. Specifically this agreement called for Robinson to play for the Montreal Royals. If he signed, he would be paid an immediate bonus of $3,500. His monthly salary would be $600. This time Rickey was neither expecting nor desiring a reply. None was forthcoming. Ballplayers, black or white, rookies or veterans, didn't negotiate contracts with Branch Rickey or with anyone else among his generation of baseball owners. They simply signed them. Which is exactly what Jackie Robinson did.

Oh, yes, there was one more thing. Until they were told otherwise, neither Robinson nor Sukeforth could tell anyone anything about this meeting. To make certain that his point was completely understood, Rickey pledged both to secrecy. With that, the Dodger boss restored the cigar to its rightful place, glanced at his watch, and ushered his veteran scout and newest employee out of his office.

Better than three hours had passed. Not bad for a partial day's work, especially considering that a little history was in the making. But a lot more history was yet to be made, and a lot more fireworks were set to explode. Once word of Robinson's signing escaped that office, there was no way of knowing just how explosive things would become.

Robinson kept his part of the bargain. He told no one of the meeting or his signing, though he immediately telephoned his girl to say that "something wonderful" had happened, something that would "affect us both." Then he returned to Kansas City and the Monarchs. His original absence had gone unexcused and unexplained. It remained just that. Monarch management learned only that Robinson had gone to New York City. The team's starting shortstop then punctuated his return by declaring that he intended to end his season early. He let it be known that he would play only until September 21, at which point he planned to return home to California.

The owner of the Monarchs, J. L. Wilkinson, was one of the few white men in Negro League baseball. White or black, Negro League owners had precious little control over their players. Contract jumping was the order of the day. Such leaps took place within individual Negro Leagues and between them. Now Wilkinson faced the additional complication of having his players jump to an entirely new Negro League (to be headlined, as announced by Rickey, by the Brooklyn Brown Dodgers). Little did Wilkinson know as of early September 1945 just how complicated Branch Rickey was about to make his baseball life. Wilkinson knew nothing about Rickey's larger agenda. And he certainly did not know that Robinson's departure would be a permanent one, one that would ultimately destroy the future of all Negro League teams. The issue at hand, therefore, was an irritant, not a major concern. And. Wilkinson could only deal with the problem as he understood it. Robinson wanted to go home early; Robinson had to be stopped. But what leverage did he have? All he could do was issue a threat of his own. Through his son, Richard, Wilkinson chose a Monarch team meeting to respond to Jack's request: Robinson would play "all the remaining games or none." The younger Wilkinson went on to inform Jack that if he left the Monarchs before the end of the season he would never again play in the Negro Leagues. Robinson was unfazed. Given the agreement that he had just signed with Rickey, he had reason to think that his future extended beyond Kansas City and Negro League baseball. In fact, he was so confident of that future that he didn't bother complaining or protesting. He simply kept his mouth shut, called Wilkinson's bluff, and promptly left the Monarchs for California and home.

Once again surrounded by his family, Robinson couldn't resist dispensing broad hints about his baseball future to his mother, brothers, sister, and friends. No one really wanted to listen to him, much less to believe him. As far as they were concerned, white people were untrustworthy at best and downright sinister at worst. But Jack's world was no longer his family's world. To be sure, he had dealt with his share of racist cops and exploitative coaches. But as an athlete he had come to understand that dependence was a two-way street. White coaches did have plenty of power, especially when it came to taking advantage of their black players. But they also offered opportunities to be seized. A veteran of collegiate and professional sport, Jack knew all of that—and more. After all, he had been around long enough to realize that white coaches and athletic directors needed him as much as he needed them.

All that said, Jackie Robinson had never met anyone quite like Branch Rickey. Following their marathon meeting, Robinson had not dropped all of his considerable guards. Nonetheless, it is safe to conclude that Rickey had greatly impressed the not-so-easily impressed Robinson. No white man had ever seemed so sincere, so committed to racial justice, so full of passion on the twin subjects of winning baseball games and making history. To be sure, Rickey had not dispelled all of Robinson's doubts about the white power structure that controlled major league baseball. But for the time being, at least, he was willing to give Branch Rickey the benefit of the doubt.

For his part, Rickey had to believe that he had been taken at his word. His more immediate worry was not that Robinson would think that he was the victim of a cruel publicity stunt, but how to control the public relations of what he had done and intended to do. The brief fireworks in the Monarchs' clubhouse were small fare compared to those yet to explode. At the time, Rickey knew nothing of the Wilkinsons' threat to their star shortstop. Nor did Robinson think it necessary to inform Rickey of it. But the Dodger president could be certain that there would be aftershocks aplenty once the white baseball world learned of his true intentions. Therefore, he wanted to control as much of the process as possible. Luck may have been the residue of design, but no one, not even an ever-plotting and generally lucky Branch Rickey, could design what was to come in the months and years ahead.

The First Inning

For the time being, Branch Rickey kept his meeting with—and signing of—Jackie Robinson entirely to himself. When he finally did break his silence, the first people he told were not fellow members of his Brooklyn Dodger baseball family, but his wife and six children. While he wanted to have all of them on his side, Rickey was especially anxious that his wife, Jane, and his only son, Branch, Jr., understand and share his dream. He needn't have worried, for both would understand and each of the seven would stand by him.

Family had always been important to Wesley Branch Rickey. Born near Stockdale, Ohio, five days before Christmas, 1881, Rickey spent a secure if impoverished childhood in the small farming community of Duck Run in the hills of southern Ohio. His father, Frank, planted corn and sorghum, raised hogs and cattle, and did his best to teach his sons the rudiments of farming and reading. His mother, Emily, taught him much as well. One lesson in particular, Rickey recalled, had a "deep effect on me for ever after." Having done something wrong (Rickey could not remember just what), he was taken into her bedroom, where he fully expected to be punished. Instead, "she asked me to kneel with her at her bedside [where] she asked for God's forgiveness." In exchange for that forgiveness, "she promised to be a better mother . . . and said she would try never again to commit the sin of letting me misbehave." Whether this was unvarnished piety or canny psychology, it worked. "I felt as though I had hit her, and I was thoroughly chastised."

In the household of Frank and Emily Rickey, each parent reinforced the religious teachings of the other. Though Frank had been raised a Baptist, the couple joined the local Methodist church following their marriage. The impact of Methodism on Rickey family life extended to the naming of their children. The "Wesley" of Wesley Branch was in honor of Methodism's founder, John Wesley. By age twelve the young Rickey had dropped "Wesley," but the effects of his Methodist upbringing did not—and would not—drop out of his life. And the accompanying revival and camp meetings were by this time just as much a part of his young life as planting and harvesting. To top it all off, gospel singing, whether to or from or during those gatherings, was a Rickey family tradition. The citizens of Duck Run always knew when the Rickeys were in the vicinity, because four-part harmony versions of such staples as "When the Roll is Called Up Yonder" could be heard over considerable distances. When his father wasn't singing, he was farming, and when he wasn't farming he was scouring the Ohio countryside in search of religious converts and theological discussion. (Years later, when Frank's baseball executive son wasn't talking baseball to anyone who would listen, he was talking religion to his baseball players, who had no choice but to listen to him.)

Frank Rickey was not an educated man, but he was determined that his sons would be. This was especially so in the case of Wesley Branch, for his father could see early on that his second son had little knack for farming and even less interest in it. Nonetheless, that second son was anything but a rebel. He did what he was asked to do and continued to perform his daily chores without complaint.

Reading was something young Wesley Branch Rickey did not have to be told to do. In his one-room schoolhouse he memorized *McGuffey's Reader.* At home he devoured the few books that the family owned, including once-drenched copies of Dante's *Inferno* and the stories of Washington Irving, which his father had retrieved from a fire sale.

In 1892 the Rickey family moved again, this time to a small farm near the town of Lucasville, Ohio, where Emily gave birth to a third son. Once again Frank Rickey hoped to escape rural poverty. And once again he failed. That this last move took place on the eve of the general economic collapse of the mid-1890s did not help. Despite ongoing hard times, the middle son of Frank and Emily Rickey managed to continue his formal schooling in Lucasville. At about the same time, through sheer force of will, he also managed to overcome a tendency to stutter. Not long after conquering what might have become a severe speech impediment, Branch Rickey decided that he had had enough of school. The year was 1895, and he thought the time had come to confine himself to the farm, where he thought he "belonged."

Fourteen-year-old Branch Rickey's renewed commitment to farming lasted approximately one week. It wasn't just that the world of learning retained its hold on him. It was something more: his brother Orla had introduced him to baseball. A left-handed pitcher and a great fan of the professional Cincinnati Reds, Orla Rickey returned to his parents' home from his first teaching job with time on his hands and a desire to teach his younger brother the rudiments of a game that was already well on its way to capturing the imagination of the entire country.

The modern game of baseball had been around in one form or another since the middle of the 1840s, but only at the end of the nineteenth century did it really become the "national pastime." This was especially so in the large cities of the East and Midwest, where the game experienced its most rapid growth. There the amateur game attracted young men who found it cheap to organize and compelling to play. And there the professional game was beginning to draw crowds that reached 5,000 people or more. Life in these cities could be difficult and routine, whether one was a part of the rising middle class or the new working class. The former were confined to desks and offices; the latter were trapped by machines and factories. Once in an urban setting migrants from rural America or from Europe were forced to carry on work lives that differed markedly from their days on the farm. Instead of cultivating a crop and watching it grow, they tended to paper or machines, all the while being watched by their superiors. Instead of working by the sun and the seasons, they labored according to the demands of the clock.

No wonder young Americans found baseball so liberating. Here was an agrarian game, even a pastoral game, one played on an expanse of green grass surrounded by sooty factories and gray office buildings. To add to this contrast, here was a game during which one's life was not governed by time. No factory watch tower loomed over the baseball park. And at least for the time that it took to play or watch a baseball game, there were no reminders that one's life was not one's own. That magical time usually began in the middle of the afternoon when factory shifts ended and offices emptied.

While two hours was the typical length of a baseball game, in theory a game could go on forever. So could fair territory—at least until ball parks began to install outfield fences. But even if the foul lines placed limits on the sea of green, they themselves extended into infinity. Here was potential boundlessness in a world increasingly hemmed in by boundaries. Here was expansiveness in a world increasingly delimited. And here was a world where urbanites, be they middle class or working class, could find real enjoyment and genuine release. At least there was a chance of finding one or both for a few hours on many a late summer afternoon in city after city from the bustling East Coast to the burgeoning Midwest.

In those same cities the playing of the game had an attraction all its own. This was especially the case for young men and boys fresh off the farm or the boat, many of whom could find no work at all. Many others quickly discovered that the work they could find, especially factory work, was incredibly boring. Baseball provided them with a critically important outlet. It required little money and no adult supervision. It also gave these young men a chance to impress young women. It was at once fast-paced and orderly. Speed was essential in the field and on the bases. Finally, the game guaranteed each player his turn at bat, the very nature of the game assuring everyone almost the same number of chances to be the hero of the day.

The players in the field had a similar opportunity. In its early years baseball was essentially a fielders' game. The role of the pitcher was to serve the batter, not to fool him. The idea was to put the ball in play and let the defense do its work. The original premium was placed on the skill of the fielder, not on the strength or guile of the pitcher, and not even on the strength or speed of the batter. But that was changing. As of the late nineteenth century, baseball was well on its way to becoming a game featuring the confrontation of pitcher and batter. Fielding remained an important ingredient, but there was an increasing balance among these three aspects of the game.

Indeed, as the century turned the noted professional baseball players of the day were likely to be pitchers and batters, not fielders. There was the pitcher Denton "Cy" Young, who won a still unsurpassed 511 games between 1890 and 1911 and for whom the Cy Young Award, given annually to the best pitcher in each league, is named. And there was "Wee Willie" Keeler who amassed 2,962 hits in the process of "hitting them where they ain't" between 1892 and 1910. Great fielders remained a part of the game as well, but as the game evolved they were less lionized and became largely unrecognized.

By the mid-1890s Branch's older brother Orla entertained dreams of having a major league career. Orla Rickey did not want to become a great fielder. In 1895 he was a nineteen-year-old pitcher who thought he could one day compete at the major league level. Home for the summer, he knew that he needed to sharpen his skills. To do so he needed a catcher. After surveying the local prospects, he decided that the best available target was his younger brother, Branch. Toughened by farm work and growing rapidly, Branch Rickey was developing an athlete's body. In 1895, however, few teenaged boys, especially farm boys, had reason to think that they were—or ever could be—athletes, much less professional athletes.

Older brother Orla did. By the end of that summer he was not ready for the Cincinnati Red Stockings, but he had established himself as the town's best pitcher. Branch could make no comparable claim, but he had begun to learn the game from the best vantage point: squatting behind a makeshift home plate on their parents' farm or catching in organized games when brother Orla pitched.

Much later, Branch Rickey, the veteran scout, provided this assessment of Branch Rickey, the novice player: "I was a natural left-handed hitter with fair power. I had an excellent throwing arm, but I threw a heavy ball. My speed was a shade better than average." While these were not exactly Hall of Fame credentials, they were enough to keep this fledgling catcher attached to the game that had caught him in 1895 and never let go.

No matter how intriguing baseball might be to young Branch Rickey, there remained the not so small matter of making a living. With farming out of the question, he tried peddling books door-to-door. After discovering that his potential customers were as poor as he was, he turned to his brother's occupation of teaching. Lacking so much as a high school diploma, Branch managed to pass an exam that qualified him to teach everything from arithmetic to physiology. By this time he was all of seventeen.

The product of a one-room schoolhouse soon found himself teaching in one. For $30 a month Branch Rickey was the sole instructor for the youth of Turkey Creek, Ohio. Home to more than its share of hidden stills and brazen bullies, Turkey Creek was overflowing with many things besides a desire for learning. Soon after his arrival Rickey learned that one of his predecessors had been savagely beaten by one of his so-called students and another had fled after a number of that same student body had seen fit to spit tobacco juice on his shoes.

On his first day in front of a class, a nervous Branch Rickey steeled himself for the worst. Under no circumstances would he permit himself to be driven off. If he could face his brother's fastball and runners bound for home, he could stand his ground against whatever his new charges could throw at him. And he did. Rickey's teaching career was only hours old before he moved to evict a "roughneck" who smelled of corn liquor. Momentarily taken aback, the accused recovered in time to challenge his teacher to a fight. He promptly received a second surprise when Rickey departed from his lesson plan long enough to administer a bloody beating.

More fights followed before Rickey was able to establish at least a measure of discipline in the classroom and win the respect of both his students and their parents. Word of the exploits of this pugilist-teacher quickly spread to neighboring communities, one of which offered him a job the following year for the hefty sum of $65 a month. Turkey Creek responded with a $5 a month raise and a pro-Rickey petition signed by "just about everybody who could write and a few who couldn't."

Torn and tempted, Branch turned to his father for advice. Complicating everything was the fact that the young man had fallen in love. The object of his affections, Jennie (she would later go by "Jane") Moulton, was the daughter of the owner of the Lucasville general store. Though still in his teens, Branch wanted to marry her as soon as possible. But because she was still in her teens, Jennie Moulton was not as anxious to join Branch Rickey at the altar, principally because her father was totally opposed to the union. A baseball player without any formal education was not Chandler Moulton's idea of a prospective son-in-law.

Rickey's own father was no more enamored of baseball than was Mr. Moulton, but he did have considerable faith in his middle son. The trick was to convince Branch to have faith that his intended bride-to-be would wait for him. That issue seemingly resolved, Frank Rickey turned to the matter of where his son should teach the following year. Money had never mattered much to the senior Rickey. What did matter was honor. And honor dictated that his son should not leave a job half done. Impending marriage or no, returning to Turkey Creek was more important than earning more money. A second year at Turkey Creek it would be.

The discussion between father and son had been a long one, but it was not quite over. If Branch was going to win Jennie Moulton he would have to persuade her father that he was not just a ballplayer. What about college? asked Branch. At the turn of the century, college was only for the well-to-do. It was not a viable option for an eighteen-year-old son of a farmer, especially one lacking even the minimum requirement, namely a high school diploma. And it certainly was not an option for any son of Frank Rickey. Money was only part of the problem, and in the father's mind it was not even the most important part. The larger issue revolved around what happened on college campuses—or, more accurately, what Frank Rickey thought happened there. To the elder Rickey, colleges were little more than dens of iniquity. What with the drinking and gambling and the general carousing, college life would be nothing but a corrupting influence on this good son of a good Methodist layman.

For a long while Branch had tried to put college out of his mind. Nonetheless, Jennie urged him to seek admission to the U.S. Naval Academy. If college was beyond a poor boy's reach, perhaps a military career was not. Plus, admission to the academy might well impress her father enough to change his mind about Branch Rickey and give him his daughter's hand in marriage. Following his first year at Turkey Creek, Branch took the admission exams for Annapolis. His scores were not high enough to win an appointment. If he was going to attend any college now, it would apparently have to be the very sort of place that Frank Rickey held suspect.

In the end the father decided to trust his middle son—and make a deal with him at the same time. If Branch completed a second year at Turkey Creek, he could then enroll at Ohio Wesleyan University in nearby Delaware. It was not the Naval Academy, but at least it was a Methodist institution. Besides, it was not that far away from home.

With money borrowed from his father, Branch Rickey enrolled at Ohio Wesleyan for the spring term of 1901. Though tuition was only $10 a year, the adult Rickey recalled that "no boy could have had fewer clothes than I had my first year in school, and no boy could have had less money." It's also unlikely that any turn-of-the-century freshman made more out of his initial college experience than Branch Rickey. He got better than good grades, found time for chapel and YMCA lectures, and signed on to catch for the school baseball team. By the fall he was a member of the football team as well. Far from a scrub on the gridiron, Rickey gained the starting halfback position and scored the winning touchdown in a late season game against archrival Ohio State.

The following summer Rickey joined the semi-professional Portsmouth (Ohio) Navvies. The $25 per month the team was willing to pay for a starting catcher beat anything anyone in Lucasville might have offered him. But the decision to accept it cost an innocent Branch Rickey his amateur status. When he returned to campus in the fall, the college president called him into his office. News reports of his baseball exploits had reached the president's desk. So had a letter from the owner of the Navvies: "Dear President, whoever said I had paid Branch Rickey any money was a Goddamned liar. I never paid him a damn cent."

Was the letter accurate? the president asked.

No, confessed the student-catcher.

The president had no alternative but to ban this admitted professional from varsity sports. But that was it. He made no move to suspend Rickey from college. Rickey was doubly relieved. Not only could he stay in school, but he could still play for money away from it. This time the squad was the Shelby Steel Tube Company, whose going rate for a Saturday afternoon football game was a whopping $50. This arrangement was lucrative while it lasted, but it didn't last for long. Three games into the season Rickey broke his ankle against Ohio Northern University. Almost exactly a year later a second broken bone effectively ended his football career.

In the interim, his baseball career began to flourish. Had the president relented? No, but in the spring of 1903 Ohio Wesleyan found itself without a baseball coach. Would Rickey be interested in the job? Yes, provided that he would be paid for his services. By this point the once skeptical Frank Rickey had mortgaged the family farm so that his son could concentrate on his studies. To contribute what he could, the son had held down a number of part-time jobs. Dropping any of them to become an unpaid baseball coach was out of the question. The president understood. As a result, Ohio Wesleyan, having lost a student-catcher, acquired a student-coach.

The first baseman (and occasional catcher) on Coach Rickey's first baseball team was Charles Thomas. One of a handful of black students at Ohio Wesleyan, Thomas aspired to a career in dentistry, but he was also handy enough with a bat and glove to win a starting position on the team. All during the spring his coach couldn't help but hear the racist taunts. Nonetheless the games were played, and played on time. This changed when the prospective opponent was the University of Kentucky. No sooner had the Kentucky coach learned of Thomas's presence in the starting lineup than he pulled all of his players from the field. With a determination to match his rival's, Rickey set out to make certain that the game was played—with Charles Thomas at first base. The starting time came and went, while the two coaches argued. Finally, the game was played, but only because of Rickey's persistence and only after it was agreed that Charles Thomas would take the field with his team.

The following spring Coach Rickey and his first baseman faced yet another challenge. This time the culprit was not an opposing coach but a hotel manager. When checking into a South Bend, Indiana, hotel prior to a game against Notre Dame, Rickey was told that Thomas would not be able to stay with the rest of the team. Overhearing the exchange between his coach and the hotel manager, Thomas offered to return to Ohio. Rickey wouldn't hear of it and sat down to negotiate with his newest adversary. The two finally agreed that Thomas could wait in Rickey's room until a place was found for him at a nearby black hotel. While the manager searched for such lodging, Rickey secured an extra cot for Thomas in his own room. When the hotel manager learned what Rickey had done, he complained that the coach was out of line. Rickey responded that "under no circumstances" would he allow Thomas to be "put out." This time there was an argument rather than a negotiation. In the end another Rickey antagonist was forced to relent: the player could remain with his coach and his team for the night.

Later that evening Rickey called all of his players to his room for a strategy session. As the meeting began, Charles Thomas sat silently in the corner. Try as he might the anxious young coach could not take his eyes off his somber first baseman. Nor would he ever forget what he saw. As Rickey recalled the scene years later, "tears welled in Charles' large, staring eyes. They spilled down his black face and splashed to the floor . . . his shoulders heaved convulsively, [as] he rubbed one great hand over the other, muttering, 'black skin . . . black skin. If I could only make 'em white.' He kept rubbing and rubbing as though he would remove the blackness by sheer friction."

For the moment Rickey could do little more than tell Thomas to "buck up." But even then he must have known that more than that would be required before the shackles of segregation could be removed. For probably the first time in his life Branch Rickey had been forced to ponder the problem of race and the impact of racial segregation on American life. It would not be the last time. Nor would this be his last chance to do something about segregation in the country he loved. Whether he suspected that it was his last chance is impossible to say, but the "recurrent vision" of Charles Thomas vainly trying to "wipe off his skin" no doubt had something to do with his subsequent determination to change the face of major league baseball.

In the spring of 1904 Branch Rickey left his Ohio Wesleyan coaching job and returned to Lucasville. He was not fired, and he did not resign. Having graduated from the university (and a year early at that) he simply presumed that his baseball coaching days were behind him. His playing days were not. That very day he received a telegram from a Portsmouth Navvies teammate informing him that the Dallas team in the Texas League needed a catcher. Was he interested? Yes and no. Texas was a long way from Ohio and his family. It was also far away from Jane Moulton. Furthermore, playing minor league baseball was not going to impress Jane's father. Though he figured that a law degree might well do the trick, he also knew that law school was costly, and right now he needed to make money, not spend it. Dallas was offering him $175 a month for the rest of the summer. With that kind of money he could live on his own and still be able to repay his father. Dallas and professional baseball it would be.

Young Branch soon learned that life on the road in the minor leagues was far removed from any life he had known—in college and especially in the Frank Rickey household. Shortly after he joined the team, Branch wrote his parents to inform them that he was "just about ready to declare [him]self something besides a ballplayer." The "profession" itself was "sort of disgraceful"; and the life of a ballplayer was dangerously "monotonous." The problem was twofold. The "baseball business" cultivated a life of "ease, laziness, and extravagant tastes." Worse than that, "church-going and ball playing don't dovetail by any means." The young catcher had learned something else as well: "Don't tell anyone you are a ballplayer, if you want to meet good people." Branch wanted to believe that he was still a good person, even a religious person, but he also wanted his parents to know that he was "feeling sore on baseball. It makes me worse than I really am, worse than I ought to be—worse than I otherwise would be."

On the field, Rickey proved to be better than he thought he would be. In fact, the reserve catcher performed so well during his two months in Texas that the Cincinnati Reds purchased his contract. The Cincinnati Reds! This had been his and brother Orla's favorite team. Now they were simply his team. There would be no more letters home filled with second thoughts about his chosen profession. Not yet twenty-three, Branch Rickey was headed for the major leagues.

The new backup catcher did not expect to play immediately upon arriving in Cincinnati. And he didn't. No matter. For the time being, his presence on a major league roster was reward enough for this reserve. He'd never even seen a major league game before. Now he was watching them from the dugout.

Player-manager Joe Kelley essentially ignored his new catcher for the better part of a week. Following a Saturday game, Kelley happened to overhear Rickey tell a teammate that he'd see him "bright and early Monday morning." A stunned Kelley couldn't believe his ears. This was Saturday, wasn't it? There was a game the next afternoon, wasn't there? Where did Rickey think he was going?

"I don't play Sundays," was the rookie's candid response.

Kelley was equally to the point. "Busher," he roared, "beat it over to the owner's office and get your release." Rickey was stunned. He thought that the Dallas club had informed Cincinnati of his self-imposed ban on playing ball on Sundays. He learned otherwise when he went to see August "Garry" Herrmann, owner of the Reds.

The conversation between player and owner was longer and calmer than the exchange between player and manager had been. Herrmann was a powerful local businessman, one who also happened to like baseball. Nothing terribly unusual here. What was somewhat more unusual was that this owner actually liked baseball players. At the turn of the century, Herrmann and his fellow owners were intent on establishing baseball as America's national game. But there were roadblocks. Gambling was one of them. So was general rowdiness among the fans. And so was the background and demeanor of many of the players. In truth, *professional* baseball players were not held in particularly high regard. They may not have been criminals or near-criminals, but many were regarded as suspicious characters at best. And most of those who held the contracts of these players didn't just share these suspicions; if anything, they helped foster them.

Young Branch Rickey was hardly among the players that Herrmann held suspect. This teetotaling straight arrow was almost too good to be true. Hence an intrigued Herrmann decided to press his catcher for an explanation. At first, Rickey refused to answer, but Herrmann persisted. More squirming ensued before the player finally relented. It wasn't that Sunday ball was immoral. It wasn't even something he personally opposed. It was just that his mother had been so upset by his turning pro that he had promised her that he wouldn't play ball on Sunday. More than that, he had promised that he wouldn't even set foot in a ball park on Sunday. That may have been "all" that was at stake here, but it meant everything to the resolute young man. Because it was a promise to his mother, it could not be violated.

Herrmann was impressed with Rickey's unvarnished sincerity. He also knew well enough that his fellow National League owners had banned Sunday ball until very recently. And then only a few upstart midwestern cities, brewery towns cities such as Cincinnati, St. Louis, and Chicago, had decided to risk the wrath of puritanical traditionalists by taking the field on the Lord's Day.

What would Rickey do if he were released, wondered Herrmann?

The young catcher replied that he would go home for a few days to see Jane and his parents before leaving for Allegheny College, where he had been offered a job coaching football and teaching. Besides, Rickey added, he hadn't planned on making baseball a career anyway. He was just saving money in order to marry and pay for law school. Soon Garry Herrmann learned what others—specifically that baseball coach in Kentucky and the hotel operator in South Bend—had learned before him, that Branch Rickey was not about to budge. Having absorbed his lesson, Herrmann told Rickey to join the Reds in Pittsburgh and "report to the team every day—except Sunday."

Herrmann might have been able to order Rickey to rejoin his teammates, but he would not order manager Kelley to play him. In short order the benched Branch Rickey found himself back in Garry Herrmann's office. This time the conversation was brief. Very brief. The owner simply announced that he was prepared to pay Rickey a month's salary and return his contract to Dallas. The rookie catcher never appeared in a game in a Cincinnati uniform.

With baseball over for the year, Rickey decided to accept the Allegheny College offer. As it developed, his coaching responsibilities included both football and baseball. But that double duty did not quite constitute a full-time appointment. In his spare time Coach Rickey was also assigned to teach English, German, and Greek drama. For the time being, playing professional baseball was placed on the back burner, even as he was being shifted from roster to roster. First Dallas sold him to the Chicago White Sox. Then the Sox promptly turned around and traded him to the St. Louis Browns.

Rickey was on the Browns roster for much of the 1905 season. Officially, he agreed to play only between June 15 and September

15, and never on Sunday. Actually, he appeared in only one game, following which his major league slate remained clean: no hits, no runs, no errors. His major league debut behind him, Rickey returned to Allegheny for another school year of coaching and teaching. By this point Chandler Moulton was so impressed with Rickey's energy that he finally agreed to let him marry his daughter. (Perhaps his future father-in-law had also glimpsed enough Browns' box scores to conclude that his future son-in-law had no future in baseball.) The date was set for June 1, 1906. But Mr. Moulton extracted one final promise: 1906 was to be Branch Rickey's last season as a professional baseball player.

It wasn't. Not only did Rickey have a surprisingly good year on the field in 1906, but his new wife came to appreciate—and share—his passion for baseball. Back with the Browns, Rickey played in sixty-four games and batted .284 (on the basis of what would be a career-high 201 trips to the plate). He also hit the only three home runs of his major league career. With his career on the upswing, with Chandler Moulton no longer in a position to make demands, and with his new bride coming to love the game nearly as much as he did, it suddenly seemed possible that baseball was going to remain a big part of the new couple's life. Or so they thought until Branch injured his throwing arm during the winter of 1906–07.

The newlyweds had been looking forward to a new season and a new town. Traded to the New York Highlanders (later the Yankees) during the off-season, Rickey had every reason to expect that his career would continue to progress. But the injured arm did not come around. Manager Clark Griffith suggested several remedies, including a stint in the mineral waters of Hot Springs, Arkansas. Nothing worked. His once powerful right arm was apparently beyond repair. Faced with the prospect that he was permanently damaged goods, Rickey chose to try to play anyway. The results bordered somewhere between futile and amateurish. His batting average for the season was a dismal .182 (on a paltry 137 at-bats). What's worse, he suffered the embarrassment of setting a major league record; base runners, taking full advantage of the catcher's bum arm, stole a total of thirteen bases against him in a single game. Though not yet twenty-six, Branch Rickey's major league playing career was effectively over. (There would be one more single-game season with the Browns in 1914 in which he went an inglorious 0-2.) Perhaps Jane's father had been right all along. Baseball was not going to provide for his daughter. Maybe it really was time to grow up.

Rickey spent the winter of 1907–08 in Delaware, Ohio, preparing for law school and pondering his future. Since neither activity was a paying proposition, he took a job with the local YMCA. At this time YMCA groups across the country were deeply involved in the Social Gospel movement. Reform under the heading of "Christian social responsibility" was the order of the day in many cities and towns across the East and Midwest. Steeped in his Methodist upbringing, Wesley Branch Rickey had no difficulty taking that order—or giving it.

To help promote the Social Gospel, Rickey brought such noted reformers as Hull House founder Jane Addams, muckraking journalist Jacob Riis, and black educator Booker T. Washington to his Delaware YMCA. He became a spokesman for a variety of reform causes, most prominently the growing campaign against alcohol. For $10 a talk Branch Rickey would address gatherings across Ohio on behalf of the YMCA and the Anti-Saloon League. The former ballplayer was on his way to becoming a traveling evangelist. In the fall of 1908 he added politics to his list of causes by signing on to do volunteer work for the local William Howard Taft for President committee. For the time being, it was just one Ohio boy helping out another, but for the rest of his life Branch Rickey would align himself with the Republican Party.

All of his traveling, speaking, organizing, studying, and pondering proved to be more draining than any season behind the plate. Branch Rickey may have been a strapping farm boy who made himself into a well-conditioned athlete, but early in 1909 he contracted tuberculosis. This was a disease that afflicted Americans of all ages during the first half of the twentieth century. Those who caught it, even rugged baseball catchers, had to be very concerned, if not just plain terrified, about their future. Branch Rickey was no different. For more than the moment, all of his many dreams had to be put on hold while he and Jane retreated to a sanitorium in the Adirondack Mountains of New York. There this advocate for the Anti-Saloon League found himself on a most embarrassing diet. In order to build up his weight he was under doctors' orders to drink a daily ration of beer.

By the end of the summer Rickey was nearly back to his fighting weight and ready for a different challenge: law school at the University of Michigan. But as luck would have it, Branch Rickey would not be spending all of his time in the law library. He arrived on the Ann Arbor campus just as the university athletic director was looking for a new baseball coach. Upon learning of the opening, Rickey approached the law school dean. Would he permit a first-year law student to lead at least a double life? Yes, came the reluctant reply, but only if each of his teachers called on him every day—and then only if he could answer whatever question they might choose to throw at him. Coach Rickey must have done just that, because he completed his law degree a year ahead of schedule, with time left over to run his team and lecture his players on everything from "astronomy to Sanskrit."

The year was 1911. If Branch Rickey was ever going to put baseball behind him, this was the moment to do it. He had graduated from law school near the top of his class. His family was growing. He needed money, and he needed it quickly. A law practice had to be more promising than a baseball career. But where to begin a new career? Rickey's answer was Boise, Idaho. He and two fraternity brothers from Ohio Wesleyan settled on Boise because they anticipated that an economic boom was about to hit the town. The word was that a new railroad line was to go right through Boise. Rickey's still precarious health also contributed to his decision. Given his recent bout with tuberculosis, the clean mountain air was a real attraction. In the end, it proved to be Boise's only attraction for this member of the fledgling law firm. Rickey's health improved dramatically, but his finances did not. Within the year the entire Rickey family had retreated to Ann Arbor and the head of the household had returned to coaching baseball.

Here he was again. Which would it be? Law or baseball? Rickey was still not prepared to make the final call, even if the choice was clear to everyone around him. Branch Rickey found the game of baseball utterly fascinating. More than that, he found it intellectually stimulating. Certainly there was little money to be made as a college coach, but there were problems to solve and students to teach. And Branch Rickey was a teacher before he was anything else.

He was also a perfectionist. Hour after hour he would drill his players on the intricacies of the game. This was the "dead ball" era at all levels of baseball. Because the ball wasn't lively, the minds of the game's practitioners had to be. No coach or manager could afford to wait around for a batter to sock a three-run homer, for a home run of any sort was a rarity. Two to one was a very common final score. Put simply, every run was precious, and virtually every run had to be manufactured. Therefore, bunting was an art to be mastered; squeeze plays had to be rehearsed repeatedly; runners had to be advanced methodically, one base at a time.

The pleasure of the game was in the details, as were victories. In order to secure the greatest pleasure—and the most victories— Rickey instructed his charges to concentrate on the little things. He taught his base runners how to take just the right lead, how to get the jump on the pitcher, and how to slide effectively. On offense, he encouraged his runners to steal bases. On defense, he ordered his catchers to guard against the stolen base and called for pitchouts on a regular basis. Above all, he urged every one of his players to gamble on the diamond, to take risks whenever they could to score those hard-to-come-by runs.

"Adventure," he repeated endlessly, "adventure." It was his message for baseball and for life.

In 1912 Branch Rickey had to force himself to listen to one of his own lectures. He also had to stop and pay attention to what was driving his daily life. And it wasn't the law. It was baseball.

There would be just one more detour to Boise before he was finally convinced.

The owner of the American League St. Louis Browns helped as well. In the spring of 1912 Robert Lee Hedges traveled all the way to Ann Arbor with a proposition for the University of Michigan baseball coach. A millionaire carriage manufacturer, Hedges had owned the Browns for better than a decade. During his tenure the team had never finished better than fourth place. It was time to change that. Hedges remembered Rickey from his days with the Browns. The plan was to offer his former catcher the job of running his minor league team in Kansas City by way of grooming him for a top post with the Browns.

Though flattered by Hedges's proposal, Rickey decided to decline it. He had promised his law partners that he would return to Boise by June. Though disappointed, Hedges refused to leave without some sort of a commitment. Would Rickey at least agree to scout for him while he was in the West? That much, and that much only, he would do. By August of that same year the frustration of a fourth straight losing season had convinced Hedges to up his ante. With his Browns on their way to a seventh-place finish (and a dismal 53-101 record), Hedges presented Rickey with a new offer. How would he like to be Hedges second in command in St. Louis?

The Browns were not a very good team, but they were a major league team. This time Rickey wasn't being asked to leave his university post for the minors. This time he was being offered a chance to take his baseball talents to the American League. As Hedges spelled out his duties, it became clear to Rickey that he was to have effective control of the Browns' baseball future. Specifically, he would be in charge of finding and developing talent. He would also have a significant role in trading players and negotiating contracts. For all this he would be paid $7,500 a year. To sweeten the pot, Rickey would be permitted to keep his Michigan coaching job (and its $1,500 salary) for one more season. This time he was floored. And this time he accepted.

Nine thousand dollars a year was a lot more money than the son of Frank Rickey ever thought he would make. It was also more than he thought he deserved. After all, he *was* Frank Rickey's son. But he was also facing new demands as a husband and father. "Adventure" was not a word that sprang to Frank Rickey's lips. Certainly, it was not the way that the elder Rickey had lived his life in rural Ohio. But his baseball-coaching son was about to practice what he had been preaching to his players. He was about to have his own adventure, an adventure that would last for better than half a century. And if it wasn't directly concerned with his life on the base paths, it had everything to do with taking the path that would marry him to the game.

Almost immediately, Branch Rickey's new life became more adventuresome than either he or Hedges had planned. During his first season with the lowly Browns, Rickey had to face a series of crises, the most serious of which concerned player-manager George Stovall. On a hot August afternoon in the midst of yet another Browns' losing streak, Stovall was ejected after protesting a close call at first base. This was nothing new for someone known as "Firebrand" to his players and opponents alike. What was new was Stovall's response to his most recent dismissal. This time his parting shot was a stream of brown tobacco juice that soon adorned the umpire's white uniform as well as his red face.

American League President Ban Johnson promptly fined the expectorating Stovall. Surprisingly, Johnson did not tack on a suspension as well. Stovall, for his part, presumed that the Browns management would at least appeal the fine. No one did. In fact, neither Hedges nor Rickey could conceal his disgust with Stovall's behavior. The St. Louis owner had long thought that baseball needed to present a more wholesome image. Rickey agreed. Baseball, he believed, ought to do everything possible to make itself attractive to the rising middle class. Women ought to be welcome at major league ball parks. And ballplayers should be role models for young people everywhere. Three strikes and "Firebrand" Stovall was out. Besides, the Browns' losing streak had reached seven games.

Stovall's initial replacement was Jimmy "Pepper" Austin, a Browns infielder. But Hedges was not quite through shuffling his managerial deck. A bare fourteen games into Austin's tenure Hedges walked into the Browns clubhouse and announced that general manager Branch Rickey was taking over as field manager, effective immediately.

There was nothing that Manager Rickey could do to salvage the 1913 season. But ideas were already percolating in his head for 1914. He would begin by taking his squad to Florida for spring training. No team had ever done that before. But Rickey's stream of innovations did not stop there. To match the team's three batting cages he installed three handball courts, not only to better condition his players but to "brighten their eyes, and make them alert." Besides, in Rickey's book, hitting was overrated. Speed and defense won baseball games. Therefore, his players would run wind sprints every day. When it came to offense, however, speed was not the total answer. Therefore his training camp would come equipped with another Rickey invention, a sliding pit. While raw speed could not be taught, how to arrive at the next base could be, and manager Rickey would be the teacher.

In fact, every day of spring training began with a Branch Rickey lecture. Promptly at 9 A.M. the Browns gathered around their manager. With a blackboard behind him, a cigar in one hand and a piece of chalk in the other, Rickey always came armed and ready to talk. Seldom was there a single topic of the day. Instead, Rickey expounded on everything from his players' sliding techniques to their moral development.

If anyone might have accused Rickey of being too much the cerebral revolutionary, another Rickey, an earthier Rickey, was ready to plead guilty. Of course he was a theorizer, but "Judas Priest," it was "blamed good practical theory." And the Browns initially responded to his practical theorizing by moving up in the standings. In his first full season at the helm, Rickey coaxed the team from seventh place to fifth and finished with a record of 71-82. While encouraging, the improvement was not sustained. Despite acquiring his first bona fide star, first baseman-outfielder George Sisler, Rickey could lead the Browns to no better than 63-91 and sixth place in 1915.

Hedges had finally had it. Tired of losing, he decided to sell the team. If the Browns owner had any second thoughts, he put them aside when competition from the upstart Federal League began to drive up player salaries. If he needed a clincher, it came when he learned that the new league had sued major league baseball over its allegedly monopolistic practices. To escape what he was convinced was imminent financial disaster, Hedges sold his team to Philip Ball, who also owned the St. Louis entry in the Federal League. Like Garry Herrmann, Ball was a rags-to-riches millionaire who simply could not resist the lure of baseball. Unlike Herrmann, Ball was a more confrontational sort, whether he was dealing with his employees or his enemies. And unlike Rickey, Ball was no friend of the Anti-Saloon League, having made some of his fortune in the brewery business.

"So you're the goddamned prohibitionist," were the first words out of Phil Ball's mouth when he was introduced to Branch Rickey. Had Ball had his way, Rickey would have been out of a job immediately. Hedges, however, had already given his primary baseball man a contract for 1916. Ball decided to honor that agreement, but at the same time he reduced Rickey's responsibilities by removing him as the Browns field manager.

Out of one half of his job, and thoroughly out of favor with his new boss, Rickey wanted out, period. He got his wish sooner than he could have imagined and without having to leave St. Louis. In 1916 the National League St. Louis Cardinals were not the team they would one day become. In fact, they had just struggled to a last place finish and bankruptcy all in the same season. A group of St. Louis businessmen approached the Cardinal management about initiating a recovery process. The obvious first step was to infuse much-needed cash into the operation. That was also the easy step. But what to do next? The new owners did not have a single baseball man among them. While their lack of baseball knowledge was conspicuous, it did not prevent them from searching for the same. Among those consulted were local sportswriters, whose recommendation for that next step was immediate and unanimous: hire Branch Rickey. This time Rickey was not just floored, he was delighted. At hand was the opportunity that he had been waiting for. Without either the detestable Ball or the meddlesome Hedges looking over his shoulder, Rickey was finally given the authority to run a major league baseball operation entirely as he saw fit.

And that was exactly what Branch Rickey would do for most of the rest of his baseball life. At the outset, however, on-field success proved elusive. The 1917 Cards jumped to third place, but in 1918 they again landed unceremoniously in the NL cellar. But the team was not without prospects, the most impressive of whom was a young shortstop by the name of Rogers Hornsby. In Rickey's glowing estimation, Hornsby was "an exemplary hitter, a remarkable batter, indeed." Little did Rickey then realize just how accurate that assessment would be.

The end of the baseball season came early in 1918. With the world at war and with the United States now a full-fledged belligerent, the War Department issued a "work or fight" order in June of 1918. Where did that leave baseball players? Unlike those whom the government defined as "entertainers" (meaning actors, etc.), most ballplayers were forced to choose between signing up for the armed services or latching onto an approved "essential" civilian job. Baseball owners tried to do their part—and keep the Wilson administration off their collective back—by linking what was unofficially America's game with highly official displays of American patriotic fervor. Suddenly American flags were flying everywhere in every ballpark. Something approaching a national anthem (there would be no official version until 1931) opened nearly every game. The owners' final entry in this patriots' game was to end the season a month early in the name of sacrificing for the war effort. (Unofficially, this decision had more to do with sagging attendance than with surging patriotism, because the owners also saved a good deal of money by not having to pay their players for the missing month.)

Branch Rickey's sense of patriotism, however, extended well beyond his pocketbook. Nearly thirty-seven and the father of four young children, the Cardinal executive was exempt from the draft on multiple grounds. Still, he thought he ought to do his part, and do it more directly than by simply unfurling a flag or singing an anthem. An old friend, one time Harvard football coach and current president of the Boston Braves, Percy Haughton, suggested to Rickey that he join the chemical warfare section of the U.S. Army. Without consulting Jane, Branch enlisted and was immediately commissioned as a major, thanks to Haughton's intervention. Though a good Republican, Branch Rickey was ready to join Woodrow Wilson's army and his cause. "Making the world safe for democracy" was not just a Democratic slogan; to Rickey it was an *American* principle.

Major Rickey made it to France before the war ended, if barely. Many soldiers left the war zone flat on their backs—on a stretcher or in a coffin. Having caught a severe case of the flu while crossing the Atlantic, Branch Rickey managed to *arrive* at the front on his back. Once on his feet again, the new officer joined Captains Christy Mathewson and Ty Cobb and Lieutenant George Sisler. These four baseball men were among a small cadre of officers assigned to explain the dangers of mustard gas to American troops. In early December 1918, Rickey returned to American soil, having completed his brief tour of duty without injury or incident. (During his service in France a less fortunate Christy Mathewson accidentally inhaled mustard gas. The incident may well have led to his subsequent bout with tuberculosis, which in turn led to his premature death in 1925.)

Branch Rickey returned to an America that was poised to enjoy the fruits of its victory. It was also an America on the verge of experiencing its first "golden age" of sport. Much of this sporting activity was professional, for it was during the 1920s that almost all of the remaining barriers against professionalism in sport came tumbling down. It hadn't been all that long ago that President Theodore Roosevelt, another Republican Rickey greatly admired, was publicly appalled that American athletes were being paid to play games, especially baseball, which he regarded as a much less "manly" sport than football. His youngest son Quentin loved baseball, but football was the official sport of this Roosevelt father and his four sons—especially collegiate football—which officially was amateur football. When it came to any sport, Roosevelt declared, professionalism a "sin." Because Roosevelt died in 1919 he was spared having to witness the proliferation of this "sin," and the country was spared his harangues against the professionalism that accompanied the "golden age" of American sport during the heyday of Babe Ruth, Red Grange, and Jack Dempsey.

Branch Rickey was highly attuned to the wonders of professional sport (especially baseball) and to the evils of sin (in all its forms). He had done his best to stay away from both while he had been Frank Rickey's son and Chandler Moulton's son-in-law to be. Having finally broken free from the Rooseveltian edict that equated professionalism with sin, Rickey always did his best to keep his near-sons, meaning his ballplayers, amateur and professional, away from sin as he defined it. As might be expected, this combination preacher and businessman had a broad definition of sin, but in the final analysis accepting money to play baseball was not on his lengthy list of evils. Of course, what players did with their money might well be. Hence this preacher's morning lectures. And in any event, paying people *too much* money to play baseball surely bordered on the sinful. Hence this businessman's reputation as a cheapskate. For the moment, however, Branch Rickey of the St. Louis Cardinals was content to do his best to take advantage of a postwar period that promised great things to those involved in professional baseball. All of a sudden great numbers of Americans would have a good deal more money—and time—to spend on leisure activities. And what better leisure activity could there be than watching skilled young men play baseball?

Little did Rickey know that baseball's coming "golden age" would be tarnished before it could truly begin. No doubt he was aware that some players did not think they were making nearly enough money. No doubt he was also aware that gambling existed on the major league level. He may even have been aware of just how serious a problem gambling was. But certainly he could be excused for not grasping the lengths to which some ballplayers would go to correct this perceived imbalance between their salaries and the owners' profits.

Few baseball owners circa 1919 were loved by their players. After all, each player had no choice but to play for the team that held his contract. Because of the infamous "reserve" system, major league franchises potentially controlled their players forever. More accurately, each owner owned his players for as long as *he* chose to do so. The owner could cut loose a player with a bare ten-days notice. But the system didn't work the same way in the other direction. Once a player signed a contract with a team, he was never at liberty to negotiate with any other team. Free agency for players was a thing of the future, and the far distant future at that.

If few owners were loved by their players, many were hated. However, no owner was hated more than Charles Comiskey of the Chicago White Sox. The "Old Roman," as he was known to friend and foe alike, paid his players a pittance—especially if he thought they had no good alternative but to play baseball. "College boys," such as second baseman Eddie Collins, drew higher salaries from the White Sox management, who reasoned that these young men might have been able to command more money in other lines of work. Non-college boys were treated very differently, which meant that most of the White Sox players were poorly compensated. Among those non-college boys were the eight White Sox who became the notorious "Black Sox," so named for conspiring with gamblers to throw the 1919 World Series to the Cincinnati Reds. Angered by the stinginess of Comiskey and the haughtiness of Collins, the eight chose to make up for lost wages by taking money to deliberately lose what was then a nine-game national fixation. They succeeded in doing so in eight games, even as they failed to collect everything due them from the gamblers.

If the plot had a ringleader, it was the barely educated first baseman Chick Gandil, who was the initial contact with the gamblers. If it had a victim, it was the completely illiterate outfielder, "Shoeless Joe" Jackson, who tried to return the tainted money but who ultimately sacrificed the rest of his illustrious baseball career and his spot in the Hall of Fame.

If any team had the potential to become a dynasty at this moment in baseball history, it was the Chicago White Sox. They had won the World Series in 1917 only to slump badly the next year.

But in 1919 they returned to the top by winning the American League pennant and were the prohibitive favorites to take the series as well. Such was not to be, thanks in equal parts to a penny-pinching Comiskey and his crooked players. Still, a year would pass before the full dimensions of the scandal were revealed. Ultimately, there would be a trial, which resulted in a "not guilty" verdict by a home-town (Chicago) jury. But that was not the end of that. Ten months later baseball's first commissioner, Judge Kenesaw Mountain Landis, ignored the jury finding and threw the eight "Black Sox" out of baseball for good. Landis had been hired to clean up the game and was given considerable leeway when it came to accomplishing the task. This would not be the last time he would wield his authority dictatorially, but no instance of his power at work was more important than this one. There would be other low points in baseball history, but none lower than the "Black Sox" scandal that had its origins in the poisoned atmosphere and murky plotting of 1919 and did not end until Landis handed down his final verdict in 1921.

Baseball would recover—and sooner rather than later thanks to an imperious Landis, the end of the "dead ball" era, and the dominance and charisma of Babe Ruth. But the immediate postwar era was a troubled time for the nation's game.

It was also a difficult time for the ever-struggling St. Louis Cardinals. Branch Rickey may have hoped to cash in on the anticipated postwar bonanza, but the team finished a distant seventh in 1919, $40\frac{1}{2}$ games out of first place. And general manager Rickey need look no further than the mirror to find someone to take most of the blame for the sorry state of his team's affairs. That's because this general manager had agreed to a series of cost-cutting moves, including his appointment as the Cardinal field manager for the 1919 season. Rickey was reluctant to return to this role, but the Cardinal hierarchy figured that this move alone would save the team at least $10,000. And this was a critical sum, for only 173,604 fans found their way to Sportsman's Park during that entire season. To everyone concerned, that paltry attendance figure could not justify having both a general manager and a field manager on the payroll, not to mention paying certain Cardinal ballplayers as much as $7,500 a year.

It was a long way up from all those empty seats and all those games behind the pennant-winning Reds for Rickey and his victory-starved Cardinals. But Branch Rickey was not the long-suffering sort. Things would get better, and soon. After all, he did have the "remarkable" Hornsby anchoring his batting order, and Branch Rickey was never short of new ideas, even for a team short on victories as well as cash. A man of consuming ambition, he was perennially committed to fielding a competitive team. An inveterate plotter, he was forever trying to figure out how to win today's game. A natural schemer, he was forever trying to figure out how to match tomorrow's competition. A practical dreamer, he was forever planning for the day when fellow competitors would be trying to figure out how to catch up to him.

Every successful enterprise has within it those who tinker, those who dream, and those who are able to convert their dreams into realities. Branch Rickey was all three. Figuring out how to win today's game was just as much fun for him as trying to build tomorrow's team. And as Rickey looked toward the future, he knew that his Cardinals needed more than a minor adjustment. He knew that he was going to have to be downright inventive if the team was ever going to be the on-field equal of John McGraw's vaunted New York Giants. That, after all, was his goal. Escaping the cellar wasn't good enough. Winning pennants was an improvement. But a string of World Series titles, that was the dream. Achieving it required a leader able to tinker, plan, and innovate.

Rickey believed that the scheme he was about to hatch was better than most, but he also estimated that the interval between its incubation and any payoff was bound to be a long one. Would Cardinal fans wait much longer? Would his boss? After inching to sixth place in 1920 the Cardinals jumped all the way to third the next year. Then, however, they settled into the middle of the pack, where they stayed all the way through the 1925 season. Unfortunately, Rickey had been right; there were no immediate dividends to be reaped. Still, a persevering Rickey was convinced that his idea was an excellent one, if only everyone would just be patient for a while longer.

The Second Inning

For many black Americans in 1919 the three "p's" of patience, perseverance, and persistence were less virtues than an enforced way of life. Surely this often was so for sharecropper Jerry Robinson, who worked the land of a white plantation owner in what was called the Velvet Corridor of southern Georgia. And this was always the case for his oft-forgiving wife, Mallie. Jerry had left her more than once, whether for another woman or for whatever else the nearby city of Cairo had to offer. But he always managed to return. And when he did Mallie often managed to become pregnant. As 1919 began, the Robinsons had three boys and a girl—and Mallie was expecting once again.

Though Mallie Robinson was the prayerful sort, she had little reason to be the hopeful sort. Still, she found it in her heart to be both when she went into labor on January 31, 1919. On this day she prayed—and hoped—for a second daughter. Once again, her prayers were not answered. By nightfall her fourth son was born. She named him Jack Roosevelt Robinson. The middle name was for former President Theodore Roosevelt, who had died a few weeks earlier. Mallie was not an educated woman, but she knew enough to look upon the Republican Roosevelt as a friend to black Americans. Early in his presidency he had created a stir by inviting none other than black educator Booker T. Washington to the White House. Throughout his presidency he appointed blacks to various low-level offices, as he tried, however vainly, to maintain a semblance of a Republican Party in the South on the basis of an interracial alliance of whites and blacks. And as president, Roosevelt sought to remake his party once again into the party of Abraham Lincoln. The first Republican president had signed the Emancipation Proclamation, which paved the way for the elimination of slavery. Intervening Republican chief executives had gradually forgotten about black Americans. President Roosevelt would remind his party and his country of what the Republican Party had stood for in its infancy. Mallie Robinson did not have to know very much about any of that to be convinced that Theodore Roosevelt was a good man who had been a good president. So Jack *Roosevelt* Robinson it would be.

Mallie had a second wish as well. With the "Spanish flu" raging across the country—killing hundreds of thousands of Americans in the process—she prayed for deliverance from this plague. This prayer was answered, for in their sharecropper's log cabin Mallie Robinson gave birth to a healthy baby boy. What's more, the delivery itself was relatively easy. It also happened to be her first with a doctor in attendance. This was highly unusual in the southern black belt. While the doctor had not been needed during what turned out to be a smooth delivery, it must have been quite comforting to have had him on the scene.

When it came to family finances, Mallie did more than pray. A strong, God-fearing woman, she had tried to pass her strength and her faith on to her irresolute husband. For whatever reason, she failed. As a husband, Jerry Robinson was absent more often than not. As a sharecropper, he was little more than a slave. Years later his son, Jack, would characterize the sharecropping system as a "kind of slavery" and look upon his father as a "victim of oppression." For his father's labor the Robinson family received a place to live, provisions, and the equivalent of $3 a week in "chits" redeemable only at the landowner's store. Mallie thought they could do better than that, if only she could prod her husband into obtaining what was called a "half crop." Under this system the family would be able to keep half of whatever it produced. But the owner refused all of Jerry's pleadings. Only when Mallie herself took up the family's case did the landowner relent, pressured, as he put it, by "about the sassiest nigger woman ever on this place."

Jack was only weeks old at the time of Mallie's victory. Though there was another mouth to feed now, Mallie thought that the family finally had good reason to anticipate better times ahead. If they could sell half of what Jerry cultivated, she estimated, family income might reach as much as $350 for the year. Jerry, however, remained more interested in cultivating the attention of other women. By July he was gone again, this time for good. The word was that he had headed for Florida with another man's wife, but Mallie never learned the full truth about his whereabouts or his liaisons. In fact, she never heard from him again. Neither did her youngest son, who despite never really knowing his father retained feelings of bitterness about his disappearance.

Not long after Jerry Robinson abandoned his family for the final time the landowner withdrew the "half crop" arrangement and began to force Mallie and her five children into smaller and smaller quarters. He had never forgiven her for trying to pry more money out of him in the first place. Now he held Mallie responsible for Jerry's absence as well. When she refused to concede any measure of responsibility for her husband's disappearance, the landowner responded by ordering the entire Robinson family off his plantation.

Mallie Robinson dealt with her eviction by looking for domestic work in Cairo. When that proved as unappealing as life on the plantation, she decided to join the growing exodus of black Americans who were leaving the South. With jobs to be had in the cities of the North and with the Ku Klux Klan on the rise throughout the South, blacks were leaving the states of the Old Confederacy by the hundreds of thousands during and following World War I. Mallie, however, did not go north. Instead, she packed up an extended family of thirteen and bought train tickets to Pasadena, California, where one of her brothers lived.

The Robinson family soon discovered that life in southern California was all too much like life in southern Georgia. The only employment that Mallie could find was as a domestic servant. And racial segregation in the city of Pasadena closely resembled the system they had experienced in the post-Reconstruction "Jim Crow" South.

Following the end of Reconstruction and the final removal of all federal troops in 1877, the Democratic Party regained full power throughout the states of the old Confederacy. At this time in American history the Democrats were essentially a "whites only" party. This was especially so in the South, where the party also endorsed states' rights. After Reconstruction that doctrine readily translated into policies that assured white dominance and the virtual re-enslavement of many blacks. Economically, former slaves and children of former slaves were kept in "their place" by having to sharecrop on white-owned land. Politically, black males were stripped of the right to vote that had been granted to them by the 1870 ratification of the Fifteenth Amendment to the Constitution. Socially, all blacks were subjected to strict and strictly legal systems of intense and intensely enforced segregation.

Outside the South, black Americans were better able to obtain and hold economic and political freedoms. But racial equality did not exist, and life was seldom easy. Whether *de jure* or *de facto,* segregation was the order of the day most everywhere. The Robinsons quickly found this to be the case in their adopted city of Pasadena. In this suburb of Los Angeles, the housing and job markets were thoroughly segregated. The public swimming pool was open to blacks only one day a week. Movie theaters had separate sections for blacks and whites.

Nonetheless, the Robinsons were able to rent a house in an all-white neighborhood. Mallie was not a pioneer for racial integration. It was just that this house was good-sized and available. It also came with a story. Not many months earlier the house had been purchased by a black woman who naively thought that there would be no hostile reaction to her presence in the neighborhood. But hostility from her white neighbors was what she got. As a result, she moved out, preferring to leave the place vacant and suffer the financial loss rather than face the daily abuse. Soon thereafter, a crafty black real state agent rented the home to Mallie Robinson and her family. The agent was well aware of the

Robinsons' needs, but he did not have their best interests at heart. What governed his thinking was his own financial profit. He calculated that the presence of yet another black family would cause panic among neighboring whites, thereby creating a bidding war that could only drive up the price of the house. The agent's craftiness was not rewarded. There was no panic, whether spontaneous or orchestrated. In the end, there wasn't even the hint of a white campaign to obtain the property. The Robinsons simply stayed put.

All, however, was not peace and tolerance between the Robinsons and their new neighbors. Stones were thrown at Robinson family members. A cross was burned on their lawn. But having already journeyed 2,500 miles, Mallie Robinson was not about to move another inch. The house at 121 Pepper Street in Pasadena was her home. It was also home to an ever-fluctuating number of relatives and friends. (Originally one of fourteen children, Mallie Robinson always maintained an open-door policy for her siblings and any of their children who found their way to the Robinson "hotel" at 121 Pepper.)

Jack's best recollection is that he was eight when the first stone was hurled in his direction. He was sweeping the sidewalk in front of the Pepper Street house when a neighbor girl began taunting him with shouts of "nigger, nigger." He responded with the best insult in his limited arsenal: "cracker." When the girl's father heard this he bolted out of the front door. Before long stones replaced words—in both directions. No blood was drawn on either side, but this incident became part of a pattern that infected Jack's growing up years in Pasadena.

Despite violence and threats thereof, Jack did grow up with a sense of security. The geographic center of his young life was indeed the house on Pepper Street, where his mother served as the emotional and spiritual center of the entire family. For five days a week and fifty-two weeks a year, Mallie Robinson toiled as a domestic. But she was a presence at 121 Pepper Street even when she was not present. So was her God. The Rickey family had nothing on the Robinson family when it came to the importance of religion in their daily lives. "She brought us up," her famous son later recalled, "believing in God, knowing there was a God and also a true hell."

Jack may not have had a Frank Rickey in his life, but he did have an older brother. Edgar Robinson, "Papa" to his younger siblings, was the next best thing to a real father in Mallie's brood. What's more, he was just as religious as his mother and more physically imposing than most anybody's father. Not that he had to use physical force to enforce his mother's dictates. The children respected her wishes even in her absence. But Edgar as well as his brother Mack did have occasion to use their fists against certain neighborhood bullies in defense of younger brother Jack.

But Jack's small world was hemmed in by much more than a few local toughs. Despite his mother's generosity and optimism, despite her insistence that hate could be overcome by love, his future was far from assured. And despite his obvious—and multiple—athletic abilities, he had no reason to think that the future was his to shape. If it was apparent to anyone who watched him that young Jack was a marvelous athlete, it was not yet apparent to Jack himself that athletics was his ticket to a successful life beyond 121 Pepper Street.

Despite almost daily affronts, Jack still found time to play. There was always time to play. The game didn't matter. Whether it was marbles or soccer, Jack was ready to compete—and determined to win. By the time he was in junior high his games of choice were more likely to be baseball and basketball, or football and track. And more often than not, he was the one to watch, whether on the diamond, the court, the gridiron, or the oval.

By this point in his young life Jack Robinson was being watched by the Pasadena police as well. It seems that athletics was not his only team activity. Barely into his teens Jack joined something called the "Pepper Street Gang," an organization that included not just young blacks, but Mexican and Japanese youths as well. Before long, he was the gang's acknowledged leader. Much of its activity was confined to harmless pranks. No doubt some of it was grounded in the members' frustration and anger against the restrictions imposed by segregation. But petty thievery was also on the agenda of the Pepper Street Gang. All of this activity soon made it the target of the police. While no police dragnet ever landed Jack in jail, on more than one occasion he was brought into the station for questioning.

Luckily, someone besides the police had his eye on Jack Robinson. His name was Karl Downs. A new minister in town and not far into his twenties, Downs fancied himself an athlete in his own right. He also suspected that his only chance to hook the Pepper Street Gang on a life beyond petty thievery was to offer organized sports to Robinson and his pals. Not everyone accepted Reverend Downs's overtures, but Jack did. In this regard, young Jack was both lucky and smart.

Together Karl Downs and Mallie Robinson did what they could to steer Jack away from gang activities and away from the tempting, if ultimately troubling, example of another older brother. Mack Robinson was four years Jack's senior. A gifted athlete in his own right, Mack was idolized by his younger brother. But just as Mack's own athletic career was about to blossom, doctors discovered a heart murmur. Their verdict was that he ought to confine himself to non-contact sports. Down, but not defeated, Mack decided to concentrate on track. With talent and hard work, he made the 1936 American Olympic team.

This was the Berlin Olympics of Jesse Owens and his four gold medals. Owens, not Robinson, would be the black American hero of this historic "Nazi" Olympic Games. But Mack Robinson had more than a small part to play in the larger Jesse Owens story. Robinson almost qualified to be a member of the winning 400-meter relay team (for which Owens ran the first leg). He did qualify for the finals of the 200-meter and ultimately finished second to Owens in that race. In fact, Robinson was actually leading Owens in the 200 until he made the fatal mistake of checking on his competition. This brief glance broke the cardinal rule for runners: never look back. To the day he died, Mack Robinson lamented that fleeting look, one which he was convinced had cost him a gold medal.

Initially, Mack Robinson was not able to parlay his silver medal into anything other than a job as a street cleaner in Pasadena. But within the year he accepted an athletic scholarship offered to him by the University of Oregon. His departure left Jack as the lone Robinson on the local athletic stage. It also placed the younger brother in a position to emerge from his older brother's formidable shadow.

The relationship between the two had long been a difficult one. Their story was not simply one in which a younger sibling stood in awe of his older brother. Jack, for his part, *did* idolize Mack. But Mack did not bask in Jack's glorifying gaze. Instead, he deeply envied his younger brother. Difficult as it was to admit, Mack was coming to realize that Jack was the better athlete—and the one whose best athletic days lay ahead of him. At the same time, Mack set a double example for Jack. On the one hand, he badly wanted to outdo his older brother. On the other hand, considering Mack's experiences, Jack could see what brother Mack did not want to: that success on the playing field did not necessarily give a young black man a leg up on, much less a guarantee of, success anywhere else. Nonetheless, for the time being Mack was gone, leaving Jack poised to have his own day in the local athletic sun.

Jack Robinson might have learned a different lesson from his Olympian brother. He might have decided to abandon sports entirely. Instead of persisting with baseball or football, he might have returned to his old gang or opted to turn himself into a serious student. But each of those alternatives was completely out of the question. Jack knew that he was too much of an athlete to be content with the life of a gang leader; he also estimated that he was not a strong enough student to achieve real success in the classroom. Moreover, he could be excused for thinking that concentrating on the books was a dead-end all its own for a young black man in depression-ridden America. Sports it had been, and sports it would be.

In the fall of 1937 Jack enrolled at Pasadena Junior College. Trouble loomed almost immediately. Soon after reporting for football practice he found himself in the middle of an unwanted controversy. Some of the white players, most of them recruits from Oklahoma, made it clear to the coach that they would not play on the same squad with blacks. Robinson was one of three black players on the team. With the coach on their side, none of the trio quit in the face of this threatened boycott and nothing came of it. But something did come of the season. Everyone learned a valuable lesson, and the coach was able to create a truly integrated team. Jack was the starting tailback, but all three black players contributed. And all three became the first members of their race to be elected to the school's student honor society.

Honors aside, Jack's life at college was not without its difficulties and failures. Despite his elusiveness on the gridiron, he could not shake the Pasadena police. Part of the problem was racial. Part of it stemmed from his own penchant for skirting the edge of the law. Another part of it stemmed from his own refusal to take the academic side of college life very seriously. There were simply too many nights on the town and too few nights with the books. Given those priorities, incidents with the police were all too common and good grades all too rare. This pattern began during Jack's last two years at Pasadena Junior College and continued after he transferred to UCLA.

By the spring of 1939 Jack Robinson was one of the most highly recruited football players in the country. He easily could have had his pick of colleges, but he preferred to stay close to home. This was his brother Frank's choice as well. Frank was Jack's most loyal fan, as well as his self-appointed counselor. He was also the least athletic of Mallie Robinson's boys. Perhaps because of his own lack of talent, Frank took a great deal of joy in Jack's athletic success. All that came to an end on May 10, 1939, when Frank Robinson was killed in a motorcycle accident. The death of this older brother devastated Jack, even as it redoubled his resolve to attend nearby UCLA.

This decision kept his family (including Frank's widow and children) in Jack's life, but it also meant that he would keep too many of his old pals and practices as well. There would still be frequent joy rides through the city's streets followed by occasional, and occasionally tense, encounters with the local police. One night's escapades in October 1939 finally landed Jack in jail and almost cost him the rest of his college football career. After exchanging racial slurs with a passing white motorist, Jack and his friends found themselves in a small-scale race riot. When the police arrived to question the participants, Jack was his usual defensive self. Before he could calm down, he was taken to headquarters, where he was booked for blocking a street, suspicion of robbery, *and* resisting arrest.

Despite this blot on his record (and despite many near-misses with the police for ticket scalping), Jack made a good name for himself at UCLA as a star athlete. On the football field—and he was recruited primarily to play football—Jack initially had to be content with the number-two position among UCLA Bruin runners. At the time, UCLA was one of the few major colleges in the country to recruit black players. This meant, among other things, that Jack was far from the lone black on the team. It also meant that he was not even close to being the black star on the team. Those honors went to seniors Kenny Washington and Woody Strode, both of whom helped shatter the NFL color line by playing for the Los Angeles Rams.

Given his stardom at Pasadena, Jack must have had a difficult time adjusting to a lesser role with the Bruins. What made his lot even more difficult was that Washington was both a great running back on the gridiron and an outgoing fellow with a winning smile and easy manner off of it. In short, among the three dozen or so blacks on the UCLA campus, Kenny Washington was the polar opposite of Jackie Robinson. Washington was openly warm and friendly; Robinson was often angry and withdrawn. Still, Jack did play an important role on a Bruin team that went undefeated (but had four ties) during the 1939 season. Used primarily as a decoy by Coach Babe Horrell, Jack still ran for 519 yards during his junior season. What was more impressive was that he reached this total on only 42 carries, meaning that his average gain from scrimmage was better than 11 yards.

In the spring of 1940 Jack joined the baseball team almost as an afterthought. His maiden season on the college diamond was far from spectacular. In ten games he compiled a meager batting average of .097. And the man who would become a defensive standout in the major leagues was not any better in the field as a UCLA Bruin. Not exactly a "no hit, good field" player, Robinson averaged nearly an error a game, no matter which position he played.

In the fall Robinson resumed his stellar football career, even as his team plummeted to the bottom of the conference. The Bruins' 1-9 record may have been abysmal, but it was not a reflection of Jack's contribution on the field. He gained 875 yards of total offense, placing him second in the Pacific Coast Conference in that category. Following the completion of the football season, Jack decided to give basketball a try. While not an immediate star, his success (and better than 11 points per game scoring average) established him as a force within the league and far exceeded his fling with baseball during the previous year. Nonetheless, football was clearly his best sport at this stage of his athletic career.

At both Pasadena Junior College and UCLA Robinson also found time for track and field. The broad jump was his specialty. While at Pasadena, he set the national junior college record in that event. In 1940 Robinson topped that accomplishment by capturing the NCAA crown. The list went on. As a UCLA student, he won golf and swimming titles, and not at the intramural level, but in Pacific Coast League conference meets. He even managed to add tennis to his athletic success stories by advancing to the semifinals of a national tournament for black players. It is no wonder that Jackie Robinson was being called the "Black Jim Thorpe," specifically by sportswriters and within the white sporting establishment generally. If Native American Jim Thorpe was the country's first minority multisport sensation, Jackie Robinson was coming to be seen as his logical successor. Early in the century, Thorpe had excelled at football, baseball, and track (which included multi–gold medal success at the 1912 Olympic Games). As of the early 1940s, Robinson had not yet come close to equaling Thorpe's exploits, but he seemed to be well on his way to doing just that.

All of this threatened to come to a sudden end in the spring of 1941. For young men everywhere, even in that land of perpetual springtime known as California, spring has a way of turning hearts and heads to thoughts of love and baseball. In the case of Californian Jackie Robinson it turned out to be a matter of love *or* baseball. Just as his UCLA Bruin teammates began to contemplate their spring season, Jack's heart led him to fall in love and his head told him to drop out of school. Gone for the moment was his immediate opportunity to redeem himself on the collegiate baseball diamond. In point of fact, as it turned out, gone for good in the young life of Jackie Robinson was college sport, college life, and the immediate possibility that he would earn a college degree.

If it is true that opposites attract, Rachel Isum and Jack Robinson were the perfect match. She was the straight "A" student that he never desired to be. She followed the straight and narrow path that he could not always find. She was as consistently reserved and unassuming as he was alternately cocky and sullen. Finally, she was the product of a middle-class upbringing that included both a mother *and* a father.

And Charles Isum had no desire to be the father that Jackie Robinson never had. For that matter, he was not at all anxious to become Robinson's father-in-law. A second-generation black Californian, Isum was a retired military man who had established himself in a second career as a bookbinder for the Los Angeles *Times*. By the time Jack and Rachel had begun to date, Isum was largely housebound, owing to a serious heart condition. Like Chandler Moulton, Charles Isum was not about to stand idly by while his daughter was swept off her feet by a ballplayer. Unlike Jane Moulton, Rachel Isum was not inclined to let anyone lead her where she did not wish to go. For that matter, Jack Robinson, unlike young Branch Rickey, had his guard up when it came to members of the opposite sex in general. Most of the women he had dated were white, and most of them had wanted just one thing from the Bruin star. Rachel was not at all like that. As Jack came to see this about her, he was better able to relax around her. Before long, he was more than relaxed; he was deeply in love. The feeling was mutual. If Rachel had initially been put off by a public persona that exuded cockiness, she was eventually won over by a combination of Robinson's respect for and devotion to her. Her father was not. In fact, there was nothing about Jack Robinson that remotely impressed Charles Isum.

The problem was not only that Jack was a ballplayer, and a nonstudious one at that. No, to Charles Isum there were more basic problems. His daughter's suitor was both too black and too far down the social scale. What made this even worse was that Jack fully realized why Mr. Isum objected to him. He could, of course, do nothing about the shade of his skin, save lament the fact that degrees of blackness not only constituted divisions within his racial world, but established hierarchies there as well. At the same time, he might have stayed on track for the day when he would begin to climb the economic ladder had he been convinced that obtaining a college degree would make any real difference. (Here was yet another disparity between Charles Isum's daughter and Mallie Robinson's son.) In sum, Rachel Isum and Jack Robinson had grown up in two different worlds. He came from the proverbial "wrong side of the tracks" and both of them knew it, thanks at least in part to Charles Isum's constant reminders.

Still, Jack might have tried to overcome his prospective father-in-law's objections by at least continuing to work toward that elusive college degree, but in the early spring of 1941 he decided to quit the university entirely. Ostensibly his reasons were entirely financial, but in truth he had not been terribly interested in his studies at any point. Hence his decision to liberate himself from the books that he was ignoring anyway. At the same time, however, Robinson was also cutting himself off from sports, especially a second Bruin baseball season. A worried Rachel tried to convince him to stay in school, both to obtain a degree and to continue his athletic career. Mallie Robinson and Karl Downs chimed in with similar advice. Charles Isum simply kept quiet, hoping all the while for what he thought was best, namely an end to his daughter's relationship with a young man who had no real future.

In the end, only Rachel seemed to understand Jack's reasoning. She had thought that a degree in physical education would open the way for him to land a job as a coach or possibly as a youth worker. Either career path might be enough to win the approval of her father for their marriage. But Jack could not be persuaded. Besides, what he had already seen of life in general convinced him that a black man had little chance at any kind of a professional life. Rachel did not want to believe him. After all, she was not just training to be a nurse, but fully expected to earn her living as one. Nonetheless, at some level she understood why he thought the way he did, even if she could not condone his decision to drop out of college.

But Jack was not dropping out of life. Instead of staying in school and playing baseball for the UCLA Bruins, in the spring of 1941 he signed on with a National Youth Administration (NYA) camp located halfway between Los Angeles and San Francisco. A New Deal creation, the NYA was designed to provide temporary employment for young people, especially college students or those who had abandoned college for whatever reason. Run nationally by a southern liberal named Aubrey Williams, the NYA was committed to serving as a model for an integrated America. Young Jack Robinson was associated with this New Deal organization long enough to get a glimpse of Aubrey Williams's ideal world. He had a number of duties, but his primary assignment was to play shortstop for the camp team. On the field Jack was more teacher than student. Everywhere else, he quickly discovered, he had much to learn. Not only was Jack Robinson a novice NYAer, but for the first time in his life he was living away from home.

This learning experience was brief, because the camp closed not long after his arrival. Like many New Deal programs, the NYA was a victim of the Roosevelt administration's mounting effort to mobilize the country for war against Nazi Germany. The Japanese attack on Pearl Harbor was still a few months away, but "Dr.

Win-the-War" (as FDR would come to call himself) was already beginning to shoulder aside the Roosevelt who portrayed himself as "Dr. New Deal."

Out of a job and out of the public eye, the athlete who continued to be called the "Black Jim Thorpe" continued to command attention in sports circles. In August he was invited to play in the College All-Star football game against the NFL champion Chicago Bears. Barnstorming with a semi-pro team called the Los Angeles Bulldogs had not prevented him from signing on with other ex-collegians to take on this professional team. And little could get in the way of better than 20,000 blacks who paid their way into Soldier Field in Chicago to watch their hero play. Jack did not disappoint any of the 98,500 fans who watched this late summer football spectacle. Although the Bears won the game by a final score of 37-13, early in the fourth quarter Jack helped make the contest close by catching a sideline pass and racing into the end zone to make the score 16-12. According to the Chicago *Tribune,* this play was "easily the most thrilling of a thrilling game." It might also have been a much closer game. The Bears did, of course, score three more touchdowns to ice the victory, but twice Jackie threatened to break away for a long touchdown run. In the eyes of the *Tribune* reporter on the scene, Robinson was "as fleet a halfback as ever sped over stadium turf."

A month later Jackie Robinson managed to double Branch Rickey's initial pay-for-play football career by accepting $100 a game to play halfback for a makeshift professional team called the Honolulu Bears. The squad was far removed from the National Football League, both in terms of talent and geography, but the money was decent and the location desirable.

Jack spent the entire fall of 1941 in Hawaii before finally hopping a steamship for the return trip to the mainland. The date was December 5, 1941. Two days later Jack was in the middle of an intense poker game when the captain called all passengers on deck to announce that the Japanese had bombed Pearl Harbor.

Jack had already escaped the military draft once. In the fall of 1940 Congress passed legislation creating the first peacetime conscription in American history. At that moment the twenty-one-year-old Robinson was a prime target of the new "selective service." For a time he was able to take advantage of the system's selectivity by obtaining a deferment on the basis of his family's economic needs. With the country now at war, however, that status was likely to change.

In the spring of 1942 Jack received his draft notice while playing semi-pro basketball for an outfit called the Los Angeles Red Devils. This "greeting" from Uncle Sam was not a welcome one. Jack's desire to stay close to Rachel was much stronger than any patriotic urge to join the fight against fascism. Initially, he did not think he would have a difficult time remaining a civilian. After all, his mother was still counting on at least some of the money he was earning on the basketball court. And if that wasn't enough to convince the local draft board, Robinson thought that he might be able to obtain an exemption for physical reasons. Any multisport athlete had to have sustained an injury or two of some seriousness. In Jack's case he could point to bone chips floating around in an ankle that he had broken a few years earlier.

Jack floated both excuses past Rachel only to have her reject each of them. He was stunned and hurt. Formal engagement or no, this was the girl he was hoping to marry—Charles Isum's continuing objections notwithstanding. But now Rachel Isum suddenly had objections of her own. More than that, she was willing to risk Jack's wrath by voicing them. As a young black American, he may have had reservations about fighting in any war—especially one against other people of color across the Pacific or in Europe against racist Germans on behalf of a country that continued to treat him and his race as second-class citizens. As a budding athlete, he may have sustained his share of debilitating injuries. As a dutiful son, he may have had good reason to be concerned about his mother's finances. But nothing, Rachel reminded him, should get in the way of his doing his patriotic duty. In stating her case, she may also have been thinking about something other than patriotism—especially if her future husband was to have a future as a professional athlete. Imagine the "blow up," she warned, if a "big strong halfback" tried to wriggle his way out of the draft.

It's hard to say whether or not the man who would become *the* Jackie Robinson was thinking about his athletic future—and especially how he would be perceived by the American public—as he listened to what Rachel had to say. What is beyond dispute is his immediate disappointment at her response. Didn't she realize that a stint in the army meant time away from her and certain postponement of any marriage ceremony? Yes, she did. But didn't he understand that more pressing duties to his country ought to take precedence over their marriage?

In the end, Jack decided to follow Rachel's advice. Having been patient for quite a while as it was, he concluded that he could wait a while longer. Little did he know at the time how much longer that wait would be—or how important this decision was. Not only did it improve his standing in Rachel's eyes, as well as in those of her father, but his military service would one day have an impact on someone he had not yet met.

As of the winter of 1942, Branch Rickey and Jackie Robinson were operating in very different worlds. As of that winter, it is possible, even probable, that each man knew who the other was. What was then highly improbable was that either could have imagined their eventual meeting, much less the circumstances surrounding it. Nonetheless, Jackie's decision to fight for his country would one day constitute one more reason for Mr. Rickey to think that he, Jackie Robinson, would be the best possible candidate to break major league baseball's color line.

The Third Inning

By 1942 Branch Rickey had grown increasingly impatient with his situation in St. Louis. For a quarter of a century he had been the mastermind behind the unlikely success of the Cardinals. Patience had been key to that success, patience along with Rickey's shrewdness when it came to adding or subtracting baseball players from his Cardinal roster. "Addition by subtraction" was a favorite Rickey expression, and one which he employed whenever he thought he had improved his team by eliminating a player or players via the trade route. But patience was no longer something that he possessed—that is when it came to thinking about his own future with the Cardinals. By all outward appearances that future seemed very secure. His '42 Cardinals had just won 106 games and the National League pennant, en route to defeating the New York Yankees four games to one in the World Series. But Branch Rickey was not a happy man in 1942. The source of much of that unhappiness was Cardinal owner Sam Breadon. Impatient by nature, Breadon was no longer willing to permit Rickey to run the team the way he saw fit. Nor did he want Rickey to receive the lion's share of the credit for the Cardinals' on-field success. His impatience fed Rickey's impatience. It was time for a change.

In truth, Rickey's thoughts about making a change had been brewing for quite a while. Twenty-five years is a long time to be in one place in any profession, let alone a profession as volatile as major league baseball. That Branch Rickey stayed in one place as long as he did was even more amazing given the increasing volatility of his relationship with this boss.

An easterner who had followed the Horace Greeley maxim and headed west, Sam Breadon was a New Yorker who had found a home and made a fortune in St. Louis. The source of his wealth was a booming automobile business. But with that wealth came a sense of restlessness. Having made a great deal of money, this millionaire was on the lookout for new challenges. As a self-proclaimed self-made man, Breadon was the sort of fellow whom Branch Rickey at once admired and sought to manipulate. Rickey did not automatically regard such men as intruders on his baseball turf, but he did expect them to defer to his expertise. Having been willing to give them their due for making their mark in the business world, Rickey thought it only fitting to expect no less in return when they stepped into his world of baseball. At the very least they ought to understand that baseball was a unique business, one with rules all its own, and one well suited to his specific talents, especially his eye for scouting potential major league players.

Sam Breadon fully entered Branch Rickey's baseball world in 1919 by acquiring nearly three-quarters of the team's stock. Suddenly, the Cardinals had a single dominant owner and a new team president. Officially, Rickey was slotted to be a vice president. But real questions remained. For starters, who would actually run the baseball operation? Here Breadon was a complete novice. As the season began to unfold, the new Cardinal owner seemed to be signaling that he would be the sort of novice who was anxious to learn and willing to defer. At this point, Branch Rickey was equally anxious to be his teacher—and quite receptive to the idea of being the object of Breadon's deference. But not everything was as simple or straightforward as it appeared. Despite his love affair with baseball, Sam Breadon soon made it clear that he was not anxious to spend his money on either baseball talent or on front-office executives. Hence his decision to assign Rickey dual roles as vice president and field manager. Rickey's preference at this point in his career would have been to concentrate fully on the larger job of running an entire baseball operation, rather than managing the team. But for the time being he would at least try to make the best of what seemed to him a less than perfect situation.

Thus began the rocky history of the Sam Breadon–Branch Rickey partnership. At the time, neither would have guessed that it would last as long as it did. From Rickey's standpoint, things began to improve as soon as he realized that Breadon genuinely admired his baseball knowledge. Sam Breadon may have forever resented Branch Rickey's formal education, but he gradually came to respect Rickey's thorough grasp of the game. Perhaps, surmised Breadon, that grasp was so firm that Rickey could actually build a good team on a low budget. Little did Sam Breadon realize just how accurate his hunch would turn out to be.

Though not an educated man, Sam Breadon was both smart and shrewd. He knew his limitations, and he had enough self-confidence not to be threatened by the skills and intelligence of those around—or under—him. When it came to the game that both he and Rickey loved, the Cardinal owner gradually decided that his role should amount to getting out of his V. P.'s way. Only on the issue of hiring and firing his managers would Breadon consistently intervene. That meant that for the foreseeable future his vice president could also be found managing the team from the Cardinal dugout.

The problem was that as the 1920s began Vice President Rickey thought of himself as a greater innovator than Manager Rickey. Perhaps he was even beginning to regard himself as a baseball revolutionary. If truth be told, Branch Rickey had never been exactly shy about attaching the visionary label to himself. Suddenly in 1921 a new opportunity to demonstrate his inventiveness almost literally dropped into his lap. In that year the two major leagues signed a new National Agreement that permitted both American and National league teams to own minor league clubs directly. The agreement did not cover all of minor league baseball, since five leagues chose to opt out of the new pact. Nonetheless, this was all Rickey needed to put in place a system that would eventually enable the Cardinals to compete against wealthier teams, most prominently the then dominant New York Giants. Thus began the St. Louis Cardinal farm system, a system that its many critics would soon be derisively calling "chain store baseball."

Though Rickey had long prided himself on having a thick skin, he was actually highly sensitive to criticism. And much criticism came his way for his decision to resort to "chain store baseball." But he would not be deterred. His Cardinals could not compete against clubs that either had more money to spend or were owned by men who were willing to spend more money than Breadon. Therefore, his Cardinals needed to develop their own players. Rickey estimated that this could be done without making a huge initial investment. A little money up front, he surmised, could mean a lot of victories—and a lot of money—down the line.

Rickey's basic idea was to create and own a series of minor league teams. At this point in baseball history minor league owners were essentially independent agents. They signed and developed ballplayers whom they eventually sold to the major leagues. Rickey wanted to eliminate this middle man by building a vast network of teams owned and operated by the St. Louis Cardinals. Each team would be stocked with players signed by Cardinal management, developed by Cardinal coaches, and trained according to the Cardinal system.

Was this a stroke of genius? Not according to Branch Rickey. Was it the mark of a revolutionary? Perhaps. "It was a case of necessity being the mother of invention," according to the not-always-modest inventor of baseball's farm system.

By the end of the 1920s the Cardinals owned seven minor league teams, ran dozens of baseball camps across the country, and controlled over 200 minor league players. A decade later the number of farm clubs reached thirty-two and the number of players under contract approached 1,000. Over the course of the twenty years between 1922 and 1942, it is estimated that the once bankrupt St. Louis Cardinal organization made more than $2 million on player sales alone. Most of that money was added to the Cardinals' profit ledger. But approximately 20 percent of it went directly into the pocket of Branch Rickey.

Both the system and the money soon attracted the attention of the first commissioner of baseball, Judge Kenesaw Mountain Landis. Hired by the owners to refurbish the image of the sport following the Black Sox scandal, Landis had been a federal judge with a reputation for being more than slightly judgmental. Appointed to the federal bench by President Theodore Roosevelt, Landis could be a judicial loose cannon. According to none other than President Roosevelt himself, Landis had the "face of a fanatic—honest, fearless, well-meaning, but tense to a degree that makes me apprehensive." He had a way of making others apprehensive as well. This was especially the case for John D. Rockefeller, for prior to his 1921 appointment as baseball commissioner Landis was best known for presiding over the successful antitrust prosecution of Rockefeller's Standard Oil Company. During World War I, Landis also gained a measure of notoriety for being a "hanging judge" during the treason trials of antidraft protesters. Whatever the case he was hearing, the stern-faced Landis, with his impressively shaggy mane of snow white hair, looked the part of the judge. And he played the part to the hilt. As one sportswriter put it, Kenesaw Mountain Landis owed his success to being an "actor who had the presence of mind never to go on stage."

Whether playing the role of judge or commissioner, Landis was a man of genuine hates. He hated big business pirates and antiwar radicals for what he thought they had tried to do to his country. He hated gamblers and crooked ballplayers for what he was convinced they had already done to his game. Though a powerful man himself, he was also very capable of hating the powerful—especially those who thought that they were powerful enough to corrupt baseball.

When it came to levels of power, Branch Rickey was not in the same league as John D. Rockefeller. But Landis was not always able to choose his enemies. Sometimes they were simply handed to him. There were also times when the commissioner allowed himself to be governed by his patriarchal urges. And sometimes those urges had a way of running up against would-be enemies. After all, if there weren't lowly people in need of his protection, there were always powerful people who deserved to be brought lower. While it was unlikely that Landis ever wanted to be caught consorting with those he considered beneath him, he did not mind being cast as their representative or stepping up to fight the battles that they could not fight on their own. And in the commissioner's battles with Branch Rickey, the lowly and oppressed fell into two categories: ballplayers who were trapped in the Cardinal farm system and local owners of minor league teams who had lost both their independence and a major source of revenue with the introduction of the major league farm system.

Landis liked to talk at length about the virtues of the "free market in players," although his commitment to player freedom did not extend to ridding baseball of the restrictive reserve system. While he liked to pretend that he was an impartial arbiter, he never forgot that it was the owners who paid his salary. Hence his silence on the subject of the reserve system, a system that inevitably ensured one-sided salary negotiations between owners and players. But the extensive Cardinal farm system was a case apart. After all, differences in degree can amount to differences in kind. More to the point, Rickey's "chain store" operation presented Landis with an opportunity to revive his reputation for independence and fairness. Besides, the commissioner didn't much care for Rickey. "That hypocritical preacher" or "that Protestant bastard [who's] always masquerading with a minister's robe" was Landis at his most generous on the subject of Branch Rickey.

Perhaps the two men were simply too much alike. After all, neither was above striking a pose when it served his purpose, especially when that purpose involved claiming the moral high ground. Perhaps it was Rickey's reputation for rectitude that rankled Landis. After all, the judge commissioner had long thought that he possessed exclusive rights to that elevated territory. Or perhaps it was Rickey's tendency toward sanctimony that ate away at the equally sanctimonious Landis. Then again, it might have been this: Kenesaw Mountain Landis had often been accused of hypocrisy, but he was convinced that Branch Rickey was the genuine article. How else to label a good, Christian prohibitionist, who was determined to keep his Cardinal ballplayers forever chained to his Cardinal farm teams?

Landis was not one to engage in much self-evaluation. He would never have seen himself as sanctimonious, much less as hypocritical. But he certainly thought he could spot such traits in others. For his part, Rickey fought his war with the commissioner by keeping as silent as possible and going about business as usual. Until mid-season 1925, that business included managing the Cardinals. He was a mediocre manager at best. Over six full seasons from 1919 through 1924, Rickey's Cardinals had never finished higher than third place. Part of the problem was Sam Breadon's shallow pockets. Another part of the problem was Branch Rickey's declining commitment to this phase of the game. He hadn't wanted the job of manager when Breadon handed it to him in the first place. And he didn't seem to generate a great deal of enthusiasm for it over the course of a half dozen campaigns.

Outwardly, Manager Rickey conducted himself as he always had. He continued to wear street clothes while managing. He could even concoct another innovation now and again. Never a fisherman, he nonetheless had an idea that employed fishing cord. To two upright posts over home plate, he attached two horizontal cords thirty-six inches apart and two vertical cords seventeen inches apart. He then instructed his pitchers not just to throw the ball through this makeshift contraption, but to hit the cords as often as possible. As Rickey put it, "Anybody can put a ball through the rectangle, but when you've hit the strings, you've caught the edge of the plate." Rickey not only demanded accuracy from his pitchers, but he continued to demand punctuality from all of his players, whether it was time to hear a Rickey lecture or time to play a major league game. The manager might have been willing to surrender his post, especially if the decision was his alone to make. But as long as he was the manager, he would not surrender any opportunity to lecture his players, complete with chalk and cigar in hand. And in those lectures, he persisted in emphasizing the fundamentals of the game and the necessity of living a fundamentally clean, Christian life. Finally, he let it be known that he preferred to hold on to his managerial job until he alone had decided that he had had enough.

The Rickey regimen did not sit well with all of his players. Especially not with his hitting star, second baseman Rogers Hornsby. Despite cultivating good habits to protect his batting eye (including a personal ban on watching movies), Hornsby had developed more than a few bad habits that rankled Rickey. He would show up late for practices, lectures, and occasionally even for games. Despite their differences, Rickey and Hornsby found themselves thrust into the uncomfortable role of allies early in the 1925 season. It was late May and the Cardinals were mired in last place with a record of 13-25. Sam Breadon had finally decided to change managers. The "Sunday school teacher" wasn't going to run his team any longer. His idea of a replacement was the twenty-nine-year-old Hornsby (who was anything but a Sunday school teacher). The only hitch in this plan was that Breadon's second baseman didn't want an additional job.

Rickey learned of Breadon's scheme from an agitated Hornsby. When his star player broke the news to him, Rickey's first thought was that the second baseman might be able to talk Breadon into changing his mind. At least that was Rickey's hope, as he dispatched Hornsby off to a meeting with the Cardinal owner. But Breadon was unmoved. Hornsby was in and Rickey was out.

Given his preference for front-office work, it's surprising that Rickey didn't simply agree to relinquish the manager's post. But no one ever likes to be fired—especially not when one is convinced that he is on the verge of success. Finally, there was the matter of *how* Rickey had been dismissed. In his own carefully chosen words, the treatment that he as the Cardinal manager had received from the Cardinal owner was both "brutal" and "callous."

It was a smoldering, even resentful, Branch Rickey who chose to remain with the Cardinals after Hornsby had replaced him as field manager. To be fired was an insult. But it also proved to be an adventure. And by agreeing to stay on as strictly a vice president, he left the door open to more adventures, even if one such endeavor depended more on patience than on derring-do.

In 1926 the Cardinals won not just their first National League pennant, but the first Cardinal title of any sort since the team took home the American Association crown in 1888. Branch Rickey could take most of the credit, because it was players from his farm system who were primarily responsible for the Cardinal victory.

But he couldn't take all of the credit for winning the World Series from the New York Yankees. The 1926 series was both marvelous and suspenseful. Both teams were on the rise. Each team had a great star, Hornsby for the Cards and Babe Ruth for the Yanks. Therefore, it was only fitting that the contest went the full seven games.

The deciding seventh game was played in Yankee Stadium. With the Cardinals leading 3-2 in the bottom of the seventh, the Yanks loaded the bases with two outs. Hornsby could see that his starter was exhausted, but he wasn't sure that he had anyone in the bullpen who could do any better. After considerable hesitation and not just second but third guesses, he sent to the mound a forty-year-old pitcher who the day before had gone the full nine innings to win and square the series at three games apiece. That ancient pitcher was the great Grover Cleveland Alexander, who had joined the Cardinals in mid-season. By the time he put on a Cardinal uniform, Alexander had already won 315 major league games over the course of sixteen seasons. If Rickey the baseball purist had to be impressed with Alexander's record, Rickey the Anti-Saloon League puritan was not. For along the way to his eventual appointment with the Hall of Fame, the marvelous pitcher had also become a serious alcoholic. Unknown to Rickey, Breadon and Hornsby had approached the Chicago Cubs about buying Alexander for the stretch run to the 1926 pennant. Fully aware of his drinking problem and convinced that he was washed up, the Cubs happily sold Alexander to the Cardinals for $4,000. The ever "dry" Rickey was not pleased when his boss and his replacement informed him that they had added the often "wet" Alexander to the Cardinal roster. Rickey remained displeased during what was left of the 1926 season. But on a drizzly fall afternoon in St. Louis, as he huddled near a radio to listen to the last game of the World Series, he was about to change his mind.

In the seventh inning of that seventh game, Branch Rickey was in an understandably agitated state. Leading by a run, his Cardinals were on the verge of winning their first World Series ever. The Yanks, however, were not quite finished, having loaded the bases with two outs. But what could Rickey do? No longer in the dugout, the former manager's agitated state was exacerbated by the knowledge that the situation was completely out of his hands. At the very least the Cardinal vice president might have accompanied the team to New York. Instead, Rickey chose to remain in St. Louis, where all he could do was listen to the game at a neighbor's house—his own radio having picked a lousy time to go dead.

Alexander had not only pitched a complete game the day before, he had also put in a full evening of celebrating. Rickey could not have known this, but he still had every reason to be concerned. So did Hornsby. Instead of waiting on the mound for his relief pitcher, the Cardinal manager walked toward the bullpen to meet Alexander. "I wanted to find out if he could see," Hornsby later told Rickey. The manager also wanted to make sure that Alexander's hip pocket did not contain a flask of liquor. His reconnaissance mission completed, Hornsby returned to the dugout to await the result of his move.

At the plate was rookie second baseman Tony Lazzeri, whose season RBI total of 114 had been topped only by Babe Ruth's 155 among Yankee hitters. Lazzeri and Alexander could readily see what adding to that total would immediately accomplish. Whether Alexander could actually *see* Lazzeri is somewhat less apparent. What is certain is that Lazzeri had trouble seeing what Alexander was throwing. He went down in three pitches. Even more amazing, Alexander handled the Yankees with ease in the eighth and ninth innings. The pitcher whom Rickey had not procured and did not want had just delivered the Cardinals the world championship of professional baseball.

But success did not bring peace and harmony to the Breadon-Hornsby relationship. By November they were arguing over Breadon's refusal to pay Hornsby what the player-manager thought he was worth. Within the month, the owner was ready to trade his star to the New York Giants for their second baseman, Frankie Frisch. Rickey tried to talk Breadon out of making the deal but failed. On Breadon's orders, Rickey reluctantly dispatched Hornsby to the Giants. Cardinal fans and St. Louis baseball writers were uniformly livid. Rickey thought their anger was justified. "Had I been in sole charge," he ruefully recalled years later, "Hornsby never would have left St. Louis. Depriving the Cardinals of a known quantity of greatness in batting and competitive spirit wasn't right." The reason for the deal, Rickey conceded, was the ongoing feud between Breadon and Hornsby, and a "personal affront is never enough to justify a move of such magnitude."

But the move was made, and it was Rickey who took the heat for making it. In the end he had little choice other than to play the part of Breadon's designated fall guy. And Breadon himself? For the time being, he was nowhere to be found. This retreat was probably unnecessary, because Cardinal fans always tended to forgive the plain-spoken Breadon more readily than they reconciled with his congenitally evasive general manager. It wasn't that Branch Rickey deliberately lied to the fans or the press. He took justifiable pride in his integrity. It's just that he liked to make what he thought was an important distinction between integrity and "mere honesty." To him, integrity dictated a "refusal to cut corners . . . or avoid responsibility." In the case of the Hornsby trade, Rickey's definition of integrity meant that he was willing to take full responsibility for the deal even when it did not belong on his shoulders.

Rickey's real problem with fans and writers was that he was never one of the boys. He was forever the resident intellectual in a game dominated by men who distrusted and derided intellectuals. To them, baseball was simply a game. As such, it was supposed to be fun and not to be overanalyzed. Rickey, of course, had plenty of what he regarded as fun. He loved being the mastermind of his team's fortunes. To him, baseball was a game of chess, whether it was being played on or off the diamond. On it, pieces were to be moved around or removed from it. Away from it, pieces were moved to and from the Cardinal roster and throughout the sprawling Cardinal farm system. This was all serious business and great fun to Branch Rickey. (Well, almost all of it, given the occasional blockbuster deal that was consummated without his seal of approval.) But fencing with the press was never his idea of fun. Nor was defending himself against criticism, whatever the source.

As Branch Rickey began to settle into middle age, he was not above thinking that he was above it all. If his integrity was beyond reproach, so was his sense of loyalty. And if his loyalty was unimpeachable, so were his decisions. The idea that he, Branch Rickey, had to defend those decisions before lesser mortals held very little appeal for him. Of course, the public relations game was also a part of the baseball game. It might even be thought of as a game within the game. But it was a game that Rickey played with less and less relish, less and less verve, and less and less success.

He was an expert in a game filled with self-styled experts. What fan didn't have an opinion on this or that trade? What sportswriter lacked for words when it came to Rickey's latest controversial maneuver? Each one of those writers would have loved being able to move ballplayers at will. But they also loved to talk about these moves—and write about them—and drink while they were doing both.

Branch Rickey still didn't drink. But he did like to open his mouth. And when he did he invariably talked down to both fans and writers. Getting rid of a ballplayer who was not performing up to the Rickey standard was his "addition by subtraction" realized. Being forced to fashion a team without a star player (such as Hornsby), was "quantitative quality." And if Rickey wasn't tossing out multisyllabic one-liners he was thumbing through his copy of *Bartlett's Quotations* in search of instant erudition. As a result, whatever he said—or did—was somehow condescending to those who watched or covered his Cardinals.

But he did remain with the Cardinals—despite the ire of Cardinal rooters and writers, despite Breadon's penchant for hiring and firing managers, and despite grousing from players over the lowly state of their salaries. There was fun to be had, even if nothing could quite equal the fun and success of 1926. The Cards won the pennant again in 1928 and 1930, only to lose both World Series. They even won it all a second time in 1931 by defeating the Philadelphia Athletics in another tense seven-game match. But not until 1934 did Branch Rickey and the Cardinals recapture the fun of 1926. This was the "Gas House Gang" Cardinals, the Cardinals of Jerome "Dizzy" Dean, Joe "Ducky" Medwick, Leo "the Lip"

Durocher, Frankie "the Fordham Flash" Frisch, and Johnny Leonard Roosevelt "Pepper" Martin, who also answered to the "Wild Hoss of the Osage."

To Rickey, Dean was "Jerome," Medwick was "Joseph," and Martin was "John Leonard." Wesley Branch Rickey preferred to call all of his players by their Christian names, and never by their nicknames. This was not false piety or phony formality on Rickey's part. This was just Branch Rickey being Branch Rickey. Whatever he called them individually, collectively "they were the best team I ever had." He didn't stop there: "The 1934 'Gas House Gang' was a high class team, with nine heavy drinkers who were paid more money over a period of ten years than any other club in the National League." If the old Anti-Saloon Leaguer could not resist a jibe at his imbibing players, he also could not resist a brief reference to the not so small matter of money. If Breadon was the official "penny-pincher," Rickey never quite managed to dodge the label either, his occasional reminders of Cardinal generosity notwithstanding.

And as much as he sometimes might have wished to do so, Rickey couldn't dodge the "Gas House Gang" either. They were his creation. He had initially scouted and signed most of them. He had devoted his considerable energies to developing them as ballplayers and as men. By 1934 he had helped mold this group of Cardinals into a unit on the field, even as he convinced himself that he had finally learned to tolerate their excesses away from it. In the end, the "Gas House Gang" was more than just a baseball team; it was a show, and Branch Rickey was the impresario. The irony is inescapable. The teetotaling Rickey had put together a team of serious drinkers before settling back to take pride in his creation. It was as though a silent deal had been struck between Rickey and his "gang." If he would conveniently forget that they liked to play games other than baseball, they would not forget how to play the game that mattered most to him.

But they did press him to his limits, no one more so than his star pitcher, Jay Hanna Dean. "Dizzy" Dean could never make up his mind whether his parents had named him Jay Hanna or Jerome

Herman. In any case, Rickey preferred "Jerome." So Jerome it was. And whatever his name, no player was more crucial to the success of the Cardinals in 1934 than this flamboyant young fireballer from Lucas, Arkansas. Or was it Bond, Mississippi? Dean was never exactly sure of his birthplace either. What he did know for certain was what to do with a baseball when it was his turn to pitch. In 1934 Dean won thirty games for the first and only time in his all too brief career. He also won the two games he started in the seven-game World Series against the Detroit Tigers. In fact, a pitcher named Dean won all four games for the Cardinals in the 1934 World Series. Jerome's brother Paul "Daffy" Dean won the other two (as well as nineteen during the regular season).

But all the while Dizzy Dean wore a Cardinal uniform he tested Rickey's legendary patience to the limit. Dean liked to spend money that he didn't have and expected the Cardinal front office to make good on his debts. He liked to pretend that he had ailments; therefore he liked to be "coaxed" into taking his next regular turn on the mound. Finally, he liked to puncture Cardinal protocol by calling Rickey "Branch" whenever he entered the vice president's office. Once comfortably settled, Dean would invariably lean back, stretch out his legs, and plunk his oversized feet on Rickey's oversized desk.

"Judas Priest," Rickey would shout to no one in particular after a Dean exit or Dean escapade. "If there were more like him in baseball, as God is my witness, I'd get out of the game." Here was someone who was proud to be a "Doctor of Jurisprudence" someone who held an honorary "Doctor of Law." How, he wondered, did he ever land in a profession that now and again required him to spend "four mortal hours conversing with a person named Dizzy Dean?" The answer, of course, had everything to do with something that Rickey and Dean both loved to do: win baseball games.

Jerome Herman Dean was in full command of two qualities that Wesley Branch Rickey knew were vital to greatness. He also had the good sense to know that those qualities could never be taught. Dean, the pitcher, was a born competitor and a natural showman. Rickey, the impresario, was now twice removed from the game itself, but he still had a role to play in Dean's success, even if he was less a professional teacher than an amateur psychologist. There were occasions when Rickey, the cajoler, had to appeal to his star pitcher's sense of showmanship in order to draw out Dean, the competitor. On the day of a critical 1934 game against the Pirates, Dean complained to Rickey that his arm was sore. This was not unusual. In fact, Rickey once reminisced that he never saw Dean "feeling right on a day he was supposed to pitch." On this day the mayor was scheduled to be in attendance. Or at least this is what Rickey told Dean. More than that, he went on to inform his star pitcher, aching arm and all, that "hizzonner" was coming specifically to see the great Dizzy Dean pitch. Well, in that case Dean agreed to give it a try, if only "for your sake, Mr. Rickey."

The cajoler wasn't quite finished. Just warm up, he advised. "If you only pitch one ball in the game and then retire, that'll leave me all right with the mayor." Dean went slightly longer than that. He hurled a three-hit, complete game shutout, striking out a dozen Pirates along the way.

Dean was more than a natural. He was a learner as well. Rickey ranked him with Giant great Christy Mathewson when it came to adding pitches to his repertoire. By exercising their powers of observation, both acquired screwballs and knuckleballs, which, marveled Rickey, they proceeded to unleash with "all kinds of speeds and deflections." And, a team with such a pitcher was a team with a "new pitcher, someone you didn't even see before."

As long as Dizzy Dean was a dominant pitcher, new or old, Branch Rickey found a way to get along with him. The year after the glorious 1934 championship season Dean went 28-12. In 1936 he dipped ever so slightly to 24-13. In retrospect, Rickey thought that he should have traded Dean right then. Rickey had long prided himself on knowing just when a player was beginning the downside of his career—or what he referred to as the "twilight zone of stardom." One of his most critical jobs was to "know ahead of time who is failing," to seize the right moment for taking the right risk. When he judged that that moment had arrived, Rickey's next task was to figure out how his team could get along *without* that player— and how to obtain maximum value for him. In Dean's case, Rickey was off by a year. The Cardinal pitcher took a line drive off the foot during the 1937 All-Star game. He tried to come back too soon and failed, finishing the season at a mediocre 13-10. By the next spring Rickey had dealt Dean to the Cubs for two players and $185,000. Dean would never regain his past greatness. After winning 134 games for the Cardinal between 1930 and 1937, he would win only sixteen for the Cubs over the course of his final three major league campaigns.

To Rickey, cash was the critical element in the Dean deal. At the onset of the 1930s the Great Depression had hit the country hard, and even as late as 1939 there were only fleeting signs that it was releasing its grip. St. Louis was not exempt from any of this bad economic news. In fact, as the depression decade ground on, the Cardinals found themselves heading into serious financial difficulty. What made things even more precarious in St. Louis was that Rickey's current team (the Cardinals) had to compete with Rickey's old team (the Browns) for fans. Two major league teams was one team too many in a small city like St. Louis.

Early in the depression years Cardinal annual attendance peaked at just over 600,000. By 1934 not even the colorful "Gas House Gang" and a triumphant season could draw people to Sportsman's Park. Total attendance for the year stood at the astoundingly low figure of 335,000.

Despite plummeting attendance—and despite Breadon's public threats to move the team—the Cardinals did continue to make a small profit. The answer to this paradox was Rickey's practice of selling ballplayers. The Dean sale was perhaps the most famous, but it was far from unique. The list of players sold was long and steady, but there was never a "fire sale" mentality to what Rickey was doing. Instead there was a design and a pattern. He was never in the business of summarily ripping apart a team that he had carefully stitched together. Nor was he simply in the business of putting together a winning, which is to say a profitable, team. Instead, he was always in the business of putting together winning, which is to say profitable, deals.

Rickey's deals kept the Cards barely solvent and reasonably competitive. They also kept Rickey himself financially secure. By the late 1930s his salary had leveled off at approximately $50,000 a year. Even for what had become a family of eight, this was a very comfortable figure for those hard economic times. And added to it was a reduced, but still substantial, 10 percent cut he received on each player sale. If Branch Rickey always remembered that baseball was a sport, he never forgot that it was a business as well.

Commissioner Landis was not without his own powers of memory. He never forgot to continue waging his war against the source of Rickey's personal wealth and his team's narrow profit margin: the highly productive Cardinal farm system. As far as Landis was concerned, the Cardinals were "raping" the minor leagues, thereby destroying minor league baseball in the process. Rickey, however, would not back down. In fact, he argued that the Cardinals were helping the minor leagues by investing a great deal of money in what was a notoriously undercapitalized business.

Actually, the war between the two men on this front began in earnest as early as 1928, when Landis forced the Cardinals to surrender a future Hall of Famer, outfielder Chuck Klein (later of the Phillies). During the 1928 season Klein signaled his potential greatness by hitting twenty-six home runs (in only eighty-eight games) for the Fort Wayne Chiefs of the Class B Central League. That the Chiefs were a Cardinal farm club was not at all a problem. That the parent Cardinals owned another team (the Dayton Aviators) in the same league was a *considerable* problem in Landis's mind. To solve it, the commissioner ordered Rickey to sell every player on the Fort Wayne roster.

A year later Rickey chose a winter baseball meeting in Chattanooga to lash back at Landis:

> The farm system is not an ideal system; and nobody is talking
> about whether it is ideal or not. When people are hungry they eat
> food which may or may not be ideally cooked and served. No

questions asked because it is not an issuable point. The point is, do we have food and can we live on it?

Is it all right to have a physician who will feel your pulse and look at you and say 'You are a sick man; I think you are going to die.' He offers you no medicine, none at all. He says you are just sick . . . Then along comes somebody else who says you've got epizootic and he doesn't have to cut out the epi. He can make you live. Here's pill number one and here's pill number two. . . .

I claim that such a doctor in a hopeless case should be acceptable both to the patient and to the helpless doctor. . . . In no way should it be said that anyone should say to the new physician who is offering assurance of a cure [that] "You can't give him those pills! You can't give him anything!"

. . . Golf, motoring, economic conditions and bad management have played havoc with our minor league operations. Our farm clubs have been hurt, but we have not suffered at all in comparison with those who are unable to continue. . . . I deplore the philosophy of indifference to what is going on. For without the minor leagues, baseball can get nowhere.

Baseball is bigger than any one club. I owe much to this game. It is bigger than I am. It is bigger than any one man.

The "one man" whom Rickey had in mind was, of course, Commissioner Landis. And, of course, Rickey sought to convince his listeners (and perhaps even Landis) that he had the best interests of the minor leagues at heart. Nonetheless, Landis was correct in assuming that Rickey was acting in other than a selfless manner on this issue. In addition to controlling more than one club at a time in more than one minor league, Rickey also had a penchant for hoarding players in the minors. As a result, historian Neil Sullivan has concluded that "by the late 1930s the farm system had failed any reasonable moral test."

Matters between Landis and Rickey came to a head in the spring of 1938 when the commissioner called the Cardinal vice president to a meeting at his Florida headquarters. At issue was the Cardinals' continuing ownership of multiple teams in more than one minor league circuit. Rickey emerged from the session declaring that "Landis has nothing on me." But two months later the commissioner had the final word. He unilaterally released seventy-four Cardinal minor leaguers from their St. Louis contracts. His investigation had discovered that the Cardinals not only owned or had "working agreements" with more than one team in the same league, but actually controlled two entire minor leagues. Rickey, according to Landis, was the chief sinner, and his "sins," Landis declared publicly, were "as big as the universe."

"Big" as the Cardinal "sins" might have been, neither Rickey nor Breadon was ever given a formal statement of the charges against them. Nor were they given a chance to present their side of the case. In this instance Commissioner Landis proved to be just as arbitrary as Judge Landis had ever been. This "trial," such as it was, was a highly one-sided affair. The commissioner constituted the sole judge and the lone juror. The dual defendants (Rickey and Breadon) could neither mount a defense nor issue an appeal.

The reactions of the two Cardinal executives were very different. Rickey was dazed and more than a little alarmed. For all he knew, the commissioner was on the verge of banning him from baseball. Landis was that unpredictable. He was also that vindictive—at least in Rickey's worried mind.

Breadon, on the other hand, was more embarrassed than he was frightened. He was also angry. In his mind, the Cardinals had been caught cheating. Therefore, the only honorable course was to accept Landis's verdict and move on. Rickey urged his boss to sue Landis, but Breadon refused. He also refused to come to the support of Rickey in the court of public opinion. What seemed at the time to be a temporary rift turned out to be much more than that. Not only was Breadon persuaded that Rickey *had* broken rules, he was also convinced that he now knew enough about baseball to run the team by himself. It was only a matter of time before Rickey's long tenure with the Cardinals would end. The clincher came when Breadon negotiated a contract with a local beer company to sponsor Cardinal games on the radio. Years earlier Sam Breadon had ousted the "Sunday school teacher" from his managerial post. Now he was on the verge of jettisoning the "prohibitionist" from his front office as well.

In the midst of his battles with Breadon, Branch Rickey contemplated getting out of baseball entirely. By 1940 there was talk among Missouri Republicans that he would make a good candidate for high political office. Both the governor's chair and a Senate seat were mentioned as possibilities. Rickey was more than mildly interested. Having long been a loyal Republican, he cordially despised Franklin Roosevelt's New Deal, which he defined as the "Dole System." But in the end he rejected all overtures to run for elective office. In fact, as 1941 unfolded, Rickey began to distance himself from many Republicans, especially midwestern isolationists, by endorsing lend-lease military supplies to Great Britain in its fight against Nazi Germany. "I prefer a dangerous freedom," he told a Republican gathering, "to permanent slavery." Rickey did not see himself as an apostate or a heretic. Only on this single issue of support for the British would he align himself with the Roosevelt administration. Nonetheless, for all practical purposes his decision to endorse a Roosevelt initiative ended his career as a Republican office-seeker before it could begin.

What to do next? Rickey's contract with the Cardinals was set to expire at the end of the 1942 season. Already a lame duck in St. Louis, he had to wonder whether he had a future anywhere else in organized baseball. At sixty, Branch Rickey also had to wonder whether he was too old to start over with another team. But at only sixty, he could reasonably conclude that he was too young to retire. Following the Cardinals' pennant-winning season of 1942, Rickey's speculations about his future gave way to a decision. In mid-October he learned that Larry MacPhail had resigned as president of the Brooklyn Dodgers. Here was more than an intriguing opening. Here was a job that he could not help but covet.

Three years earlier MacPhail had lured Branch Rickey, Jr., away from his father and the Cardinals to run the growing Dodger farm system. The senior Rickey was sorry to see his son leave St. Louis, but the junior Rickey was not at all reluctant to go. Working for his father had never been easy. Working for someone other than his father, he figured, would by definition have to be better. It wasn't. Larry MacPhail proved to be just as overbearing as Branch Rickey, Sr., had ever been.

Rickey had done his best to accept his son's departure. He also tried hard to maintain personal and professional contact with him. More than once he must have entertained the possibility that they would eventually be reunited. That possibility became less remote with MacPhail's departure from the Dodgers. Within days of MacPhail's resignation the Dodgers announced that his successor would be Branch Rickey . . . Senior. If the son had reason to be disappointed, the father had at least three reasons to be absolutely delighted. He was going to stay in the game that he loved, he was now in full command of a major league team, and once again he would be working right beside his only son (who was known as "Twig" within the baseball world). Who said life couldn't begin again after sixty?

But this was not exactly 1917 all over again. Unlike the Cardinals of that era, the Dodgers of the early 1940s were no longer the doormats of the National League that they had been for two decades. For much of the interwar period the Dodgers, or the "Bums" as they were affectionately (and derisively) known, had been the laughing stock of the National League. That ended in 1941 when the Dodgers won their first NL pennant since 1920, defeating the Cardinals by $2^1/_2$ games. Though Brooklyn failed to repeat in 1942, they did win 104 games that year. The only problem was that Rickey's last St. Louis team won 106 games. Clearly, Larry MacPhail was a genius of sorts in his own right. When it came to baseball under the lights and on the radio, MacPhail was both a pioneer and a revolutionary. Another of his bright ideas was as incendiary as it was revolutionary. MacPhail decided to install a microphone under home plate so that his radio audience could listen to arguments with the umpire. This experiment lasted all of a single game before the National League ordered his eavesdropping device removed. Not all of this pioneer's experiments had such short lives. While running the Cincinnati club he brought night baseball to the major leagues in 1935. Three years later MacPhail was calling the shots in Brooklyn, where one of his first decisions as the Dodger boss was to install lights in Ebbets Field. If those lights burned brightly in Larry MacPhail's new baseball home, he did not. By 1942 Macphail had managed to burn himself out in Brooklyn, thereby opening the way for one Branch Rickey to begin burning himself into the memory of Dodger fans everywhere.

Initially, this was not thought to be a marriage made in baseball heaven. As historian Jules Tygiel wryly put it, Branch Rickey and Brooklyn fans were at best an "imperfect match." To hard-edged Brooklynites, Rickey seemed to be a certifiable phony. To working-class baseball fans, he was sanctimonious and hypocritical. To those whose knowledge of baseball surpassed their command of English, he was a long-winded snob. To ethnics throughout the borough, he was a puritanical WASP of the worst sort. To his new ballplayers and to the manager (Leo Durocher) he had inherited, Branch Rickey was a potential scourge. Actually, Commissioner Landis hoped such would be the case, for in his mind the Brooklyn club had become a "nest of horseplayers and card sharks." In the name of eliminating both groups Landis summoned Rickey to his Chicago office just before he was to take control of the Dodgers. This time Landis was not out to dismantle something that Rickey had created. This time he simply ordered Rickey to do something about the gambling that had infested the Dodger clubhouse. "Clean house" or else was the Landis command. And at least on this single occasion Branch Rickey both listened to and agreed with the commissioner.

Once in Brooklyn, Branch Rickey soon proved to be more than the sum of all these parts. Yes, he proved to be a scourge, and a successful one at that. Yes, he continued to be verbose and puritanical, not to mention sanctimonious (but never in his own mind hypocritical). But he also turned out to be a reborn revolutionary. In fact, the story of Branch Rickey replacing Larry MacPhail was a story of one revolutionary replacing another. And once installed in Brooklyn, Rickey would not be that far away from orchestrating the most revolutionary act of his baseball career.

The Fourth Inning

In the spring of 1942 Jackie Robinson was undergoing basic training at Fort Riley, Kansas. Draftee Robinson was anything but a happy young man. He was especially perturbed with the army's segregationist practices and the daily reminders of unequal status that accompanied them. One escape route was Officer Candidate School (OCS), but that outlet apparently had been sealed off when his application was rejected. It would take the intervention of another black soldier at Fort Riley to give Robinson a second chance. That man was heavyweight boxing champion Joe Louis. Curiously, it was the internationally famous Louis who first approached Robinson. Upon learning of Jack's OCS disappointment, Louis put in a call to a War Department friend. A few days later Robinson was admitted to the program.

On January 28, 1943, Jackie Robinson was commissioned as a second lieutenant and assigned to an all-black unit. His official responsibility was to serve as the unit's morale officer. In that capacity Second Lieutenant Robinson decided to take it upon himself to build morale by challenging the fort's entrenched system of racial segregation. Fort Riley had an athletic program with a double standard. With football and baseball on its list of offerings, Robinson had thought he would have an opportunity to keep his hand in both sports, but only the football team permitted black players (apparently because it played against racially mixed teams from other military bases, as well as local colleges). Robinson's decision to challenge policy by attempting to join the baseball team was met with a firm "no." Pete Reiser, who would later play with Robinson in Brooklyn, was a member of the camp team. He would never forget the first time he saw Jackie Robinson: "I didn't know who he was then, but . . . I can still remember him walking away by himself." Football was another matter. In the fall of that year, the coach recruited Robinson to play halfback on the team, but Jackie would have none of it. Angered by his treatment on the diamond, he refused to join the football squad—even after an officer ordered him to suit up.

The army eventually responded to Lieutenant Robinson's behavior, on and off the playing field, by transferring him to Camp Hood in Texas. This was a post that had a reputation for taking a hard line against those who challenged the racial status quo. Assigned to the 761st Tank Battalion, Robinson discovered that black soldiers at Camp Hood were routinely used as "school [enemy] troops" for the training of white soldiers. Initially, Robinson did nothing to rock the boat. But once Robinson discovered that Camp Hood had no baseball team, he set out to change things. With the help of a white second lieutenant, Robinson gathered what money he could to buy uniforms and equipment. Having taken the initiative to organize the team, he was the central figure on it. For the first time in his baseball life, Jackie Robinson pitched on a regular basis. All this transpired without the help of Camp Hood brass, but without their interference as well. Ironically, the camp with the reputation for taking the racial hard line was the camp where Jackie was able to play baseball. Only then did the lieutenant with the reputation for challenging the racial status quo begin to emerge from his shell.

If baseball raised slightly the curtain of obscurity surrounding him, it was completely lifted on July 6, 1944. There is still some confusion about the events of that day, but whatever happened confirmed the accuracy of Robinson's subsequent assessment of his military career: "I learned that I was in two wars, one against a foreign enemy, the other against prejudice at home." Confusion and conflicting stories aside, the essence of what happened on that summer day in 1944 is this: Robinson boarded an intracamp bus and took a seat near the front. When asked by the civilian driver to move to the black section in the rear, Robinson refused to comply. (He may have known that a Pentagon order banning segregation of military vehicles was about to go into effect.) The driver ordered him off the bus. Again, he refused. This time the driver called the military police, who promptly took Robinson into custody. Following a hurried investigation, Second Lieutenant Jack Roosevelt Robinson was charged with three counts of insubordination.

Faced with an impending court-martial, Robinson decided to contact Joe Louis. He also sent a letter detailing his version of events to the national headquarters of the NAACP. That combination of moves had some effect, because his commanding officer decided against proceeding with the court-martial. But instead of dropping the charges entirely, the army transferred Robinson to a unit headed by a commander who was willing to prosecute him. The trial was brief, but conclusive, as Robinson was acquitted of all charges. However, it is apparent that this case—and the accompanying negative publicity—was more than the army wanted to handle. Although Jackie Robinson was an athlete of some note, and although the army was in the process of revising the bus seating rules that Robinson had challenged, the contentious lieutenant was "honorably relieved from active duty" in November of that year.

Effectively, Robinson was granted an honorable discharge. But technically, the terms of the order did not constitute a *full* honorable discharge (meaning, among other things, that he would not be eligible for veteran's benefits). This decision grated at Robinson for years afterward and would soon anger an unlikely Robinson ally: the Communist Party.

Back in civilian life, ex-serviceman Jackie Robinson was not exactly flooded with job opportunities. The lone professional offer came from Sam Houston College, a small black school in Texas, which was looking for a basketball coach at the last minute. Robinson did not have to think twice before accepting. At the end of the hard court season, Robinson was approached by the Kansas City Monarchs to play Negro League baseball. Initially, he hesitated. The Monarchs may have been one of the top teams in the Negro Leagues, but the prospect of playing the game at this level did not hold much appeal for the ex-college player. Jackie did not claim to know a lot about the Negro Leagues, but what he did know he didn't much like. From what he had been told, the general atmosphere was bad, the money was not much better, and the playing conditions were appalling.

Ironically, Negro League baseball was enjoying its first and only period of financial success about the time that Jackie Robinson was trying to make up his mind about joining the Monarchs. World War II was a major factor in bringing about this sudden burst of prosperity. Negro League pitching great Satchel Paige remembered it as a time when "everybody had money and everybody was looking around for entertainment." This included African Americans, courtesy of high levels of wartime employment. It was also a time when "entertainment" was easy to come by and relatively inexpensive. Negro League baseball fit the bill, as it was both highly entertaining and downright cheap. Whether it was the pregame showboating or the game itself, a few hours at the ballpark was a good investment.

The history of African Americans and professional baseball is both lengthy and complicated, as well as consistent with what was happening in the larger culture. With the end of Reconstruction came the end of any commitment on the part of the federal government to ensure a racially integrated society. At the same time, the post-Reconstruction South was back in the hands of white Democrats who were determined to solidify their power by imposing a system of legal segregation. As a result, "Jim Crow" segregation came to life throughout the South during the 1880s. But segregation was far from limited to state policy or the South. During the 1880s it took on a life of its own outside the South and within private institutions as well. Baseball was one of those private institutions that was soon subjected to "Jim Crow"–style restrictions.

Before baseball's color line hardened during the 1880s a handful of black ballplayers dotted the rosters of teams in the National League and the American Association (which was then consid-

ered to be the second "major league"). Once blacks were effectively banned (by way of a silent agreement, rather than any formal edict), all-black teams began to crop up in northern cities,
especially those along the East Coast. For such teams, barnstorming was a way of life. Teams existed, but leagues did not, so games
were played on a catch-as-catch-can basis. To be sure, some scheduling did take place, but the idea was that individual teams would
play individual games, not that teams would join together to play
for championships. Instead of set seasons pointing toward a title,
there was only endless travel pointing toward the next pay day.
More often than not, these for-pay games pitted one black team
against another, but barnstorming did include black-white competition as well. And once the major league season was over many
barnstormers were white major leaguers looking to supplement
their incomes.

Not until after World War I did organized black leagues come
into existence. The first on the scene was the Negro National
League, which began play in 1920. The Eastern Colored League
followed three years later. By 1932 both had fallen victim to the
Great Depression. A year later Gus Greenlee, owner of a team
called the Pittsburgh Crawfords, played a key role in establishing
a second Negro National League. Four years later a rival Negro
American League was formed. Both of these leagues were still in
existence as of 1945, but neither made much money until the war
was drawing to a close.

For most of its history Negro League baseball continued to rely
on barnstorming to survive. Teams and players had no choice. They
had to play hard and often if they expected to earn anything approaching a decent living. Until the late 1920s many of those barnstormed games were played in the fall and winter against major
league teams looking for extra revenue. Commissioner Landis finally banned such competition, no doubt because the result was
often embarrassing to the white teams. He did continue to permit
post–regular season games involving major league all-star contin-
gents, but always with a limit on the number of players from any
one team.

On average Negro League teams would play upwards of 200 games a year, but only one-third of these contests would count in league standings. In order to squeeze in as many games as possible, Negro League owners pioneered night baseball. In fact, Robinson's future team, the Kansas City Monarchs, participated in the first professional game under the lights. The year was 1930.

Despite the crowded schedule, most Negro League players only earned between $125 and $300 a month, approximately half of the average income of white major leaguers. To further economize, black teams usually carried only seventeen or eighteen players (as opposed to the normal twenty-five-man major league roster). Because of such restrictions, a premium was placed on versatility in the field. Generally, this meant that infielders and outfielders were interchangeable, but no Negro League player could match the many-sided skills of Ted Radcliffe. Better known as "Double Duty" Radcliffe, he would often pitch the first game of a double-header and catch the second. Such multiple talents made for great stories, even if they did not always make for great baseball. By Radcliffe's own admission the Negro League teams of his era performed at "about Triple-A level." More often than not the problem was one of depth. "The big leaguers were strong in every position . . . most of the colored teams had a few stars, but they weren't strong in every position."

But what teams and what stars! The Pittsburgh Crawfords and the Homestead Grays went head-to-head and finished at or near the top on a regular basis. The Baltimore Elite Giants, the Chicago American Giants, the New York Black Yankees, the Newark Eagles, and the Indianapolis Clowns also joined the Kansas City Monarchs among the strong squads of the Negro Leagues. And if these teams were not uniformly deep, each had a number of front-line performers. With a fastball that blazed and darted, Satchel Paige held his own against the best of the white big leaguers. Devastating with the bat and solid with the glove, Josh Gibson was the equal of any major league catcher. The more-than-fleet James "Cool Papa" Bell patrolled centerfield (and beyond), while running the bases with the speed and savvy of the swiftest National or American league player. And slick-fielding, dependable-hitting Judy Johnson and Ray Dandridge rivaled any third baseman in the game.

In many respects Negro League baseball was a throwback to the "dead ball" era of the white major leagues. Between 1900 and 1920 every team in each major league was forced to rely on scoring runs one at a time. Negro League teams of the 1920s and 1930s did not ignore the bunt. Speed and daring base-running were also essential components of what their players liked to call "tricky baseball." But Negro League teams also featured players who could both run the bases and hit for power. Jackie Robinson himself would prove to be one of those players during his single year in the Negro Leagues. But he was far from alone. By the time that Robinson was ready for professional baseball both white major leagues had long since abandoned the "one run at a time" philosophy. The transitional figure was, of course, Babe Ruth, whose home-run swing and home-run trot were a staple at American League parks throughout the 1920s. (But even Ruth had five seasons in which his stolen base figure reached double digits.) By World War II Babe Ruth had long since retired, but he had clearly put his mark on the major league game, where resorting to the home run took precedence over manufacturing individual runs. Not so with the Negro Leagues, where individuals players were adept practitioners of both "tricky baseball" and the long ball.

And pitching—and hitting—in the Negro Leagues was especially tricky business. It could also be highly dangerous. According to Robinson's future Dodger teammate, catcher Roy Campanella, "anything went" in Negro League baseball. The spitball may have been banned from the major leagues, but Negro League pitchers lived by it. Scuffing the ball was done early and often. And given the paucity of baseballs, scuffed balls generally remained in the game. So did pitchers who threw at batters. Again, if Campanella's recollections are accurate, brushbacks and even beanballs were vital weapons in a pitcher's arsenal. White major leaguers were not immune from throwing close to or even at hitters, but Campanella was probably correct to note a decided difference between the two operations on this score.

Had any of these pitches actually been outlawed, Negro League umpires would have had a difficult time enforcing such bans. For that matter, they were rarely in a strong position to police much of anything. Poorly paid by the owners, they were treated with contempt by many players. Physical attacks on umpires was an all too common occurrence, whether during or after games.

Unruliness on the part of players was more than matched by shadiness on the part of owners. Those who ran Negro League teams were often involved in a variety of questionable enterprises. For example, Gus Greenlee was reputed to be the black "numbers game" boss of Pittsburgh. The seat of his empire was a black night club, the Crawford Grille (hence the Pittsburgh Crawfords). At least Greenlee managed to accumulate enough nonbaseball money to accomplish the near-impossible in the Negro League game: he was able to build a ball park for his team. And what a team it could be. At one time or another the Pittsburgh Crawfords had Satchel Paige, Josh Gibson, Judy Johnson, and "Cool Papa" Bell on its always-revolving roster.

Most Negro League teams rented the fields of major and minor league teams. For the white landlords these rental fees represented an important source of much-needed additional revenue. For the black players this arrangement was terribly insulting for at least two reasons. The best players among them felt they deserved to be playing on those diamonds on a regular basis and for a good deal more money. And all Negro League players were barred from using the locker rooms and showers of the white major leaguers who were then on the road. In a sense, Negro Leaguers were almost perpetually on the road, whether they were barnstorming on makeshift fields or renting the best that the majors had to offer.

The scheduling of Negro League games was always contingent upon the open dates on white schedules. Playing dates were also governed by white booking agents, who often demanded as much as 40 percent of the gate receipts for their services. Because of these arrangements, Negro League baseball was inevitably in a state of some confusion and disarray. And because of this sadly typical condition, Branch Rickey was quick to label the Negro

Leagues little more than "rackets." That many owners were engaged in "rackets" of their own only served to confirm the accuracy of Rickey's characterization. But "rackets" or no, this was a $2 million a year empire by the end of World War II. That figure may have been loose change to white empire builders in steel, oil, and even in baseball, but as of 1945 Negro League baseball was one of the largest black-owned enterprises in the country.

Robinson did not ask to inspect a balance sheet when considering the Monarchs' offer. His main concern at the time was not the economic status of Negro League baseball. Nor was it the future of this brand of baseball. Of immediate concern was his own future. Already twenty-six and still hopeful of one day winning Rachel Isum, he had to have been thinking about his life beyond 1945 and perhaps even his life beyond baseball. The Kansas City Monarchs may have been in the running for his services in 1945, but they did not figure prominently in his long-term thinking.

Nonetheless, Robinson might have been excused for at least entertaining the idea of a future in major league baseball. As early as 1942 he had requested a tryout with the Chicago White Sox, who were then training in Pasadena. The team did not move to sign him, but its manager, Jimmy Dykes, judged Robinson to be "worth $50,000 of anybody's money." Three years would pass before Robinson would get his second major league tryout. In mid-April of 1945 Jack and two Negro League veterans were invited by the Boston Red Sox to showcase their skills at Fenway Park. Robinson had already made a verbal agreement to play for the Monarchs, but he accepted the invitation anyway. After all, the word was out that the Red Sox were under mounting pressure from Boston politicians to sign a black player. What was not widely known was that Red Sox officials only intended to go through the motions of giving a few black players a look. That much they did. Performing before a small battery of scouts and front-office types, Jack was clearly the best of the three. But no contract was forthcoming. In fact, Robinson received no word at all from any Red Sox official until he contacted the team. At that point he was told that the Red Sox were concerned about repercussions if the Boston team was found tampering with Negro League players. And that was that. He never heard from the Red Sox again. In retrospect, he had been given the "runaround," rather than a real chance to make the team.

Only the Monarchs made Robinson an offer to play baseball professionally in 1945. But they did not sign him to a formal contract. In a letter to Branch Rickey in July 1946, Robinson reminded the Dodger president that "no contract of any kind was ever tendered to me by the Kansas City Monarchs . . . I simply received an offer in a letter and I reported to the Monarchs as a result of that letter." Robinson went on to explain that he subsequently asked for a contract, "but none was offered." In fact, he was fully aware that he "had no job at any minute they cared to dismiss me."

In the end, Robinson did decide that the Monarchs had something to offer beyond a contract or even a salary. This was, after all, Satchel Paige's team. Though nearly forty, Paige remained a formidable pitcher. A few years earlier, Dizzy Dean had deemed Paige to be "a better pitcher than I am, ever was, or will be." A few years later Paige would finally make it to the majors (where he compiled a 28-31 record, first with the Cleveland Indians, then with the St. Louis Browns, and finally with the Kansas City Athletics for all of three innings in 1965). Robinson did not know much about Paige personally, but he probably thought he could learn a few things about hitting from him. He also knew that he would be competing against superb players, including the fleet "Cool Papa" Bell, who could certainly show him a thing or two about base running. Besides, he stood to make at least $100 a week. This was far from great money, but it was more than he had been paid for coaching basketball. So what did he have to lose? To clinch matters, Jack had temporarily lost Rachel, who had broken off their engagement during his tour of duty at Fort Riley.

So, during the summer of 1945 Jackie Robinson played shortstop for the Kansas City Monarchs. In forty-five games, he hit .387, socked five home runs, and stole fifteen bases. On defense he was at least respectable. But there were weak spots. Most apparent was the difficulty he had going to his right to retrieve ground balls.

And what about that ever-suspicious arm? Could he get the ball smartly to first base from deep in the hole at shortstop?

Robinson had larger worries as the season progressed. If life in the army had been difficult for him, life in the Negro Leagues was not much better. Both were thoroughly segregated institutions, the former out of its own perversity, the latter out of sheer necessity. Having recently learned that there was no place for him in the U.S. Army, Jackie Robinson now discovered that he was an outsider in his new world. His Monarch teammates kept their distance, and he returned the nonfavor. Negro League competitors treated him the same way. The problem had many dimensions, but from Robinson's perspective too few of his teammates and his rivals were competitive or disciplined enough for him. He was the sort of fellow who took most everything seriously, including what he deemed to be a lack of dedication among Negro League players.

To other Negro League players, Jack Robinson was many things they were not. Though he lacked a college degree, he was still a "college boy" in their eyes. His scrapes with Pasadena police notwithstanding, Robinson had not remained a man on the margins of American life. As of 1945 he was a well-mannered young man in his mid-twenties with three-plus years at UCLA and a U.S. Army commission to his credit. Finally, he was not just a baseball player. He had already established himself as a multisport athlete accustomed to multisport success, one not at all willing to accept a permanent second-class status.

To Jackie Robinson, the Negro League teams were not even second-class operations. At worst, they were a poor imitation of professionalism. At best, they were a step toward something better. What that something else might be, Robinson could not be sure. But he was sure that he didn't want to stay there for long. If he did, he feared that he would inevitably be corrupted by a way of life that was not for him. To an ever-proud Jackie Robinson, too many of his fellow competitors were simply too complacent about too much that was wrong with their situation. They were too tolerant of shoddy conditions, too accepting of inferior umpiring, and too quick to engage in showboating on the field. In sum, Robinson encountered many Negro League players who were willing to accept the indignities that resulted from playing baseball as they were forced to play it in segregated America.

Those who ran the Negro Leagues were no better. Whether the owners would admit it or not, they had made a deal with the devil; they were co-conspirators (with their white major league counterparts) in maintaining an intolerable system of segregated baseball that had already been tolerated for far too long. Worse than that, their players were too willing to accept small, if fairly steady, paychecks, in return for which many of them perpetuated the worst sort of racial stereotypes. A proud Jackie Robinson was unwilling to add his name to this list of conscious or unconscious co-conspirators.

As the 1945 season wore on, Jackie grew increasingly dissatisfied with everything around him. He battled teammates and competitors; he battled white racists and symbols of racism; and he battled himself. He also drove himself. Robinson could not control the future, but he could prepare—and hope. Monarch teammates recalled that Robinson was always telling them to "get ready," that the day was coming when a major league team would "sign one of us." Little did he know how quickly that day would arrive.

Pressure to integrate the major leagues had only begun in earnest in the mid-1930s. The leaders of that campaign were not baseball men, but reform-minded journalists. Some were of a radical bent, and some of those were Communists. In fact, as early as 1933 the voice of the American Communist Party, the *Daily Worker,* initiated what would build into a steady drumbeat for the integration of the major leagues, a drumbeat that continued until Robinson's breakthrough signing and echoed for many years after that. To the *Daily Worker,* segregation in the major leagues was one more thing to "chalk up against capitalist controlled sports." It was the rare baseball article in this publication that did not make some sort of reference to the exclusion of black ballplayers. Inevitably its editors also strove to link that exclusion to an oppresive capitalist system and portray the ballplayers as underpaid workers within it.

In the *Daily Worker*'s coverage of this ongoing issue, 1936 was a critical year. Not long after the conclusion of the "Nazi" Olympics, readers of the Sunday edition of the *Worker* awoke to find a front-page article calling for the elimination of "Jim Crow baseball." Under the direction of new sports editor Lester Rodney, the *Daily Worker* ran a series of articles detailing the history of Negro League baseball and highlighting the careers of Negro League stars, players who *Worker* writers were convinced would—and should— shine in the major leagues. Subthemes running through these pieces persistently blamed major league owners for the perpetuation of "Jim Crow baseball" and absolved their employees of any measure of responsibility for the absence of black players from major league rosters.

To clinch its case, the *Daily Worker* secured quote after quote from white players who favored ending segregation in the majors. Late in the 1937 season Rodney managed to interview Yankee rookie Joe DiMaggio concerning his barnstorming days against Negro League players. According to DiMaggio, "Satchel Paige was the greatest pitcher [he had] ever batted against." Three days later Rodney ran an article titled, "Paige Asks Test for Negro Stars." What Paige proposed was a single postseason game at Yankee Stadium between the 1937 World Series winner and the Negro League All-Stars. Paige predicted that such a contest would draw a "packed house." He was also so certain of victory that he offered to play without pay "if we don't beat them." The offer was ignored. What could not be ignored was the issue.

Rodney began to establish a working relationship with black sportswriters, all in the name of promoting the integration of the major leagues. Of course, he would have been pleased to learn that any major league team had signed a black player, but he directed most of his editorial attention to the three New York teams, especially to the team whose fan base was primarily working class. That team, of course, was the Brooklyn Dodgers.

In 1938 *Worker* writers drafted antidiscrimination pamphlets for distribution at all three major league ballparks in New York City. The next year Rodney orchestrated a petition drive to achieve the desired goal. *Worker* staffers and friends gathered signatures at Yankee, Giant, and Dodger games. They then delivered the stack to Commissioner Landis, as well as to the presidents of both the National and American leagues. This campaign was repeated every year until 1947 in the hope of shaming baseball's hierarchy into finally doing what the *Daily Worker* deemed to be right and just.

The *Worker* had no single player in mind to put forward as *the* person to break the color line. But as early as 1939 it did mention Jackie Robinson as a possible candidate. In October the newspaper ran a column by a California Communist speculating on Robinson's major league potential on the basis of his UCLA career. A year later it called Robinson "one of the most amazing athletes in the land." Not only was the "20-year-old Jackie . . . the leading scorer on the Coast in basketball," but he was "a shortstop of big league caliber and a track ace."

On the opposite coast, liberals and Communists had begun to join forces on a number of fronts under the umbrella banner of the Popular Front. Spurred on by the rise of fascism, the Communist International had decreed as early as 1935 that everyone on the left ought to align together against the menace of Hitler. Though interrupted by the infamous Nazi-Soviet Pact of 1939, liberal-Communist cooperation would be revived in June of 1941 when Hitler invaded the Soviet Union. It would be cemented when the United States joined the war in the aftermath of the Japanese attack on Pearl Harbor.

Desegregating major league baseball cannot rank with defeating fascism, but it was a significant item on the Popular Front agenda. To be sure, the importance of the war, as well as the rationale behind it, gave an added push to the campaign that the *Daily Worker* had initiated when few others were paying attention to the issue. If black Americans could be asked to die for their country in a war against racist Nazis, why should they not be invited to play the American game at its highest level of competition? The *Daily Worker* had long been asking a similar question. Now they were being joined by liberal politicians in New York City and in the

New York state legislature. This budding alliance also included the black press of New York, especially Joe Bostic of the *People's Voice.*

As a result of pressure on all these fronts, the New York legislature passed the Ives-Quinn Law in 1943. Designed to end discrimination in hiring practices, it soon would be used to call attention to the failure of all three New York teams to desegregate their rosters. Republican Mayor Fiorello La Guardia added his voice to the growing chorus by delivering a radio address to plead with the owners of the Yankees, Giants, and Dodgers to drop their ban against black players. He also created a New York City Council committee whose sole charge was to monitor the owners on this issue. But highlighting—and criticizing—past practices was not enough. Nor was tracking the owners' current behavior on the subject of race. La Guardia wanted action. So did other white politicians, especially those of a liberal or even radical persuasion.

A few white columnists and sportswriters for mass circulation newspapers, especially New York City newspapers, added their lukewarm endorsement now and again. But the most forceful, most insistent, and most impassioned writing on the subject was done by black writers, most notably Wendell Smith of the Pittsburgh *Courier* and Sam Lacy of the Chicago *Defender.* Themselves victims of "Jim Crow" restrictions in the world of sports journalism, Lacy and Smith were determined to shatter this system as it operated in the world of professional baseball. They received little support from their white brethren in the print business and none from the baseball "bible," *The Sporting News.* In 1942 this St. Louis-based publication editorialized that the "use of mixed teams in baseball would benefit neither the Negro nor white professional game, because of the possibility of unpleasant incidents." It was apparent to the editors of *The Sporting News* that the most unpleasant incident of all would be the day that a black player set foot on a major league diamond. (When that day finally occurred *The Sporting News* did extend a grudging welcome to Robinson, a welcome which included a request that he be judged solely on the basis of his baseball skills. But at the same time its editors could not resist returning to the old refrain that both races would really be happier if they confined their ball playing to separate fields.)

Nonetheless, the campaign to speed the day when those fields would be integrated went forward as World War II progressed. This effort remained focused on New York City, given its heavy concentration of liberals and its large black population. As a result, it was conducted away from the reading eyes of the vast majority of white Americans. White sports fans did not ordinarily read the black press. Few Americans, black or white, bothered to read the Communist press. And very few people outside of New York City typically read that city's press.

The war itself created new opportunities for advocates of black access to the major leagues. With rosters depleted by draft calls, teams were desperate for ballplayers. What better time to ratchet up the pressure for signing black ballplayers, especially the highly skilled veterans of the Negro Leagues? In New York, the focal point of this pressure was increasingly concentrated on Branch Rickey's Dodgers. The lordly New York Yankees were not a likely target. The once lordly Giants were somehow above this battle as well. But not the Dodgers. Brooklyn was a working-class town, and the Dodgers were a working-class team. Hence a 1943 *Daily Worker* decision to draft an open letter to Branch Rickey. After calling on New York fans to write letters to all three New York teams to demand integration, the editors specifically asked Rickey to sign Negro League shortstop Willie Wells. The regular Dodger shortstop, "Pee Wee" Reese, had just been drafted into the military. Why not replace him with Wells?

Rickey officially ignored this request. But unbeknownst to any sportswriter, he was unofficially moving in this direction. The Dodger president already had privately approached the leading financial backer of the Dodgers, George McLaughlin, to sound him out on the possibility of signing a black player. McLaughlin was a banker and a major voice in the political life of the borough of Brooklyn. His support for any Rickey initiative on the integration front was absolutely crucial. Rickey let him know that he intended to search the country for the best baseball talent, adding that in the process of "beating of the bushes" the Dodgers might flush out a "negro player or two." When McLaughlin raised no objection, Rickey thought he had sufficient reason to proceed, albeit cautiously.

At the time, much was being said—or whispered—by baseball people on the subject of integration. Despite inaction, despite Commissioner's Landis's intransigence, there were many rumors and hints, even some fears and threats, that one or more teams might soon make a move to break the color line. Bill McKechnie, manager of the Cincinnati Reds, let it be known that there were "at least twenty [black] players good enough to play in the big leagues, and I would be happy to have them on the Reds, if given permission." About the same time, Giant pitching great Carl Hubbell called Josh Gibson of the Homestead Grays "as great a catcher" as there was in the game. In fact, an informal survey conducted by Wendell Smith in the late 1930s indicated that as many as four-fifths of National League players and managers did not object to the idea of their teams fielding blacks.

However, most of the pressure to integrate the major leagues did not come from major league players or managers. Most of it had been and remained political. That pressure finally forced Commissioner Landis to put the issue of integration on the agenda of the 1943 winter meetings of major league owners. Landis had tried mightily to keep that agenda and the majors as all-white affairs. But at the last minute the celebrated black singer and actor, Paul Robeson, was invited to address baseball executives. With Landis on the podium and Rickey in the audience, Robeson lectured the assembled on the need for some action, for some evidence of good-will on their part. His bottom line was that at least one black ballplayer should be signed to a major league contract before the start of the 1944 season.

Much to the amazement of baseball writers in attendance, Robeson's words received warm applause. It was left to a defensive Landis (who had introduced Robeson) to state the official party line: "each manager is free to choose players regardless of race, color, or any other condition." But nothing happened immediately to change the status quo.

During that 1944 season the seemingly interminable status quo ended with the sudden death of Commissioner Landis. The power structure of the major leagues responded by organizing an interim Baseball Council to run the game, pending the appointment of Landis's successor. That council, in turn, formed a special committee to look into the ongoing issue of integration. Prominent among its members were Sam Lacy, Larry MacPhail (now of the Yankees), and Branch Rickey.

In the meantime, during the winter of 1944–45 Wendell Smith, in league with Sam Lacy and other black sportswriters, went about the business of composing a short list of black players who would be good candidates for tryouts with major league teams. Though Jackie Robinson's name was always near the top of that master list of prospects, his was far from the only name on it. In early April of 1945, Joe Bostic of the *Daily Worker* surprised Branch Rickey by showing up at a makeshift Dodger training site in New England. With him were two veteran Negro League players. Together, the threesome confronted Rickey and demanded a tryout. As Bostic recalled the scene, the Dodger president "went berserk." But he did permit the unscheduled tryout to go forward. It lasted all of forty-five minutes, at which point Bostic and the players were told to leave. Once again, that seemed to be that. Rickey's public face was stern and unbending. When pressed on the subject of Bostic's initiative, Rickey expressed suspicion of the "red tinge" that colored it. Privately he continued to lay the groundwork for his own desegregation effort, even as he continued to resent being pressured by outsiders, whatever their politics.

Shortly thereafter, Wendell Smith asked for a one-on-one meeting with Rickey. The Dodger president liked and respected Smith. The two men were also in agreement on a major political issue. Firm anti-Communists, they were anxious to prevent the Joe Bostics of the world from taking credit for breaking the color line. During their meeting Rickey went so far as to let Smith know of his interest in signing a black player, but he also wanted Smith to understand that any Dodger pursuit of black players had to be kept quiet at this early stage. Smith agreed. Unlike the Communist press, Smith had no agenda other than that of placing black ballplayers on the rosters of major league clubs. One of those players was Jackie Robinson. At the conclusion of their meeting, Rickey agreed to have Robinson scouted.

A few weeks later Rickey held a press conference. With both black and white reporters in attendance, he blasted "Communist inspired" efforts to desegregate baseball. He then went on to announce that at the moment the Dodgers had no intention of signing a black player—especially if any such signing appeared as capitulation to Communist pressure. Finally, he took on the Negro Leagues, which were still the "rackets" he had long since labeled them as. At this point he put before the press the only bit of real news he had to offer. The Dodger president unveiled a plan to create something he called the "United States League" and to field a team called the Brooklyn Brown Dodgers. This would be a new league for black players, but unlike the existing Negro Leagues it would be organized around standard contracts, uniform schedules, and enforced rules. Finally, Rickey dropped the not-so-small hint that the best players in this league might one day perform in the major leagues.

The combination of this press conference and his earlier meeting with Rickey convinced Wendell Smith that among the small fraternity of baseball executives Branch Rickey was the likeliest candidate to take the lead in integrating the major league game. At the same time, Rickey was increasingly convinced that Jackie Robinson was worth the close attention of Dodger scouts, which included Rickey's old Browns' star, George Sisler, and Clyde Sukeforth.

It was Sukeforth who drew the task of following Robinson on and off throughout the 1945 season. In doing so, he became Rickey's eyes on that "young man from the West" (which was the Dodger boss's code phrase for Robinson). He was Rickey's agent as well. It was Sukeforth who would approach Robinson on that August day at Comiskey Park, and who would arrange Robinson's historic meeting with Rickey.

Because of Clyde Sukeforth's efforts, Branch Rickey knew quite a bit about Jackie Robinson in advance of their August 28 encounter. He had been fully apprised of Robinson's playing abilities and had also learned much about Robinson's background, his habits, his temperament, and even his private life.

As their rendezvous neared, Rickey underscored the importance of total secrecy regarding any Dodger interest in Robinson. Such a strategy, he surmised, was best for all concerned. It represented Robinson's best chance to be offered a Dodger contract—and the Dodgers best chance to sign a top prospect. Wendell Smith continued to be a party to this game. He agreed that premature publicity would "kill" Robinson's chances. So he did what he could to keep Robinson's name out of his newspaper.

Smith also continued to stay in contact with Rickey about Robinson. When word reached Rickey that Robinson had threatened to punch an umpire, the first person he contacted was Smith. Was Jackie the "belligerent type?" Smith was reluctant to tell Rickey the truth, which was that Robinson could be difficult. He didn't want to tell the Dodger president what everybody who followed the Negro leagues and the Monarchs knew, so he fudged: Robinson was not so much belligerent as he was someone who was willing to stand up for what was right.

Up went a red flag. But in their owns ways, Smith and Sukeforth did what they could to reassure Rickey that he had nothing to worry about. Not that Rickey needed all that much assurance. There was so much about Robinson that was positive. And this was something he had long wanted to do—for his Dodgers, for his game, and for his country (and, if pressed, probably in that order). Solid baseball man that he was, he appreciated the talent that was on display in the Negro Leagues. Competitive character that he was, he was increasingly anxious to secure more than his share of that talent for the Dodgers. Lincoln Republican that he always claimed to be, he could readily grasp the absurdity of the color line.

But why did he wait so long to do what he had long known was the right thing? In Brooklyn, as opposed to St. Louis, he was not only in a better position to challenge the color line but he also found himself under increasing pressure to do so. And in Brooklyn he discovered that he couldn't win with a whites-only team (if for no other reason than the whites-only Cardinals that he had put together remained the cream of the National League through 1946).

Despite internal and external pressure, Rickey still had to be sure that Robinson was *the* one. And there would be only one. Rickey might have selected two, three, or more players who would be signed, cultivated, promoted, and in position to break the color line together. This he deliberately chose not to do. In his mind it was crucial that one player be given center stage. This individual did not necessarily have to be the best black baseball player, but he did have to be the best *person*. Hence a Rickey decision to go to California on his own to investigate Robinson's background. Hence the importance of their August 28th encounter. And hence his insistence on secrecy before his meeting with Robinson—and the continued secrecy after it.

And while there is no doubt that Branch Rickey already knew a great deal about Jackie Robinson before the latter entered the "cave of the winds" on August 28, 1945, there is also little doubt that not everything he had learned about him was positive. Chief among the denizen of the cave's worries was that Robinson had "more and deeper racial resentment than was hoped for or expected." That sense of resentment, coupled with Robinson's hair-trigger temper, could spell disaster for Rickey's carefully plotted design.

But the saving grace for Robinson—and the design—was that he was, in Rickey's estimation, a "Christian by inheritance and practice." Robinson also struck Rickey as an intelligent man. As such, he seemed to have understood when Rickey explained, as only Rickey could, that his candidate needed to accept "some Booker T. Washington temporary compromises with surface inequality for the sake of expediency." What that mouthful amounted to was that Rickey remained an optimist twice over: he believed that Robinson was at heart as accommodating as Washington had been (despite Jackie's obvious feelings of resentment), and he believed that America's inequalities and racist impulses were only skin deep (despite considerable evidence to the contrary).

But even intelligence was not enough. Following their time together, Rickey thought he detected in Robinson the "great moral courage" necessary to accept the challenge and "see it through." In sum, Rickey learned enough over the course of those three hours to proceed with his design.

Branch Rickey did not like to think of himself as a lucky man. Instead, he preferred to see himself as a risk taker—not an impulsive risk taker, of course, but a risk taker nonetheless. In the late summer of 1945 he was in the midst of negotiating his way through the biggest gamble of his life. All the more reason to proceed carefully—and secretly. The world would learn soon enough about his plans. In his ever-calculating mind, Rickey always coupled "adventure" with advance planning. Even in this momentous undertaking he remained determined to control as much of the process as possible. While he would never turn down a little luck along the way, Branch Rickey did not like to depend on it. "Luck," he continued to insist, was still nothing more than the "residue of design."

The Fifth Inning

Rickey's original script called for the public announcement of Robinson's signing to be delayed until early 1946. In the interim, the Dodger executive hoped to sign other black ballplayers to minor-league contracts so that he could make a package announcement, thereby taking at least some of the pressure off Robinson. But New York City election-year politics intervened. Local liberal politicians, Mayor La Guardia included, were vying for the city's considerable black vote in citywide November elections. They wanted to be seen as holding the feet of major league baseball to the fire. La Guardia himself continued to seek specific assurances that blacks would soon be added to the rosters of the three New York teams. Had those assurances been forthcoming, the mayor would not have objected to taking some of the credit for Rickey's action before the November elections.

Branch Rickey and Fiorello La Guardia were fellow Republicans. Beyond baseball, each was sympathetic to the plight of black Americans and to the then-simmering cause of black civil rights. But Rickey did not want to be seen as caving in to anybody, especially politicians. Therefore, he decided to go public with Robinson's signing before La Guardia and others grew even more outspoken— and certainly before a safely re-elected La Guardia moved to turn the heat up even higher. Not all "designs" can be carried out exactly as planned. Therefore, on October 23, 1945, baseball fans and the world learned that Jackie Robinson of the Kansas City Monarchs had signed a contract to play professional baseball for the Brooklyn Dodger organization.

Ebbets Field in Brooklyn, however, would not be Robinson's first stop. It was announced that the team's newest recruit would begin his career in the Dodger organization with the Montreal Royals, Brooklyn's top farm team in the Triple A International League. The accompanying Dodger story line was that Robinson's signing had little to do with racial justice and everything to do with his being a fine player who could eventually help Brooklyn win baseball games. Rickey also tried to downplay the less savory aspects of Robinson's past. Missing from Dodger press releases were any references to his youthful brushes with the law, as well as his battles with and discharge from the army. Also kept from the public was any suggestion of his sometimes terrible temper.

Branch Rickey wanted nothing negative about the unfolding Jackie Robinson story to appear in print. For the most part, he succeeded. Robinson's personal history was not paraded before the public, but his plusses and minuses on the baseball diamond were scrutinized—and openly criticized. New York *Daily News* columnist Jimmy Powers thought he was at best a "1,000-to-1 shot to make the grade." *The Sporting News* scouting report rated him a "Class C" prospect, "were he white." Cleveland Indian pitcher Bob Feller added a similar note: "If he were a white man, I doubt if they would consider him big league material." When informed of Feller's verdict, Robinson retorted that he'd barnstormed against the Indian hurler exactly twice. "If you lined up ten of us (Negro Leaguers), I'll bet he couldn't pick me out of the bunch."

Sam Lacy and Wendell Smith were quite certain that every baseball fan in the country would recognize Robinson's abilities if he were given a chance to perform for the Dodgers. But they also understood that much was at stake. To Smith, the "hopes and ambitions of thirteen million black Americans [were] heaped upon [Robinson's] broad shoulders." At the same time, a columnist for the *New York Age* let his readers know that he felt "sorry for Jackie. He will be haunted by the expectations of his race. . . . Unlike white players, he can never afford an off-day or an off-night. His private life will be watched, too, because white America will judge the Negro race by everything he does. And Lord help him with his fellow Negroes if he should fail them."

At least one of Robinson's peers was less cautious than resentful. Monarch pitcher Satchel Paige thought he should have been chosen over Robinson. After all, an argument could be made that Paige was the best pitcher in all of baseball, white or black, even though he was approaching forty. Not until much later did Paige go public with his feelings of rejection and resentment, but they had been there from the beginning. Robinson's signing had hurt him "deep down." He'd been the one "who the white boys wanted to barnstorm against." But Paige had a rationalization at the ready: "Those major league owners knew I wouldn't start out with any minor league team. . . ." Still, Paige publicly supported Robinson, whom he called a "number one player."

Other Negro Leaguers were not so sure. As ten-time Negro League All-Star Buck Leonard of the Homestead Grays succinctly put it, "we didn't think he was that good." In fact, a few of the more suspicious among that fraternity thought that Rickey had signed Robinson *knowing* that the Monarch shortstop would fail, thereby quashing integration possibilities for the foreseeable future. But despite his personal hurt and disappointment, Satchel Paige never could agree with the naysayers. He too got straight to the point by saying that Rickey "didn't make a mistake in signing Robinson."

Robinson began his post-Monarch career by barnstorming with white and black players throughout Venezuela. His unofficial tutor and confidante along the way was Gene Benson, an aging Negro League player whom Rickey had asked to help Robinson improve his basic skills. This veteran of black baseball did just that, but his most important contribution to Rickey's design was what he did to improve Robinson's overall attitude and boost his confidence at the plate and in the field. He kept telling Robinson that "where you're going is easier than where you're coming from." Jackie had trouble believing what he was hearing. Was Gene Benson telling him that Negro League players were better than their major league counterparts? No, Benson conceded, the caliber of play was better in the majors. Still, he insisted, it was going to be "easier" to play the game in the majors. When pressed for specifics by a perplexed Robinson, his tutor reminded him that in the Negro Leagues "throwing at you is just part of the game." If a batter complained, the umpire would simply order him to get back in the batter's box. Once there, hitters had to be ready for anything, including a spitball. That type of pitch had been banned in the majors. Not so in the Negro Leagues, where "anybody can throw the spitter anytime he wants."

With Benson's help Robinson returned from South America armed with greater confidence in himself and a wedding ring for Rachel. On February 10, 1946, he and Rachel were finally married, with his Pasadena mentor the Reverend Karl Downs officiating. After a brief honeymoon in San Jose, the new couple began a harrowing journey to Florida en route to Jackie's first spring training camp as a Dodger farmhand. Bumped from planes and buses in favor of white passengers, the Robinsons arrived in Florida exhausted and angry. To Jackie, the trip brought back too many reminders of his life in the segregated military. To Rachel, it opened her eyes to the reality of life for black Americans in the Old South.

Wendell Smith was on hand to greet the Robinsons when they arrived in Florida. Major league teams, then and now, do not have official greeters. But both Robinsons needed that much—and more. For Smith, the realization quickly hit home that his job had just begun. The treatment the couple had received while traveling had been so terrible that Jackie was ready to quit before he had even begun. It took an all-night session with Smith to convince him that he ought to forget about his journey to Florida and report to the Dodger training camp as scheduled.

The next day Clyde Sukeforth met Robinson (and black teammate, pitcher John Wright, who at this point was the only other member of Rickey's interracial package). The Dodger scout then escorted the two rookies to their first meeting with Royals manager Clay Hopper. A white Mississippian, the forty-four-year-old Hopper brought to his job all of the racial attitudes of his past and his region. To put it bluntly, the Montreal manager did not believe that blacks and whites belonged anywhere together. But if Hopper initially resented the presence of Robinson and Wright on his squad, he kept his considerable reservations to himself. Although Clay Hopper was racist, he was also a thoroughly knowledgeable baseball man and a loyal Branch Rickey disciple. For his part, Rickey was confident that Hopper's loyalty to the Dodgers generally and to him specifically guaranteed that the Montreal manager would not derail the experiment.

Sam Lacy's *Afro-American* may have summarized the worries of black Americans with a simple, but loaded, headline that read: "Oh! Oh!" For his part, Hopper may have begged Rickey to remove him from this assignment. But before spring training was over it had become apparent that the concerns of both Lacy and Hopper were unfounded. It was also apparent that Rickey knew what he was doing when he asked Hopper to manage the Royals *after* he assigned Robinson to play for that team. Hopper had been at the helm of Rickey farm clubs for seventeen consecutive years and had developed a number of young players for both the Cardinals and the Dodgers. When it came to his handling and evaluating minor league prospects, Clay Hopper was anything but a gamble. Because of Hopper's standing within the organization, Rickey hoped that his eventual acceptance of Robinson would provide a good example to young white players in the Dodger system. Once again, here was Branch Rickey at his optimistic best.

Grounds for optimism aside, Rickey was beset by a number of potentially troubling challenges during the winter of 1945–46. Concern was ongoing that Negro League owners would file a law suit over Rickey's original signing of Robinson, even though Rickey had banked on there being no such suit given the chaotic personnel practices in the Negro Leagues. Personal financial difficulties also loomed because Rickey had gone into considerable debt to acquire a 25 percent share of the Dodgers.

With pressures building from a variety of sources, Rickey began to experience mysterious dizzy spells. Doctors were initially unable to diagnose the problem. Numerous tests were conducted before it was determined that he was suffering from Meniere's Syndrome, which stemmed from a gradual deterioration of a nerve

leading to the inner ear. Its manifestation included not just ver-
tigo, but nausea as well. While there was no permanent cure, it
could be controlled by medication. Nonetheless, Rickey experienced at least eight more spells over the ensuing two or three
years and would be plagued with the syndrome for the rest of his
life. For the immediate future he was ordered to do nothing but
rest. To help him do just that, doctors hospitalized him for five
weeks.

Rickey emerged from his doctors' care in time for spring training—and just in time to issue a few orders of his own. The initial
plan had been to break Jackie in at shortstop. But that suspect arm
grew progressively weaker with each day in camp. Because he
didn't want his charge sitting on the bench, Rickey instructed
Hopper to move Robinson to first base. The manager complied,
but Robinson had difficulty mastering the footwork required at
this new position. Fortunately, his arm had healed enough by that
time to allow him to try his hand at second base. After a few days
back in the middle of the infield Robinson began to show the very
skills that Rickey knew he possessed.

Hopper was less convinced. During an intrasquad game Rickey
and Hopper were sitting together when Robinson dove for a ball
hit up the middle. After snagging it, he made a back-handed flip to
the shortstop to force out the runner at second. Rickey was ecstatic. "Wasn't that just a superhuman play?" he roared. But Hopper responded with a question of his own: "Mr. Rickey, do you
really think a nigger's a human being?"

Rickey was silent, and no doubt pained and disappointed as
well. But he held his tongue. He didn't berate Hopper. Instead,
knowing that the Montreal manager was a sincere man whose
racial views were deeply rooted in him, he chose to believe that
Hopper's question would ultimately be answered by Robinson's
play and demeanor. Then and only then would Clay Hopper begin to change his mind. Until then, there was nothing that Branch
Rickey could say that would really matter.

Robinson's play in spring training games did begin to help erase
Hopper's prejudices. But the real story of this Florida spring was

that the rookie infielder survived the experience at all. There had been much to endure. At a pretraining camp at Sanford, Florida, Jack was ordered off the field by a delegation from the community. At Jacksonville, the Royals arrived to play a game only to find the gate to the ballpark padlocked and a police contingent on hand to ensure that the team (especially Robinson) did not take the field. A second incident took place at Sanford in early April. Rickey had ignored a demand by city leaders to bar Robinson from a game. But they did not ignore Robinson. On their orders, and with the game underway, the chief of police walked onto the field to inform Hopper that Robinson had to be removed—and not just from the diamond, but from the ballpark as well. Under the circumstances the manager and his player could do little but comply.

Throughout the spring, Robinson was repeatedly subjected to humiliation. Beyond that, he had to contend with the ongoing public glare and his own poor play. There were cheers from black fans who embarrassed him by applauding everything he did and taunts from white fans who only embarrassed themselves. Finally, there was the ostracism and the pressure, which included the terrible pressure he put on himself.

If Jackie still had any reason to think that "Mr. Rickey's" experiment was little more than a publicity stunt, such thoughts had perished by the end of spring training. Given his less-than-stellar play, Robinson might well have been cut by the Royals. In fact, he half expected as much. Instead, he made the team and would go to Montreal as planned. Errors aside—as well as the all too occasional flashes of brilliance—Branch Rickey was in this for the long haul. He had not forgotten to be patient. And he had just seen Robinson practice the same virtue under tremendous pressure.

If Dodger fans or baseball writers at all suspected that Robinson's retention was less an experiment than a stunt, their suspicions were put to rest on Opening Day, 1946. On that day Montreal defeated the Jersey City Giants 14-1, and Jackie Robinson went four for five, hitting a homer, driving in four runs, and stealing two bases. Not every day would be like that one, but his play throughout the rest of the season was generally superb. After it was over, Robinson was awarded the league's Most Valuable Player (MVP) crown on the basis of a .349 batting average, a tie for first in runs scored, and the best fielding average among all International League second basemen.

Sadly, life away from the field of play was never very easy. The people of Montreal accepted the Robinsons, but only on a superficial level. Walls of isolation and separation remained firmly in place. Jackie and Rachel were objects, not neighbors. In the clubhouse, Robinson's teammates kept their distance. On the road, Robinson's accommodations were invariably segregated. Despite his great season, life as a Montreal Royal was desperately lonely and at times potentially violent for this most isolated of rookies.

Early in the season the Royals were scheduled to play a series in Baltimore, the most Southern of the cities in the International League. Fearing the worst, league president Frank Shaughnessy phoned Rickey and begged him to keep Robinson out of the lineup against the Orioles. Rickey was unmoved. To scratch Robinson would only encourage the kind of behavior that Shaughnessy claimed to fear. Shaughnessy was not convinced. He predicted "rioting and bloodshed" if Rickey refused to change his mind. Characteristically, the Dodger president held his ground. After all, he'd been doing that for better than forty years, or at least ever since his first coaching job at Ohio Wesleyan.

Robinson played the entire series. Nothing approaching a riot ensued, though there were catcalls—and worse—from the stands and the opposing bench. But that had happened in other parks around the league. Still, Robinson had all he could do to try to ignore what was swirling around him—and dodge the projectiles hurled at him. Inside he was being eaten alive. He knew as much. So did Rachel.

Branch Rickey was kept fully informed as to what was happening on the field, even if he could never have known exactly what it was doing to Robinson. By this time Branch had assigned his younger brother, Frank, to follow the Royals through the remainder of the season. Frank Rickey's main responsibility was to send regular reports to his brother's office on Montague Street.

Those reports were confined to Robinson's play, Robinson's demeanor, and the fans' and opponents' reactions to him.

By the end of July, events had taken such a toll on her husband that Rachel insisted he see a doctor. There had been too many days when he couldn't keep any food down—and too many nights when he couldn't sleep at all. Finally, he complied with her persistent pleadings. The diagnosis was "nervous exhaustion," and the recommendation was a ten-day break from play. Jackie agreed, but less than a week later he was back on the field, fearful as he was that he would be tagged as lazy if he stayed out any longer. That *New York Age* columnist was right: he would be held to a higher standard.

Jackie Robinson's first year in the Dodger organization ended with an exciting Little World Series between the Royals and the Louisville Colonels of the American Association. Guess who scored the winning run for the Royals in the sixth and deciding game? No sooner was the game over than Montreal fans rushed onto the field to hoist Jackie to their shoulders. Hopper received the same treatment. There they were, the black player and his white manager, together being paraded around the field by joyful Royals fans. Later Robinson emerged from the clubhouse only to be engulfed in adulation once again. After accepting the fans' accolades, as well as their hugs and kisses, he politely began edging his way out of the melée. Soon edging turned into thrusting. Ultimately, Robinson made his escape by transforming himself from the baseball player he was into the football player he had once been by breaking into an open field run while being chased down the streets by hundreds of fans. A sportswriter for Sam Lacy's Pittsburgh *Courier* could not avoid noting the irony of the scene. It was, he wrote, perhaps the first time in history that a black man was hounded by a white mob "and not because of hate but because of love."

Robinson's great year meant many things, not the least of which was that his future could now be judged on his merits as a player within the Dodger organization and not on the color of his skin. But that great year did not necessarily guarantee him an automatic promotion to the Brooklyn Dodgers. While there had been some pressure on Rickey to bring Robinson up *before* the end of the 1946 season, Rickey steadfastly refused. There was still more work to be done.

Rickey's cohorts among major league magnates were no more willing to put a black player on a major league field now than they had been at the time of Commissioner Landis's death two years earlier. By the time of the winter meetings of 1946 a new commissioner was in place. His name was A. B. "Happy" Chandler. A Kentuckian by birth and a Democrat by trade, Chandler had served one term as the governor of his home state and another as a U.S. senator. There was little evidence in Chandler's personal or political past that would indicate any commitment on his part to black civil rights. There was also little evidence that he would give Rickey any encouragement following a 15-1 vote *against* permitting black players in the major leagues. (There is disagreement as to just when that vote was taken during the off-season, but there is no doubt that Rickey cast the lone "yes" vote.) Nonetheless, Chandler did respond to Rickey's request for support by telling the Dodger president to go ahead and "bring him in. He'll play if he's got the capacity to play."

Though Rickey gladly accepted every bit of encouragement that came his way, he found it necessary to issue a few discouraging words of his own. Such words came in torrents on February 5, 1947. The place was the Carlton Branch of the Brooklyn YMCA, where some thirty local black leaders had gathered at Rickey's request to hear the words of someone who had long ago traveled the YMCA circuit. Throwing aside his prepared text, Rickey sought to take his listeners into his confidence as he launched into a history lesson and a series of calculated warnings.

After broadly hinting that he was indeed considering putting Jackie Robinson on the Dodger roster, Rickey reminded his audience that he had yet to make his final decision. He wanted everyone in attendance to know that "if" he did bring Robinson up "the biggest threat to his success—and the one enemy most likely to ruin that success—was the Negro people themselves!"

As shocking as that line was calculated to be, more shocks were on the way. "Every step of racial progress you have made has been won by suffering and often bloodshed. This step in baseball is being taken for you by a single person whose wound you cannot see or share. . . . And yet, on the day that Robinson enters the big leagues—*if* he does—every one of you will go out and form parades and welcoming committees. You'll strut. You'll wear badges. You'll hold Jackie Robinson Days and Jackie Robinson nights. You'll get drunk. You'll fight. You'll be arrested. You'll wine and dine the player until he is fat and futile. You'll transform his victory into a national comedy—and ultimately into a national tragedy, yes, a tragedy!"

Having flattened his listeners, Rickey was not about to flatter them—or even revive them. Instead, he finished with a warning. "If any individual, group, or segment of Negro society sees the advancement of Jackie Robinson in baseball as a symbol of social 'ism' or schism, a triumph of race over race, I will curse the day I ever signed him to a contract, and I will personally see that baseball is never so abused and misrepresented again!"

At that moment many in the audience rose to their feet and cheered. Some even wept. Cries of "speak, brother, speak" came from more than a few. Rickey was so overcome with emotion that, for perhaps the first time in his life, he could not speak. Finally, he offered this bit of advice: organize committees of black leaders in every major city and have them take the lead in making sure that no one spoiled Robinson's opportunity. In short, "Don't spoil Jackie's chances."

Who could know what those African-American leaders were thinking as they went home that night? Middle-class men that they were, they were prone to engaging in their own form of condescension toward those less fortunate, especially toward newly arrived poor blacks from the rural South. Many in Rickey's audience were professionals who had worked hard for what they had achieved. Others were reformers who hoped to elevate the recent arrivals from the South to their own middle-class status, a status defined not simply by one's income, but by one's behavior.

At the midpoint of the twentieth century, middle-class Americans and those who hoped to become middle-class Americans were taught to abide by certain rules. Hard work and loyalty to family and country lay at the heart of respectability. Deportment was, of course, not far from that center either. Here Rickey was simply reinforcing the middle-class message. No matter their color, people ought not to drink excessively. Certainly they shouldn't fight publicly. And, most assuredly, they had better not wind up in jail. But Rickey's not-so-hidden message was that black Americans, southern and northern, had a special obligation to do everything they could to avoid even the appearance of departing from the straight-and-narrow middle-class path. The large matter of appearance included the not-so-small matter of dress. Middle-class people, especially blacks, had to dress the part—even at baseball games, and now especially at baseball games. All this in the name of doing everything possible to avoid "spoiling Jackie's chances." No doubt Rickey was preaching to the choir that night.

In any event, part of Rickey's plan for Robinson demanded that he begin to take others into his confidence. One of the most important was Dodger play-by-play announcer Red Barber. Rickey knew how important Barber's reassuring voice was to Dodger fans. He knew that those who listened to Dodger games trusted Barber, that Barber's words—and voice—would be critical to advancing fan acceptance of Robinson. What Rickey could not be sure of was Red Barber's personal reaction to his plan. Like Clay Hopper, Barber was a white southerner. The Dodger announcer later conceded that he entertained the idea of resigning when Rickey first told him of his intentions. But once he put that thought aside—and he put it aside very quickly—Red Barber became an effective Rickey ally, both on the air and behind the scenes. Barber on Barber was more retiring: "I didn't resent him [Robinson] and I didn't crusade for him. I broadcast the ball."

Rickey's careful preparations for the historic 1947 season included shifting the Dodgers' spring training site to Havana, Cuba. He also arranged for the Dodgers and Royals to play a series of exhibition games in Panama. In either locale, Robinson and his Royal (and future Dodger) teammates would not just be out of the glare of the Florida sun and the reach of Florida police, but a few more steps removed from the heat generated by the New York press as well. Safely lost in the Caribbean, Robinson and the entire Dodger organization could find relative calm and quiet. Publicity would be minimal and pressure would be manageable. Or at least that was what Branch Rickey hoped.

But luck, it seems, was not the residue of hope. While there was a method to his Caribbean madness, in one sense it was mad—especially to someone who had always scrutinized the bottom line. The most conservative estimate had it that the Cuban venture would cost the Dodgers an extra $50,000, a considerable figure in 1947. Though Rickey was willing to swallow the potential loss, he planned to offset it; he fully expected to see large crowds of baseball-wise Cubans at Dodger exhibition games. But those crowds did not materialize. Accustomed to high-caliber play, Cuban fans refused to spend money to watch out-of-shape Americans perform at something less than their best. In the end, Rickey took the loss, knowing that other goals were more important anyway.

His most immediate goal was to create an atmosphere in which Robinson would be accepted by his eventual Dodger teammates. Rickey thought that could best be accomplished some place far removed from the everyday distractions of spring training. In Cuba, his players would be forced to deal with one another. Rickey's assumption was that white racism, latent or otherwise, would melt away in the Cuban sun. Racism, he reasoned, was a product of ignorance; and ignorance was the result of the absence of contact between the races.

Branch Rickey fancied himself to be many things, among them a student of history. And his reading of history had convinced him that his theory made sense. He was especially influenced by the writings of Columbia University historian Frank Tannenbaum, who found greater tolerance in Latin American societies, where blacks and whites regularly mixed with one another. Tannenbaum's key word was "proximity." Rickey loved the word. In the first place, it was a wonderful, multisyllabic word, the very sort of word that Rickey loved to sprinkle throughout his preachings. But this word also expressed an important idea. Proximity between the races was bound to improve relations between them, because it was bound to eat away at ignorance. It was a greatly optimistic idea, perhaps even a naive one. But where better to implement it than in the very Latin culture that Tannenbaum held up as ideal?

At the same time, Rickey did not want to appear to be forcing Robinson on the rest of the Dodger team. Better that they come to see him as one of their own. Better yet, they might come to Rickey one day to *demand* that Robinson join the team. Sure, the white Dodgers might be hesitant to accept him at first. But given time—and proximity—and Robinson's great talents, the rest of the Dodger team would soon see things the same way that Rickey did. This was the plan. This was the hope.

It was Rickey himself, however, who contributed to a certain lack of proximity by insisting on segregated housing for Robinson and his fellow black players: pitchers John Wright, Don Newcombe, and Roy Partlow and catcher Roy Campanella. Once again Branch Rickey was proving to be a very cautious risk taker. Here he was, on the verge of challenging the entire baseball establishment by putting Jackie Robinson in a Dodger uniform, but he would not issue the slightest of challenges to the social convention of segregation within his own spring training camp. To Rickey this was still a "great adventure," but one that continued to require "great deliberation."

On the field of play, however, Branch Rickey wanted Jackie Robinson to be anything but deliberate. This was especially the case as the Dodgers and the Royals prepared for an exhibition series in Panama. For the first time Robinson would appear on the same field with his future Dodger teammates. Just prior to the first game of the series Rickey pulled Robinson aside to pass along a few last-minute instructions. "I want you to run wild, to steal the pants off them, to be the most conspicuous player on the field." When he spoke those words, Branch Rickey was not just thinking about Robinson's impact on the Dodger players on the field. He was also thinking about his impact on New York baseball writers and fans. And the more explosive he could be, the more likely it was that the New York fans would "demand . . . that you be brought up to the majors."

Those few words were as close as Rickey had come to revealing his hand to Robinson. Rickey had offered Robinson no guarantee that he would be wearing a Dodger uniform come the start of the 1947 major league season, but, for the moment at least, Jackie's anxiety over his future must have decreased. After all, the man who controlled it had just told him that a good chunk of his own fate was now in his own explosive hands.

If Jackie Robinson had reason to believe that Branch Rickey was his unquestioned ally, he had little reason to think that Dodger players were looking forward to his joining them. Almost to a man, they were cold to him during the initial Panama series. Jackie couldn't help but notice. In fact, he could barely contain his resentment at the treatment he received. But he did his best to keep everything to himself. For public consumption he said only that if the Dodgers didn't want him, "there would be no point in forcing myself on them." Baseball, after all, was a team game and "morale is mighty important" to any successful team. But Robinson couldn't resist making one more comment. Look at the 1946 Montreal Royals. They were successful, and they hadn't exactly "suffered by my presence."

Apparently some of the Dodger players *were* suffering—and none too silently—at the prospect of having Jackie Robinson as their teammate. Rickey had anticipated as much and was counting on his manager, the fiery Leo Durocher, to quell any potential player rebellion before it started. Durocher did his best to do so. When he learned that an anti-Robinson petition was about to be circulated among his players, he wasted no time in calling a team meeting at the unlikeliest of hours. It was midnight when the manager made his case as bluntly as he could to his bleary-eyed charges—and potential mutineers. The essence of his argument was not in Rickey's league. Nor could he match his boss in erudition. Robinson belonged on his team for the simple reason that Durocher was convinced that he could help the Brooklyn Dodgers win baseball games. From everything he had heard (and now seen) "this fellow is a real great ballplayer." And if he turns out to be half as great as he looks, every Dodger player within earshot of Durocher would make money. "I don't care if the guy is yellow or black . . . I say he can make all of us rich . . . And if any of you can't use the money, I'll see that you're traded." In the meantime, he warned, get used to Robinson's presence. "From everything I hear, he's only the first, boys, only the first."

Durocher's reference to money had nothing to do with Robinson's potential impact on player salaries. The reserve system was still very much in place. No player was going to get rich negotiating a new contract with management. What the Dodger manager did have in mind was winning National League pennants and qualifying for a share of the pot of money available to World Series winners. Untold riches were not to be had by taking home a cut of World Series money. But a player on a championship team could at least expect to add a hefty chunk to his regular season salary.

If Durocher's money talk wasn't sufficiently persuasive, Branch Rickey was right there to add more than his two cents. Having arrived in Havana a few days earlier, he was ready to inspect his charges and deal directly with potential troublemakers, should any materialize. The very next day he began to meet with his mutineers, first collectively and then one-by-one. In all, seven such players-turned-plotters had been identified. If there was a lead plotter, it was popular outfielder Dixie Walker. The Georgia-born Walker had been quite vocal about his opposition to Robinson. More than that, he was the player who had circulated the petition that had prompted Durocher's harangue. In reverse order of their importance to the team, the other six were third-string rookie catcher Bobby Bragan, reserve infielder Cookie Lavagetto, veteran pitchers Hugh Casey and Kirby Higbe, second baseman Eddie Stanky, and rightfielder Carl Furillo. All but California-born Lavagetto and Pennsylvania-born Furillo were from the South. One crucial southerner was not among the signees. That would be the Dodger shortstop, Kentucky-born "Pee Wee" Reese. Because Robinson was also a shortstop, Reese may have had more than one reason to sign the Walker petition. But he refused to do so. Having been in the navy for three years, he simply wanted to play baseball. It was time to make money, not waves. Hence his decision to reject those who would reject Robinson. And this small act of resistance may have had as much to do with the failure of the players' petition as any word spoken by Durocher or Rickey.

But Branch Rickey did indeed have his say on the matter. He began by delivering his standard sermon on Americanism. Each of them had no doubt heard the Dodger president preach on this subject many times before. This particular sermon, after all, was one of Rickey's favorites. But no Dodger player had ever witnessed Branch Rickey at this level of intensity. This was Rickey the paternalist at his most stern and Rickey the evangelist at his most intense. This was also the very same Branch Rickey who had spoken his mind to those black leaders of Brooklyn a few weeks earlier.

Furillo proved to be the easiest to handle. The Dodger boss began by reminding the second-year outfielder that his parents had come to the United States from Sicily for one reason only: to better themselves. That's all Jackie Robinson wanted to do. Why should anyone stand in the way of his journey from California to Brooklyn? Rickey then informed Furillo that he would have to accept Robinson as his teammate or find himself unemployed. The choice was easily made.

The "People's Cherce," Dixie Walker, would have been far more difficult had he actually been on the scene. The source of the problem, the author of the petition that had prompted Rickey's intervention, had been called home because of a family illness. But before departing he had written Rickey a letter in which he made his desire for a trade quite clear. A Dodger fixture since 1940 and a perennial .300 hitter, the thirty-six-year-old outfielder thought he had considerable bargaining room. Hence his ultimatum.

Rickey did not wish to part with Walker, who was a popular and a productive player. His own estimate was that Walker had at least two .300-plus season left in his bat, and he wanted at least one of those years to be spent in a Brooklyn uniform. As it turned out, Walker remained on the team and hit .306 for the Dodgers in

1947. At season's end he was dealt to the Pirates (with whom he would have his final .300-plus season in a major league uniform by hitting .316 the following year).

Despite his intensity and his convictions, Branch Rickey was not the sort of man to engage in reverse bigotry. In fact, he did his best to understand the dilemma of those white players who were in the process of having their racial world turned upside down. And this was especially the case for white southerners. They were given a difficult task: to unthink that which they had thought for a lifetime. Rickey understood that. But he still wanted to believe that time—and proximity—and a little prodding would eventually make a difference. After all, he had the Clay Hopper example to point to. Wouldn't his players be close behind?

A few weeks later, Rickey found himself sharing such thoughts and the afternoon with a Dodger associate. As they discussed the ups and downs of integrating the Dodgers, Rickey began to recite from Alexander Pope's *Essay on Man*:

> Vice is a monster of so frightful mien
> As to be hated, needs but to be seen;
> Yet seen too oft, familiar with her face,
> We first endure, then pity, then embrace.

As he pondered those words, Rickey leaned back and stared into space as he searched for just the right twist on what Pope had written. Then he spoke: "First they'll endure Robinson, then pity him, then embrace him." Branch Rickey was nothing if not an idealist. He was also nothing if not a pragmatist.

The other immediate (not to mention pragmatic) question facing Rickey and Durocher was where in the infield to play Robinson. The Dodgers seemed set at short and second with Reese and Stanky. Third was out of the question because of Robinson's still questionable arm. This left first base, a position that Jackie did not want to play and one for which he had shown little aptitude. Was this Rickey's way of getting rid of Robinson? Once again that nagging thought crossed Jackie's mind. A year earlier he had been trying to persuade skeptical family and friends of Rickey's sincerity. Now his own doubts resurfaced.

Rickey had not helped matters by dropping hints to the press that the final decision would be left to Durocher. No sooner did he mention this possibility than Commissioner Chandler dropped his own bombshell on Rickey and the Dodgers. On the eve of the 1947 season the commissioner announced that, "effective immediately," Leo Durocher would be suspended from baseball for a year because of "conduct detrimental" to the game. The charge was as serious as it was vague. Behind it was a running feud that pitted Larry MacPhail (now of the hated Yankees) against both Durocher and Rickey. In a ghost-written article, Durocher had accused MacPhail of inviting known gamblers to sit with him at exhibition games in Cuba. MacPhail responded with charges of his own against Durocher's alleged involvement with gamblers. Complicating everything was not just the Yankee-Dodger rivalry, but Larry Mac-Phail's well-known opposition to the integration of major league baseball.

Chandler heard the evidence, such as it was, and issued his less than even-handed verdict. Both teams would be fined, but only Durocher would be suspended. For the moment, any discussion of Jackie Robinson and his baseball future had been pushed aside by charges and countercharges of gambling.

Rickey had been gambling as well. He had been gambling that the mercurial Durocher was not just the man to run the Dodgers, but the manager who could best ensure Robinson's acceptance on the team. A Dodger announcement that Robinson had made the team was supposed to have been made on the day Chandler suspended Durocher. Rickey decided to wait, but only for a day. On April 10, 1947, he circulated a brief note to writers covering a Royal-Dodger exhibition game at Ebbets Field. It was all of two sentences long and signed by Branch Rickey: "The Brooklyn Dodgers today purchased the contract of Jackie Robinson from the Montreal Royals. He will report immediately."

As it happened, Robinson joined the Dodgers simply by switching dressing rooms in Ebbets Field. He was issued number 42 and told to hang his clothes on a nail. A locker would be assigned as soon as one became available.

Jackie Robinson's major league debut was by no means a repeat of his first regular season game as a Montreal Royal. With Clyde Sukeforth as the interim manager, he went hitless and rapped into a double play before being removed for defensive purposes late in the game. But the real story of that day was the fact that Robinson was in the lineup and on the field. That alone prompted a small flood of telegrams to Rickey's office. Permit one Rabbi Isserman to speak for all of them: "Congratulations on engagement of Robinson. It's good sportsmanship, good baseball, good Americanism, good religion."

During his second game as a Dodger, Robinson began to play good baseball. He also began to reveal the brand of baseball he would play. His first hit was a perfectly placed bunt single in the fifth inning. The hit itself proved meaningless, but it was a portent of the Jackie Robinson to come.

And it was this Jackie Robinson, Robinson on the base paths, whom fans came to see. Ebbets Field was only two-thirds full for Robinson's debut. (Among the crowd were an estimated 14,000 black fans.) But before the season was very old Ebbets Field was home to huge crowds. Fans, black and white, were moving through the turnstiles in record numbers to see Jackie Robinson play. The Dodger rookie was, according to Red Barber, the "biggest attraction in baseball since Babe Ruth." That attraction accounted for a team attendance record of 1,807,526. It was a record that the Brooklyn Dodgers would never break.

But Robinson's on-field exploits were far from the only story in 1947. On a cold, blustery day in late April a near full-house was on hand to welcome the Dodgers home from a brief road trip. The opposition was provided by the Philadelphia Phillies, managed by Tennessee-born Ben Chapman. What happened that afternoon made Clay Hopper out to be a model of racial rectitude. Robinson later remembered it as the day that "brought me nearer to cracking up than I had ever been."

The insults and the racial taunts began in the first inning and continued until the last out was made. As if "synchronized by some master conductor," venom spewed from Chapman and his Phillies. The next day Dodger traveling secretary Harold Parrott reported to Rickey that he had never heard such "dugout filth to match the abuse that [was] sprayed on Robinson last night."

"Hey, nigger, why don't you go back to the cotton field where you belong?"

"They're waiting for you in the jungles, black boy."

"Hey, snowflake, which one of those white boys' wives are you dating tonight?"

Jackie tried vainly to pretend that he heard none of this. As he did his best to "endure the insults," he couldn't help but wonder what the Phillies wanted from him. More than that, he asked himself whether "Mr. Rickey" really expected him to "endure" this? "For one wild and rage-crazed moment," Jackie Robinson was ready to say "to hell with Mr. Rickey's 'noble experiment' . . . to hell with the image of the patient black freak."

But at the last moment Robinson remembered not just his promise to Rickey, but his unspoken pact with black fans and black leaders. To break his word with the Dodger president, to fight back even at this "rage-crazed moment," would mean setting back for years, maybe even decades, the breaking of baseball's color line. With one ignoble punch the whole "noble experiment" would be over. Instead of throwing that punch, Jackie held back and endured the insults. Later he struck a more telling blow by lining a clean single and scoring the lone run in a 1-0 Dodger victory.

When the game was over Robinson had more than one reason to feel vindicated. Obviously, his play and his restraint had been commendable. But the insults hurled by Chapman and the Phillies had been so relentless and so cruel that they had also angered his Dodger teammates. At one point Eddie Stanky took matters into his own hands by issuing a taunt of his own: "Listen, you yellow-bellied cowards. Why don't you yell at somebody who can answer back? There isn't one of you who has the guts of a louse."

Curiously, the second baseman from Alabama, the player nicknamed "The Brat," was rapidly becoming Robinson's major defender among the Dodgers. In Rickey's judgment, Eddie Stanky had little natural ability. He couldn't hit, run, field, or throw very well. But he always managed to find a way to help his team win.

Having endured and perhaps even pitied Jackie Robinson in the spring of 1947, Stanky was now helping *their* team win by finally embracing him.

Dixie Walker would never go that far, but he was also upset by Chapman's behavior. Despite—or perhaps because—the two were friends, he confronted the Phillies' manager after the game. Having heard the venom, he felt compelled to tell Chapman that the Phillies had stepped over the line. Having endured Robinson for a few months, Walker had at least moved toward pitying him.

But the worst was far from over. Robinson completed his first month as a major leaguer with a .225 batting average, enduring not just insults, but an 0 for 20 slump along the way. If there was a low time for Jackie during the 1947 season, it was the early part of May. Threats against his life began to arrive in the mail. The abuse from rival players had not let up. He would be denied access to the visitors' hotel in Philadelphia (and humiliated by the Dodgers' bowing to the slight). And right now he was not playing all that well.

Still, there was no thought of benching him. Rickey counseled patience. And new Dodger Manager Burt Shotton concurred. Whenever writers questioned Shotton about Robinson's future he simply shrugged his shoulders and penciled him into the lineup for the next game.

Burt Shotton does not rank among the great managers in the history of the game. Perhaps his most distinctive claim is that he ended his managerial career on the same note and at the same time as the legendary Connie Mack. When both retired in 1950 they would be the last major league managers to wear street clothes in the dugout. But this long-time Rickey friend and associate was a solid major leaguer and a decent field manager. On the diamond Shotton had compiled a lifetime batting average of .270 and stolen 294 bases over a thirteen-year career. In 1926 Rickey hired him to manage in the Cardinal farm system. After a stint running the lowly Philadelphia Phillies, Shotton returned to work for Rickey in 1935, managing the Columbus Red Birds, which was the top Cardinal minor league team. There he gained a well-earned reputation for doing what Rickey wanted done: bringing along younger players. By 1947 Shotton had retired to Florida when Rickey summoned him with this terse telegram: "Be in Brooklyn tomorrow. See nobody. Say nothing. Rickey."

With that command the placid presence of Burt Shotton was thrust into the middle of what Red Barber termed the "most torn-apart ball club in history." That Shotton helped prepare the way for the calm following the chaos is a credit to Rickey's wisdom and his luck; but it is also a credit to Burt Shotton himself. Sometimes luck can be the residue of miscarried designs. Rickey had thought that the mercurial Leo Durocher was the best choice to pilot the Dodgers through the storms of 1947. He may have been better advised to have selected the placid Burt Shotton in the first place. Certainly Robinson both "respected" his substitute manager and "appreciated his patience. . . ."

By early May, Shotton and Rickey began to see encouraging signs from Robinson. Most important, Jack began to hit. But not everything that was heartening occurred on the field of play. On a bright day in May, Joe Louis happened to show up at Ebbets Field. No sooner had the great boxer taken his seat than Jackie walked over to shake his hand. And no sooner had the two black men exchanged greetings than warm applause began to ripple through the ball park. As Red Barber remembered it, "photographers sprang up around them like rain lilies after a cloudburst." It was, in the Dodger announcer's understated words, a "turning point."

But it was not the end of the ugliness. The New York *Herald Tribune* claimed to have uncovered a planned strike by Rickey's old team, the St. Louis Cardinals. Just how serious the players actually were is difficult to determine, but Cardinal owner Sam Breadon took the matter seriously enough to rush off to New York City to confer with National League President Ford Frick, even as he tried to downplay the gravity of the situation. Frick took the strike plot quite seriously. Acting swiftly, he announced that any striking player would be "suspended from the league." He went on to state that he didn't care if "half the league strikes. Those who do it will encounter swift retribution. All will be suspended and I don't care if it wrecks the National League for five years." After all, "this is America and baseball is America's game." For a baseball executive (and eventual commissioner) with a well-deserved reputation for meekly doing the bidding of the owners who paid his salary, this may have been his finest hour. No Cardinal player challenged the suddenly decisive Frick. No further strike plots surfaced. One more "turning point" had been tentatively reached— and successfully negotiated.

A few days later the Dodgers paid their first visit of the season to Shibe Park in Philadelphia. This four-game Dodger-Philly series would also be the first games between the two teams since the Ben Chapman-inspired outpouring of bigotry in Ebbets Field. This time Jackie would score no winning run (as his Dodgers lost three of the four games). This time few words were directed at him from the Phillies bench (though Robinson did recall that bats accompanied by "machine gun-like noises" were pointed at him more than once). And this time Ben Chapman was on his best behavior.

Perhaps fearful of losing his job and no doubt responding to orders from above, Chapman agreed to pose for a picture with Robinson. There would be no handshake, but the two men did agree to stand together behind home plate while each held a bat for the cameras. For the moment Robinson seemed to be in a forgiving mood. At least that was his public posture at the time. In Jackie's semi-regular column for the Pittsburgh *Courier,* which appeared on May 10, he wrote that Chapman "impressed me as a nice fellow." Moreover, he doubted that the Phillies manager "really meant the things he was shouting at me the first time we played Philadelphia." Only later, in his autobiography, did Robinson reveal what was still very much on his mind: "Having my picture taken with this man was one of the most difficult things I had to make myself do."

During that pathbreaking 1947 season there were many things that Jackie Robinson had to make himself do—and not do. He had to put up with the humiliation of staying alone in black hotels while his white teammates were housed in the best any city had to offer. On occasion, he did room with Wendell Smith, who had been hired by Rickey for the season. Smith's role was not clearly defined; he was part companion, part chaperone, and part flack catcher. In any of these roles he could do much for Robinson, but he could not eliminate the sense of humiliation and disappointment Jackie often felt. Not the least of his pains concerned the failure of his white teammates to protest his being subjected to segregated housing arrangements whenever the Dodgers were on the road. And more often than not he had to eat alone, though on occasion he was joined by another Dodger rookie, centerfielder Duke Snider.

At bat, Robinson quickly learned that one of Branch Rickey's warnings had to be taken to heart. He also learned that Gene Benson hadn't been entirely right: the majors were not necessarily easier, at least not for their lone black player. By the end of May, Robinson had been thrown at—or close to—countless times and hit six times. On each of those half-dozen occasions he could only do what he had promised Rickey he would do: shake off the sting and trot stoically to first base. Though he probably did not know this, that sixth HBP (hit by a pitch) tied the individual mark for the whole of the 1946 season. There would be only three more such incidents during the rest of the 1947 season. Did National League pitchers suddenly grow kinder and gentler? Not really: two months of the season was enough to teach them that they didn't want the explosive Jackie Robinson dancing off first base and charging into second if they could possibly help it.

If Robinson's body was increasingly off-limits to opposing pitchers, it remained the target of other opposing players. In a game against the Cardinals in mid-August, Jackie was stationed at his regular post of first base. The two teams were in a tight pennant race and Dodger pitcher Ralph Branca was working on a no-hitter, but those facts alone did not dictate the near disastrous incident that occurred on a seventh-inning throw to first. Cardinal outfielder Enos Slaughter hit a sharp ground ball and raced to first. With both the ball and Slaughter about to reach the bag simultaneously, Jackie stretched to secure the out. At that moment Slaughter landed hard, not on the bag, but on Robinson's leg. In the process, his spikes narrowly missed Robinson's Achilles tendon. Slaughter was called out, the Dodgers won the game, and Robinson was not seriously injured. But forever after Jackie was convinced that the Cardinal outfielder had "deliberately" gone for his leg instead of the bag. And forever after Slaughter denied as much: "I never intentionally spiked Jackie Robinson." Who can know the truth? But this footnote to the story is worth mentioning: Enos Slaughter was thought to have been behind the aborted Cardinal strike of early May.

There were also incidents that cut the other way. One day in Boston—or possibly Cincinnati, since the accounts vary—the foul language and general abuse was particularly offensive. This time some of the taunts seem to have been directed at Robinson's keystone partner, "Pee Wee" Reese. Of course, both Reese and Robinson knew who the real target of the animosity was. In the midst of the verbal abuse, Reese left his position, walked over to first base, and put his hand on Robinson's shoulder. Suddenly the hecklers in the stands and in the dugout grew silent. For the first time in anyone's memory a white player had touched a black player fondly—and deliberately—on a baseball diamond. Another turning point had been reached. And the season was not yet half over.

By the end of June Jackie Robinson was "far from the unhappy ballplayer" that he had been in April and May. He was also in the middle of a sizzling hitting streak. Branch Rickey tried to act as though nothing at all about Robinson's play was out of the ordinary. In fact, he kept assuring the beat writers in the press box that they had yet to see the "real Robinson." "Maybe," he added, "you won't really see him until next year." Right now he's "still in a shell. Just wait until he gets to bunting and running as freely as he should."

On July 4 the Robinson hitting streak ended at twenty-one games—one game short of the major league record for rookies. No sooner did it end than he began another streak of almost the same length. Such performances did not land him on the All-Star team, but his vote total was impressive. Over 300,000 fans had cast their ballots for the rookie first baseman. No longer did he feel quite so alone.

And no longer was he literally so alone. In early July, Cleveland Indian owner Bill Veeck added black outfielder Larry Doby to the team roster. He did so without a minor league trial run and without any Rickey-style preparations or preachings. Now each league had one black player. By the end of August, Branch Rickey made major league history again. This time he signed and promoted the first black pitcher, Dan Bankhead, formerly of the Memphis Red Sox of the Negro Leagues. Now Jackie was no longer the only black person on his team. Bankhead did not prove to be the second coming of Robinson or Satchel Paige, but he did hit a home run in his first major league at bat. Another milestone had been recorded. And more would be on the way, as Rickey also signed Negro Leaguers and future Dodger stars Don Newcombe and Roy Campanella to minor league contracts.

But the only milestone that really mattered to Robinson and his Dodger teammates was the 1947 National League pennant. After a tense race with St. Louis, that pennant fell into the hands of the Dodgers on September 22 when the Cardinals lost to the Cubs. The season was all that Rickey and Robinson could have wanted. It had been a moral success and a financial success; now it was an artistic success as well. Unfortunately, it would not be capped off with the first World Series victory in Brooklyn Dodger history. MacPhail's Yankees walked off with the championship, this time four games to three.

The most memorable game of this series was the fourth. Down two games to one, the Dodgers had to win to stay alive. They did. Yankee pitcher Bill Bevens took a no-hitter and a 2-1 lead into the bottom of the ninth (when he set a World Series record by walking his ninth batter, Carl Furillo). Two batters later, pinch hitter Cookie Lavagetto delivered a game-winning double. The veteran Lavagetto was a marginal player who had been kept on the team by Rickey at Shotton's insistence. His hit was enough to square the series, but it was not enough to win it. Neither was anything that Robinson did. Over the course of the seven games he averaged only .259 and made no significant mark in the field or the basepaths.

Despite his disappointing World Series, Jackie Robinson had every reason to be proud of what he had accomplished over the course of his rookie year. He finished the regular season with a respectable .297 batting average and led the Dodgers in runs scored (125), singles (127), and total bases (255). He also tied Reese for the team lead in home runs with 12, and topped all National Leaguers in stolen bases with 29. Almost single handedly, Jackie Robinson had brought "tricky baseball" to the National League. Called the "Ebony Ty Cobb" by members of the press, Robinson's 46 bunting attempts resulted in 14 hits and 28 successful sacrifices.

More than that, he introduced what historian David Shiner calls the "third age of modern baseball." First there was the era of the "dead ball," dominated by Ty Cobb. Then there was the era of the long ball, personified by Babe Ruth. With the arrival of Jackie Robinson in Brooklyn, the key features of Negro League baseball, power *and* speed, had come to the National League. Today it is common to find "30-30" players, meaning those who hit at least thirty homers and steal at least thirty bases in a season. But, as Shiner notes, until Robinson no player in the history of the white major leagues had ever had more than six "12-12" seasons in his entire career. Robinson accomplished this then remarkable feat in each of his first seven years with the Dodgers. And it all began in 1947.

By the end of Robinson's rookie season the "noble experiment" was no longer an experiment at all. Jackie Robinson had come to play—and to stay—and to shine.

Accolades for Robinson came from many directions in 1947. During the season he was on the cover of *Time* magazine. In the postseason *The Sporting News* named him "Rookie of the Year." (This honor was especially satisfying because this leading baseball publication had long been a foe of integration, and as recently as spring training, 1947, its editors had been more than slightly suspicious of Robinson's playing abilities.) Even Dixie Walker chimed in. Jackie Robinson, he pronounced at the end of this tumultuous season, was "everything Branch Rickey said he was. . . ." If that single line didn't constitute yet another turning point, it certainly turned a few heads, Jackie Robinson's included.

More than unadorned tributes and semi-apologies came Robinson's way following his historic rookie season. Endorsement proposals arrived in his mailbox as well. Rickey had ordered Robinson to accept no commercial endorsements until the conclusion of the 1947 season. Now released from that restriction, he signed contracts to serve as a spokesman for everything from bread and milk to cigarettes. Whatever the product, these mass-market commercials represented the first time that an African American had been used so extensively as the messenger.

Though Jackie did have to think twice before agreeing to endorse Old Gold cigarettes, he was naturally pleased to be liberated from the Rickey ban. His salary for the 1947 season had been the major league minimum of $5,000. At the same time, he was well aware that his presence on the field during 1947 spelled larger profits for all National League teams. In fact, NAACP President Walter White estimated that total league revenue went up by at least $200,000 because Jackie Robinson was in the Dodger lineup. While no one expected that Robinson would be offered anything approaching a $200,000 contract for 1948, Jackie was hoping for at least $20,000. Rickey's first and final offer was $12,500. Both Robinsons were disappointed, but Jack signed without private negotiation or public complaint.

Years later Rachel recalled the signing ceremony as "pure plantation. There was no chance to negotiate, to discuss anything." Of course, she added, "it was no different for the white players, but I never thought it was right." At the time Jack kept any negative thoughts that he might have had very much to himself. He could not bring himself to challenge the man to whom he felt so indebted. When he met with baseball writers following his signing he simply told the assembled that "Mr. Rickey and I came to terms easily. I left it all to him and he came through with a good contract." He also refused to spar with reporters over his contract or

Right: Well beyond his playing days and just beyond his bench managing days, Branch Rickey, circa 1925, is solidly entrenched as a St. Louis Cardinal executive and on his way to becoming a powerful figure in major league baseball.

Below: A proudly confident "Mr. Rickey" shows off his certificate as *The Sporting News* executive of the year for 1936.

All photos are courtesy of *The Sporting News,* unless otherwise noted.

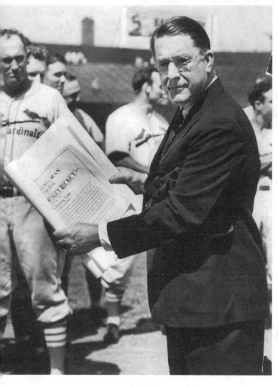

Above: Lieutenant Jack Roosevelt Robinson in the U.S. Army, circa 1943.

Left: Jackie Robinson in the uniform of the Kansas City Monarchs. The year is 1945. This was his only team and only year in Negro League baseball.

Opposite top: Jackie Robinson at first base during his 1947 rookie season as a Brooklyn Dodger.

Opposite bottom: Robinson in the Brooklyn dugout during his 1947 rookie season. Seated to his left is Eddie Stanky, whom Robinson replaced at second base in the spring of 1948.

Above: Branch Rickey and Dodger Manager Burt Shotton, who managed the team during Robinson's rookie season, confer in Ebbets Field.

Left: Jackie with the second black Dodger, pitcher Don Bankhead, who joined the team in the late summer of 1947.

Opposite top: Robinson completes a triple steal by swiping home against the Boston Braves on August 22, 1948. Dodger third baseman Billy Cox is the batter. The home plate umpire is Jocko Conlan. (AP/Wide World Photos)

Opposite bottom: Robinson testifie before the House Un-American Activities Committee on July, 18, 1949. (AP/Wide World Photos)

Above: Jackie Robinson interviewing Branch Rickey on WMCA's "The Jackie Robinson Show," circa 1950.

Left: Having left the Dodgers a year earlier, Rickey poses wearing a Pirate cap early in the 1951 season.

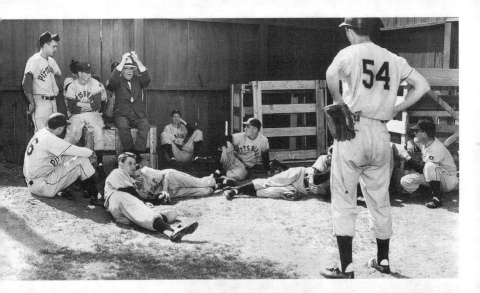

Above: Rickey lectures Pirate rookie pitcher Ron Necciai during spring training in California, 1952.

Right: The ever-present cigar in hand, Mr. Rickey surveys his diamond domain, circa 1952, as president of the Pittsburgh Pirates.

Left: A solemn Jackie Robinson is seen chatting with Dodger owner Walter O'Malley in October, 1956, or right after what turned out to be the conclusion of Robinson's major league playing career.

Below: Robinson and Rickey enjoy a good laugh at Robinson's Hall of Fame induction ceremony on August 4, 1962.

speculate as to the size of future contracts, assuming that he continued his stellar play.

Both Robinson's and the Dodgers' immediate future looked bright indeed. During the off-season the team opened up second base to Jackie by trading Eddie Stanky to the Boston Braves. (Other Dodgers who had been in on the abortive rebellion of the previous spring already were—or soon would be—ex-Dodgers. Pitcher Kirby Higbe was dealt to the Pirates early in the 1947 season. Walker followed him to Pittsburgh at season's end. Hugh Casey, too, was a Pirate by 1949.) When informed of the Stanky trade, a diplomatic Robinson did not want to appear to be overanxious. He jumped neither for joy nor at the job, saying only that "I like second base better than first . . . and hope I can do well enough to stay there all season."

After having been fêted at a parade of banquets over the winter of 1947–48, Robinson reported for spring training at a paunchy 215 pounds. Leo Durocher, back in charge after having served his year-long suspension, was incensed. One look at his new second baseman produced this explosion: "You look like an old woman . . why, you can't even bend over."

Durocher promptly ordered Robinson to undergo a rigorous exercise regimen. Jackie dutifully complied, admitting that he had made a mistake that he would not repeat. Durocher, he conceded, was right, "My speed is a big asset—without that I would be lost." The Dodger manager was far from alone in leveling criticism at the 1947 NL Rookie of the Year. Wendell Smith informed his Pittsburgh readers that a "porky-pig" Robinson was far from the "dashing, daring base runner of 1947." Sam Lacy of the Baltimore *Afro-American* also used his byline to let Jack know that he had better get himself back in shape. Robinson could do little but take his medicine. He also acknowledged that Durocher was right about more than his weight: he needed to hit more balls to the opposite field. Spring training, 1948, was shaping up to be every bit as difficult as 1947 had been, if not quite for the same reasons.

Despite his hard work, Robinson began the regular season very slowly, so slowly in fact that when June arrived he had yet to steal a single base. His batting average was a respectable if far from outstanding .270. Dodger management was so displeased with his overall performance that Rickey decided to jolt Robinson by placing him on waivers. Technically, this meant that Jackie was available to any other team. But Rickey had no intention of losing him and could withdraw his name from the waiver list at any time. His goal was simply to prod Robinson to perform better. The strategy worked. Jackie *was* stunned by the move, so stunned that he rebounded to finish the season at figures close to those of 1947. He led the Dodgers in a number of categories, while compiling a .296 batting average and equaling his 1947 home run total. Only in stolen bases did he experience a significant dip (from 29 to 22). Meanwhile, the Dodgers finished a disappointing third behind Boston and St. Louis.

Still, the 1948 season was far from a total disaster for Jackie Robinson. He not only survived the notorious "sophomore jinx," but he solidified his hold on second base. Gone was any threat that his name might again appear on a waiver list. Nor was there any discussion of a potential trade. All was relatively calm until Durocher shocked both the Dodgers and the baseball world by bolting to the rival Giants, who had fired manager Mel Ott in midseason. In response, Rickey tried to repeat his last-minute magic of 1947 by reinstalling Burt Shotton at the Dodger helm. Publicly, Jackie was sorry to see Durocher go. Privately, he was not necessarily displeased by the switch. To the press he described Durocher as a "human dynamo"; to nearly everyone else his frenetic former manager was a "holy terror."

Early in the season Rickey added another black ballplayer to the Dodgers when he called up catcher Roy Campanella from St. Paul of the American Association. Jackie Robinson and Roy Campanella had little in common beyond their baseball skills, their competitive drive to excel and win, and one-half of their ancestry. Campanella was half-black and half-Italian. He was also squat and slow—and even slower to anger. If Jackie Robinson was quick out of the batter's box and quick to take offense, Roy Campanella was forever calm and terminally good-natured. He also had the habit of good-naturedly doing what he could to calm others, Robinson included.

But no one could calm Jackie Robinson on August 24, 1948. In a game against the Pittsburgh Pirates Robinson bolted out of the dugout to protest the ejection of a teammate. Seeming to be a man possessed, he rushed up to the umpire and unleashed a string of angry words long enough to earn him a place on the bench next to his already-banished teammate. For the first time in his still young major league career Jackie Robinson had entered the field of play to argue with an umpire. And for the first time he was the victim of an umpire's thumb. Another milestone had been reached.

This incident occurred near the end of the Rickey-imposed three-year ban on Robinson's ability to challenge anyone, at least from rival players to jeering fans to hasty umpires. This was not so much a violation of Rickey's orders as evidence that the Dodger boss was gradually loosening the strings. Jackie was not completely unfettered, but on the field he was able to begin to act as a normal ballplayer.

Following the 1948 season Jackie was determined not to repeat his mistakes of the previous winter. Instead of eating his way across the country he organized a barnstorming tour of the South and Southwest with Campanella. Their off-season "season" culminated in Los Angeles, where the Robinson-Campanella squad played a series against a Negro League All-Star team led by Satchel Paige. For the first time since the 1945 season Jackie found himself on the same field with Negro League players. This was not, to put it mildly, an entirely pleasant reunion. Some Negro League veterans still thought that Robinson had not been the best choice to break the color line. A few, Paige primary among them, felt that they should have been selected ahead of him. Others resented what they saw as an attitude of superiority on Robinson's part. Still others continued to believe that Jackie had sold them out. Too old to make the majors themselves, they knew that Robinson's elevation spelled the eventual doom of the Negro Leagues—and of their baseball livelihood.

Robinson's own income jumped again in 1949. Once again, his goal was $20,000. Once again, he settled quietly for less: $17,500. This figure was far below the salaries of established stars, such as Yankee outfielder Joe DiMaggio, who had reached the $100,000 plateau, and Cleveland Indian pitcher Bob Feller, who earned $82,000 in 1948. But at least Robinson's salary was comparable to those of other front-line Dodger players.

If Robinson did not complain about Rickey's salary offer, he did feel increasingly free to assert himself off the baseball diamond. Those assertions included not so veiled criticisms of the departed Leo Durocher. In response, the new Jackie Robinson drew some negative comments from both the white and black press, most prominently Sam Lacy. The Baltimore writer used his column to lash out at Robinson for departing from the example of Joe Louis, who "NEVER criticized the people who gave him his chance . . . and NEVER blamed someone else for anything that happened."

Robinson took Lacy's admonition to heart. He also took spring training, 1949, very seriously as well. He knew that the Dodgers had the makings of an excellent team. He also knew that time was beginning to run out for him. Though 1949 would be only his third year in the majors, Jackie was already thirty years old. If he was going to make DiMaggio-like money, he was going to have to put up DiMaggio-like numbers at the plate, and he was going to have to do it soon.

Robinson was quite aware of something else as well. In the two years since he had broken the color line, major league rosters had not been flooded with black ballplayers. In fact, at the start of the season, only seven black players were spread among only three teams: the Dodgers (with pitcher Don Newcombe joining Robinson and Campanella), the Indians, and the Giants. Robinson's job may have been secure, but his race had barely been welcomed to the national game at its highest level, or for that matter, at lower levels.

Branch Rickey had long predicted that the real breakthrough for black players would come in the minors. But as of the start of the 1949 season only the St. Louis Browns had joined the Dodgers in signing black prospects for their minor league teams. Mysteriously, the two pioneers, Rickey and Veeck, each made statements during the off-season indicating there were few players left in the Negro Leagues who were good enough to sign a major or minor league contract. Baseball historian Jules Tygiel has weighed in with a different opinion. By the most "conservative estimate" there were "at least" ten Negro Leaguers who deserved a major league trial and "dozens more" who merited minor league contracts.

If 1949 would not be a critical year on the integration front, Jackie Robinson regarded it as a pivotal one for his own baseball career. With Rickey's coaxing, he placed himself in the hands of Rickey protégés Pepper Martin (to improve his sliding technique) and George Sisler (to boost his batting average). The results were electrifying. By early June Robinson possessed a .344 average. A month later he reached .361 and started at second base in the All-Star Game. (Only Ted Williams of the Boston Red Sox had garnered more votes than Robinson to start in baseball's midsummer classic.) In fact, all three black Dodgers were on that National League team, providing further evidence that Rickey's original gamble was continuing to pay rich dividends.

Baseball was not the only thing on Jackie Robinson's mind in July of 1949. Just before the All-Star Game, Georgia Congressman John Wood of the House Un-American Activities Committee (HUAC) asked him to testify at congressional hearings concerning the loyalty of black Americans. This was an invitation, not an order. His presence had been requested, not subpoenaed. Still, Jackie worried that a refusal to testify would be viewed negatively. So did Branch Rickey. But Rickey worried about something else as well. He was anxious that the HUAC invitation be treated as the opportunity that he presumed it to be. To Rickey, it was not an ominous summons but a unique chance to advance the cause of black equality *and* strike a blow against international Communism. A confirmed anti-Communist himself, Rickey viewed Robinson not just as a silent symbol of racial justice, but as a valuable spokesman for the American way of life, this at a time when the Cold War was just beginning to heat up.

A less silent spokesman for black America at this time was also an athlete. His name was Paul Robeson, the same Paul Robeson who a few years earlier had pleaded with baseball executives to desegregate the game. A football player at Rutgers University in the 1920s, Robeson had gone on to make a name for himself as a singer, an actor, and an outspoken friend of the Soviet Union. At this point in American history, Robinson and Robeson joined Joe Louis as the three most recognizable black men in the country. Given his elevated stature as an entertainer and a man of the left, Robeson had the potential to reach some Americans, white and black, whom neither Louis nor Robinson could affect. This potential was especially worrisome to conservative HUAC members. It was also more than a little troubling to Branch Rickey.

The reason for their joint worrying had little to do with Robeson's past as a football player or his present as a Broadway entertainer. Instead it had everything to do with Robeson's openly friendly relations with Moscow and his ideological commitment to some version of radical socialism, if not necessarily to Soviet-style Communism. Paul Robeson's identification with the Soviet Union can be traced to a 1934 visit to Moscow, where he was warmly received by Soviet leaders and intellectuals. That identification grew significantly stronger during World War II, when Moscow and Washington were aligned against Berlin and Tokyo.

By the late 1940s, controversy surrounded Robeson everywhere he went, on both sides of the Atlantic. It reached a peak in April of 1949 when he addressed a Paris gathering of the left-leaning World Congress of the Partisans of Peace. That controversial speech included this highly controversial sentence: "It is unthinkable that American Negroes would go to war on behalf of those who have oppressed us for generations against a country which in one generation has raised our people to the full dignity of mankind."

Robeson's speech drew heavy criticism in the United States. Among his many detractors was Walter White of the NAACP. To

White, Robeson's statement could only provide ammunition to those very oppressors he had alluded to in his Paris speech. Complicating this was White's long-standing opposition to what he perceived to be heavy-handed HUAC tactics when it came to dealing with domestic dissent. In attempting to walk a fine line between Robeson's pro-Communism and HUAC's anti-Communism, White offered to assist Robinson in preparing for his appearance before the congressional committee. Interpreting that gesture as an "attempt to keep me quiet," Jackie ultimately decided to go ahead and testify—and to do so on his own.

In any event, Robinson could not help but notice the irony of it all. Having never met Paul Robeson, Jackie had no desire to be a pawn in somebody else's war against him. If anything, he admired the noted entertainer's many talents and appreciated his willingness to speak out against segregationist practices in all of America, including major league baseball. Now he found himself being asked to condemn Robeson. The fact that the request had been initiated by a white man from Georgia and was directed to a black "refugee from Georgia" stretched beyond the realm of irony and into the land of the absurd.

There were moments in all this when Robinson didn't know whether to laugh or cry. Whatever his decision, he faced a no-win situation. To refuse to testify would disappoint Rickey. But to speak out against Robeson would risk the anger and alienation of fellow blacks. The choice was not an easy one, but the more Jackie mulled it over the more he realized that he had to testify—even at the risk of being labeled an "Uncle Tom." In Robinson's mind, loyalty to his country took precedence over any sense of racial solidarity.

In the end, he hardly needed Branch Rickey to tell him that what Robeson had said in Paris was an affront to black Americans, especially to those blacks who had served in America's wars, including, of course, a certain Lieutenant Jack Roosevelt Robinson. If anything clinched Robinson's decision to appear before the committee it was his own anti-Communist sentiments. The Dodger second baseman did not have to be a student of world politics to know that Josef Stalin was an oppressive ruler. He didn't need the Methodist Mr. Rickey to keep him abreast of the antireligious nature of the Soviet Union. Good Methodist that *he* was, Jackie Robinson wanted to believe that the vast majority of black Americans embraced God and country and rejected godless Communism.

With Rachel by his side, Jack appeared before HUAC on July 18, 1949. He began with an opening statement in which he conceded that a number of people had tried to discourage him from testifying. So why did he "stick [his] neck out?" Not because he could provide the committee with a point-by-point refutation of anything Paul Robeson said or Karl Marx wrote. And not because HUAC members wanted to hear his expertise on the proper technique for stealing second base. He was there only as an expert on being a "colored American, with thirty years experience at it." And he could only speak out of a "sense of responsibility" to himself and to his country.

In his statement to HUAC, Jackie Robinson attacked two American institutions: Paul Robeson and Jim Crow. In Robinson's estimation, Robeson was on the wrong side in the burgeoning Cold War and wrong to question the motives of black Americans. But he was not wrong to criticize the Jim Crow system of racial segregation, i.e., the legal underpinnings of American racism. To Jackie Robinson, whether or not Paul Robeson was a Communist was almost beside the point. Robeson was simply wrong to align himself with the Soviet Union. At the same time, he was right to speak out " . . . against injustices black Americans faced when dealing with the court system, the police, or even lynch mobs." Those were genuine wrongs, even if it *was* a Soviet sympathizer who happened to be speaking out against them. But were those historic "wrongs" wrong enough to convince black Americans to give up on their country? Not according to Jackie Robinson.

Rickey was completely satisfied with Robinson's performance. If he had any reason to worry about the effect that the HUAC appearance would have on his star player's game, those worries were quickly put aside. Back in uniform that same evening, Robinson stole home in the sixth inning and drove in a run with an eighth-inning triple to clinch a 3-0 Dodger win over the Cubs. To Rickey it was "as great an exhibition of baseball play as [he had] ever seen." According to the New York *Post*, Robinson's performance amounted to a "near one-man show" that came right on the heels of his "afternoon victory over Paul Robeson." It also marked the 77th game (of 83 that season) in which Robinson had been on base.

Never would Jackie Robinson permit outside factors to affect his baseball play. And never would he change his mind about his country. But he did gradually soften his criticism of Paul Robeson. That process began almost immediately. In late August 1949, he learned that a Robeson appearance at a benefit concert in upstate New York had provoked a riot in which more than a dozen people were injured. The next day Robinson told the sports editor of the *Daily Worker* that "Paul Robeson should have the right to sing, speak, or do anything he wants to." Robinson added that he still didn't believe in Communism, but he did let the editor know that he thought there was something wrong with a country in which "anything progressive is called Communism." That brand of revisionist thinking continued through Robinson's final version of his last autobiography, *I Never Had It Made,* which was published just before he died. In it, he conceded that over the years his respect for Robeson had gradually increased, given the sacrifices that the singer had made and given his own growing awareness of the "painful truths about America's destructiveness."

The most painful truth about the 1949 season was that Robinson's and Rickey's Brooklyn Dodgers once again fell short of their goal of a World Series victory. The Dodgers did win the National League pennant (by a single game over the still competitive Cardinals). And Robinson was an important cog in the Dodger machine, as he led the league in batting for the only time in his career (with a .342 average). He also topped the National League in stolen bases (with the then lofty figure of 37). That, along with 124 RBIs, was enough to earn him the National League's MVP award. But it did not serve as a prelude to a great World Series for either Robinson or his team. Two years earlier the upstart Dodgers had taken the vaunted Yankees to a full seven games. This time the

Yankees made easy work of their crosstown rivals by taking the series four games to one. Jackie Robinson may have been the 1949 National League MVP, but he collected only three meaningless hits in a less than MVP-caliber World Series. Once again the Dodger refrain would have to be "wait till next year."

The Sixth Inning

The following year, 1950, proved to be a watershed year for both Jackie Robinson and Branch Rickey. In the off-season Rickey made Robinson the highest paid Brooklyn Dodger in team history by offering the league's reigning MVP a $35,000 contract. But even more important, this was the season when Jackie finally became just another player on the field. By the end of the 1948 season Robinson had fulfilled his three-year promise to Rickey. At that point, Jackie's full "sentence" had been served, which meant that he was theoretically free to challenge both opposing players and umpires as he saw fit. Robinson had actually begun to emerge from his Rickey-designed shell late in the 1948 season. He was even more his own man in 1949. But gnawing doubts remained. How would fans respond if he revealed his naturally assertive self? And what about the man who paid his salary? Would Rickey appreciate and support him if he strayed too far from the "turn the other cheek" mandate? By 1950 Robinson was finally able to put such doubts to rest and declare his full independence.

Shortly after the 1950 season ended Robinson no longer had to answer to Rickey at all. By then, Branch Rickey was no longer the president of the Brooklyn Dodgers. As rumors about Rickey's impending exit began to circulate, Robinson claimed to be unconcerned: "I just play ball," was his commentary on the matter. But he could not have been pleased by this prospect. Rickey, after all, had been his patron and his ally. In the end Rickey's departure proved to be one more reason for Robinson to strike a more independent course. The irony of their respective situations was inescapable. Throughout the 1950 campaign Robinson had further solidified his position on the Dodgers, even as Rickey was in the process of losing his. To put it another way, just as a certain Dodger regular could finally risk behaving as a regular guy, certain irregularities in the Dodger front office dictated that the man who had signed his checks was about to be bounced.

In the meantime, there was a baseball season to play. And what a season it was! Given their performance in 1949, the Dodgers were the solid favorite to repeat as NL champs in 1950. Instead, the team sputtered and struggled for much of the campaign. What might have been the year that the Dodgers would finally "win it all" became instead the year of the Philadelphia Phillie "Whiz Kids." Led by pitcher Robin Roberts and centerfielder Richie Ashburn, the Phillies seemed to have the pennant well within their grasp as September began. Only then did the Dodgers finally begin to make their move. On September 6 Don Newcombe started both ends of a double-header as the Dodgers took a pair of games from the Phils. (In all, Newcombe hurled sixteen innings in 2-0 and 3-2 Dodger victories, with Robinson scoring the winning run in the second game.) Catapulted by that sweep, the Dodgers continued to cut the Phillies' lead. The "Whiz Kids" made their own contribution to this Dodger resurgence by losing eight of ten games during a late September slump. As a result, the Phils found themselves clinging to a precarious two-game lead with only a pair of games left on the schedule. The scene for both contests was to be Ebbets Field and a head-to-head match up between the Dodgers and the Phils. Central casting could not have planned it better.

The Dodgers won the first game handily, bringing the entire season down to sudden death. A Phillies' win and the pennant was theirs. A Dodger victory and a three-game playoff would follow. Each team had its ace pitcher ready to go. After five innings both Newcombe and Roberts were working on shutouts. Each team scored a run in the sixth, with the Dodgers' tally coming on a controversial Pee Wee Reese home run. When the ball left Reese's bat and began its arc toward right field, it looked more like a routine fly ball than a potential round tripper. Somehow the ball managed to reach the screen in right field. But it failed to clear it. Meanwhile, the right fielder waited for the carom and the chance to nail Reese at second, only to watch helplessly as the ball trickled down the screen before lodging precariously in a crack at its base. Score one for the Dodgers—and another for the idiosyncracies of Ebbets Field.

The Dodgers almost won the game in the bottom of the ninth. Outfielder Cal Abrams (then the team's great Jewish hope) walked to open the Dodger half of the inning. Reese followed with a single to left. Duke Snider matched that, only to have Abrams thrown out trying to score from second. It was an ill-fated dash that would never die in Dodger lore. And it provoked a debate that would never end. Why did the third base coach send Abrams home and risk a play at the plate with no one out? Robinson was then issued an intentional walk to load the bases. At this point Phillies manager Eddie Sawyer strolled to the mound for a conference with the tiring Roberts. Strategy and compassion seemed to dictate a call to the bullpen, where relief ace Jim Konstanty was ready and warm. But no call was made. Roberts got Carl Furillo to foul out on the first pitch before Gil Hodges ended the Dodger threat with a fly ball to deep left.

In the Phils' half of the tenth, Sawyer stunned everybody by sending Roberts up to bat for himself. Once again the manager proved prescient because Roberts promptly lined a sharp single. First baseman Eddie Waitkus then duplicated that blow. A Richie Ashburn bunt forced Roberts at third. The next Philly batter was outfielder Dick Sisler, the son of Rickey's first Hall of Fame discovery, George Sisler. The junior Sisler had already garnered three hits and scored the lone Phils' run, but he wasn't quite through for the day. On this at-bat the left-handed Sisler stroked a slicing liner to the opposite field. The ball barely cleared the left field fence. But as it did the "Whiz Kids" had a 4-1 lead that they would never surrender. The score did not change in the bottom of the tenth.

Thanks to the son of Branch Rickey's first phenom, the Philadelphia Phillies had captured the game and the team's first pennant in thirty-five years.

This huge disappointment aside, Jackie Robinson had had an excellent year. For the season, he had hit .328, cracked 14 homers, driven in 81 runs, and scored 99 times. These were impressive numbers, though not on a par with his MVP year of 1949. Still, after four solid seasons Robinson had firmly established himself as a perennial all-star and a team leader.

More crushing to Robinson than the Phillies' victory in the pennant race was the departure of Branch Rickey from the Dodgers within days of the season's end. For a number of years a rivalry had been building between Rickey and the club's vice president and chief counsel, Walter O'Malley. Matters began to come to a head in July when one of the key Dodger owners, John L. Smith, died. This set in motion an intense struggle for control of the franchise, a struggle that quickly centered on Rickey and O'Malley, each of whom owned one quarter of the team. Obviously, whoever obtained Smith's shares would be poised to gain control of the team.

For seven years the Dodgers had been run by a triumvirate put in place by George McLaughlin. Though the Brooklyn banker had no interest in operating the team himself, he did want to do what he could to put its precarious financial house in order and a winner on the field. Hence his idea of creating a three-man syndicate that included Rickey, O'Malley, and Smith. The plan was far from a ridiculous one. Rickey was to provide the baseball brains, O'Malley would handle legal matters, and Smith would be the financial wizard (largely because he had the deepest pockets). President of the Charles Pfizer Chemical Company, John Smith was an American rags-to-riches story. German by birth and shy by nature, Smith had risen to the top of the company by dint of hard work and technical know-how. Though baseball was never his passion, he did understand the importance of the Dodgers to Brooklyn.

For his part, O'Malley had no baseball background and no discernable interest in learning very much about the game. What he did possess was a consuming desire to be in total control of any enterprise in which he had a significant financial stake. Branch Rickey often stood accused of treating baseball as a business, but this was never an entirely accurate assessment of his priorities. Making a profit was important to him, but it was always a means to another, and greater, end, namely winning baseball games.

The two men battled openly and often over virtually every aspect of the Dodger operation. A New York baseball writer once dubbed Rickey "El Cheapo," but when it came to the care and feeding of his players, Branch Rickey could be downright extravagant in Walter O'Malley's narrowed eyes. Of course, Rickey carefully watched what he paid his players. Robinson could testify to that. But at the same time Branch Rickey greatly admired his athletes. Away from the diamond his young charges could be terribly foolish at times. But once on the field of play they were capable of transforming themselves into magicians whom an otherwise highly judgmental Rickey could hold in utter awe.

That sense of awe led Rickey to do things that the real "El Cheapo" in the Dodger front office did his level best to overrule. Walter O'Malley, after all, was in awe of no one, certainly not baseball players. Invariably, he objected to any significant financial investment in cultivating the talents of Dodger prospects. For example, the Dodger spring training complex at Vero Beach, Florida, was deemed extravagant by O'Malley—as was Rickey's private plane (the better to scout players); his vast Dodger farm system (the better to prepare talent); and reliance on air travel for his major leaguers (the better to put a rested team on the field).

As far as O'Malley was concerned, when Rickey wasn't concocting new ways to spend money, he was currying favor with his players. After the 1946 season he wanted to give every Dodger player a new Studebaker car to reward them for their second-place finish. When O'Malley learned of this exercise in philanthropy, he immediately set out to countermand it. And he succeeded. Three years later

Rickey ordered rings for his players following their trip to the 1949 World Series. O'Malley intervened by requiring that veterans of the 1947 Series turn in their old rings before receiving new ones.

The two men also went to the mat over the issue of lifting the ban on beer company sponsorship of Dodger games. Not surprisingly, Rickey opposed the move, while O'Malley favored it. Once again, Rickey lost. Not long after that defeat he confided to his youngest daughter that he was a "doomed" man, that sooner or later he would be "forced out."

Sooner rather than later arrived in 1950, which also happened to be the fifth and final year of Rickey's contract as Dodger general manager–president. Given his many losing battles with O'Malley, Rickey clearly was a man on the ropes. Then John Smith died. In short order, O'Malley acquired Smith's share of the team from Smith's widow and increased the pressure on Rickey to sell. By October it was apparent that Rickey's future in Brooklyn was nonexistent.

If Rickey's immediate prospects seemed dim at best, the Dodgers still appeared to be the team to beat in 1951. For the foreseeable future, the Dodgers' prospects on the diamond looked rosy indeed. Jackie Robinson and many of his teammates were in the prime years of their baseball lives. They had already demonstrated their superiority over their National League rivals, including the once-dominant Cardinals. It was only a matter of time before they would triumph over the American League Yankees as well. Or so O'Malley and Robinson—and even Rickey—continued to hope.

But the future of the Dodgers *in* Brooklyn was far less rosy. In Walter O'Malley's ever-scheming mind, the future of baseball in general and the Brooklyn Dodgers in particular was about to be governed by television. Baseball had just set a new total attendance mark in 1949, when more than 22 million fans passed through the turnstiles. O'Malley found this figure at once encouraging and somewhat irrelevant. For many years he had been content to think in terms of major league baseball in the northeast quadrant of the United States and Dodger baseball within the peculiar confines of Ebbets Field. By midcentury he was already turning his attention to the country at large, as well as to one very large, untapped *television* market in southern California. As the commercial possibilities of marrying baseball and TV loomed, it was increasingly apparent that Branch Rickey was no longer the only visionary in the Dodger organization.

Years earlier Rickey had fought the introduction of night baseball to the major leagues. "It would ruin family life," he roared to anyone who would listen. To him, baseball was as much a civil religion as it was a business. And a major league franchise was, in effect, a "quasi-public" institution. As such, the game and its major league teams played a critical role in knitting together local communities and families. Night baseball promised to damage the family connection. But radio broadcasts did not. In fact, Rickey was a pioneer among baseball executives in deciding to beam its product over the airwaves, all in the name of bringing families *and* communities closer together. "Radio," Rickey argued, "created a desire to see something." Television, on the other hand, amounted to giving fans something for nothing.

Radio not only whetted the appetite of fans, it also preserved the magic of the game—and of its magicians, namely the players. When their exploits were confined to what people read in the newspapers or heard on the radio, they remained distant heroes and somehow larger than life. Once televised, however, those same heroic players were reduced to small, flickering images. What this new medium might actually do to fan attendance remained debatable at midcentury. What it would do to the individual fan's emotional attachment to the game and to its most talented competitors could also not be known with great certainty—at least not at the dawn of the age of television.

Branch Rickey would eventually be proven wrong on the marriage of baseball and television. But at the time he remained convinced that television would break fans of the "ballpark habit" without bringing new fans into those same ballparks. He went on to argue that a "great many fans will never reacquire" that habit once they discovered they could stay at home and watch games from the friendly confines of their easy chair. But if Rickey was wrong to predict that television would kill his sport, he was right to question its impact on the game and on the fans' connections to it. And at least in the short term he was right to contend that television would do serious damage to the minor leagues and, therefore, to another of his great innovations, the farm system. In his best prophetic tones, Rickey issued repeated warnings that the "basic structure of professional baseball" was indeed threatened by this new monster called television.

The other new monster on the block was Walter O'Malley. It was he who ordered Rickey off the block—and out of his formidable office at 215 Montague Street. It was he who dismissed his bitter rival as a "psalm-singing faker." And it was he who would engineer Rickey's most ignominious defeat.

Even as the 1950 season neared its conclusion Rickey had hopes of averting his fate. In truth he was doing more than hoping. Branch Rickey, after all, was not above a little plotting of his own. Nor was he above raising his voice now and then. Red Barber remembered a late September 1950, day at the ballpark. Specifically, it was the final game of the regular season, the very game against the Phillies that had almost forced a Dodgers-Phillies playoff. It was, in short, not just another baseball game. And yet Rickey could not concentrate on what was happening on the field of play. Neither could Walter O'Malley. For that matter, the Dodger play-by-play man was having his own difficulties keeping his mind on the action before him. The distraction was traceable to the verbal fireworks that were going on right next to him. Separated from Rickey and O'Malley by only a thin partition, Barber could not help but hear the two of them "screaming at each other all afternoon."

The reason for the screaming may have had something to do with a clause in the existing contract between Rickey and O'Malley. It stipulated that if either of them would ever choose to sell their shares (assuming the existence of a genuine offer), the other would have the right of first refusal to buy those shares by meeting the offer of the outside party. O'Malley, of course, thought he had Rickey right where he wanted him. Now that he controlled Smith's shares he could outvote Rickey. But he wanted Rickey's shares as well. And he assumed that he would be able to buy them at a bargain-basement rate. He knew that Rickey was not a wealthy man, that he had gone into debt to finance his 25 percent ownership of the team and had subsequently suffered reverses in the stock market. Assuming (and correctly so) that Rickey was strapped for cash, O'Malley offered Rickey $300,000 for his Dodger shares. The Machiavellian O'Malley assumed something else as well: he figured that he would have no serious rivals for those shares, that no one would want to spend a lot of money without acquiring a controlling voice in team operations as well.

But Branch Rickey's asking price was an astounding $1 million for his 25 percent share. And thanks to an old friend, Pittsburgh Pirate owner John Galbreath, he had a legitimate buyer. It was Galbreath who put Rickey in contact with New York real estate developer William Zeckendorf. And it was Zeckendorf who not only met Rickey's price, but who demanded that O'Malley tack on an additional $50,000 for "tying up my capital." All this had to be settled in ninety days. Otherwise Zeckendorf would then own Rickey's shares and join forces with the fourth Dodger owner (a widow named Mulvey who paid no attention to the daily business of the team, but who was known to be sympathetic to Rickey). The final Rickey-Zeckendorf threat was that the new team of Zeckendorf and Mulvey would then try to rehire Rickey, leaving the Dodgers in permanent turmoil with a 50-50 split between the two sides.

O'Malley swallowed his pride and opened his checkbook. The final compromise was $1,025,000. Branch Rickey got his money, but he did not have the last laugh. Walter O'Malley had forced him out of what had become his organization and out of an opportunity to be a part of a Dodgers World Series triumph. At midcentury the Dodgers were a team with all of the Rickey essentials for playing winning baseball: pitching, speed, and power. In short, it was a team that had everything except a World Series title. Now it was a team without Branch Rickey as well.

Before leaving the organization for good, Rickey asked for a final meeting, not with the team's major league players but with the minor leaguers as they prepared for winter instructional sessions. Rickey used that meeting not to talk about baseball or their place in the Dodger hierarchy of player talent, but to talk about their lives in general and the role that Jesus Christ had played in his life.

"He left a life. He left a philosophy. He left a religion . . . and yet to me the real revelation—even if we strip him of divinity, boys [and] say there's no God in him—he's just a man like us. I don't think that. But let's say for the moment that he was. He still lived a great life—a marvelous life." Rickey could not avoid leaping from the theological to the practical. "Don't shift too much responsibility for your success in this game to somebody else. Rely pretty much on yourself. Be anxious about it. Be persevering about it. Be firm about it. Have a high purpose. Pay the price; pay whatever it takes, and you'll probably come out about where merit takes you."

Rickey had no more finished than he turned abruptly and left. As he walked away under his trademark oversized hat (the better to ward off the Florida sun), the sixty-nine-year-old enforced retiree assumed that he was walking into the sunset of his professional life. And as he strode off, each prospective member of the next generation of Dodgers spontaneously stood up and applauded.

Branch Rickey's departure from the Dodgers was a blow to every player in the organization, but it was a blow that struck with particular force against Jackie Robinson. Rickey had played many roles in Robinson's life. He had been a surrogate father. He had been a teacher, albeit an often hectoring one, whether the subject was baseball or life. He had been Robinson's patron and his defender, too. But most of all, Branch Rickey had been a fan: an everloyal, ever-marveling fan.

Shortly after learning of Rickey's departure from the Dodgers, Robinson wrote a most sincere "I hate to see you go" letter to his former boss. He thanked Rickey "for all you have meant not only to me and my family but to the entire country and particularly to the members of our race." Reflecting on 1947, he had to "admit" that it was "your constant guidance that had enabled" him to survive the experience. All in all, Robinson concluded, "being associated with you has been the finest experience that I have had."

Rickey responded in kind. "My acquaintanceship with you has ripened into a very real friendship." Furthermore, Rickey knew of no player "in the game today who could . . . manage a major league team better than yourself. I recently made this statement in the presence of several writers, but I have looked in vain for the reporting of this statement." Before signing off, Rickey reverted to Father Rickey, or at least Mr. Rickey, by counseling Robinson "to finish your college course meritoriously, and get your degree."

Rickey's relationship with Robinson transcended the ordinary. For most all of his life, in one way or another, Jackie Robinson had been testing his country and his fellow countrymen. There were many days when both had failed Robinson's severe tests. There were also days when he failed those tests himself. But Branch Rickey had never failed him. Invariably, he had justified the faith that Robinson had placed in him. Early on in their relationship there were moments when Robinson fretted that Rickey would not deliver on his promises. Later, there were moments when he feared that he was a mere token in some trivial Rickey game. But all of those doubts and second thoughts had disappeared by 1950. Branch Rickey was the genuine article.

What made Rickey's departure more difficult for Jackie Robinson was that Walter O'Malley was someone he had already come to loathe. O'Malley had no great interest in the cause of civil rights. He had played no significant role in Rickey's "experiment." He was not even a baseball man. He was simply an untrustworthy wheeler-dealer, a man who had taken advantage of the unfortunate, a conniver who had made his fortune by processing mortgage foreclosures during the depression years of the 1930s.

Robinson soon learned that Walter O'Malley was also a man who demanded total loyalty from his subordinates—meaning everyone else in the Dodger organization. The process of securing that loyalty began by purging the premises of any memory of

Branch Rickey. Over the winter of 1950–51, O'Malley ordered a total renovation of Dodger headquarters at 215 Montague. Gone were all traces of Rickey, including that trademark fish tank. Gone as well was Manager Burt Shotton. His replacement, Charlie Dressen, was an unknown quantity to Robinson. But here he would reserve judgement—and happily so, because Dressen soon proved to be Robinson's favorite manager.

There was no reason to reserve judgement on Walter O'Malley. From the outset of the O'Malley era, Jackie Robinson assumed that O'Malley's control of the club spelled trouble for him, and at no point during his remaining years as a Dodger did Robinson change his mind on that score. Difficulties between the two men surfaced almost immediately. Early in the 1951 spring training season O'Malley accused Robinson of deliberately skipping exhibition games. The new Dodger president also charged his star second baseman with trying to subvert his authority by complaining about the continuation of segregated housing at the Vero Beach facility. To his credit, O'Malley didn't simply label Robinson a malcontent and grumble behind Robinson's back. To his discredit, he called *both* Robinsons into his office not to hear their side of the story, but to administer a formal dressing down.

Jackie was furious with him. So was Rachel. If Walter O'Malley was man enough to confront them directly, he was apparently too much of a coward to face Robinson alone. Jackie took it upon himself to answer both charges. An injury had kept him out of the starting lineup and O'Malley's indifference had kept the Robinson family from living with the rest of the Dodger family. If O'Malley wanted a second opinion on the injury, he could consult the team trainer. If he wanted to know who was responsible for the Dodger housing situation—and for the Robinsons refusal to keep silent any longer—he ought to look in the mirror.

Walter O'Malley would have dearly loved to rid *his* Dodgers of every Branch Rickey protégé and supporter in the organization. The two at the top of his purge wish list were Robinson and Red Barber. Ironically, these were the two he could least afford to lose. Each was already a Brooklyn institution. Walter O'Malley may have been a man of large flaws and few virtues, but he was not stupid. He knew that Red Barber was a treasure, and that many Dodger fans were tied to their team by his vocal chords. He also knew that no single player was more important to the success of the Dodgers than Jackie Robinson.

For his part, Jackie Robinson was simultaneously in a powerful and a somewhat precarious position. He fully realized that O'Malley dared not trade him. But he also understood that there were limits to how far he could go in speaking his mind, whether to Walter O'Malley or to anyone else (umpires included). Behind closed doors, he could—and did—let O'Malley have it on the subject of continued segregation in team housing. But he knew that he could not challenge the new Dodger president publicly.

Nor could he take on other team owners on the subject of speeding up the signing of more black players. Here the irony builds. Rickey had long contended that Robinson had to stay on everyone's straight and narrow, otherwise the "noble experiment" would be sure to end in abysmal failure. His operating assumption had always been that Robinson's baseball skills would not be enough to ensure the success of that experiment and pave the way for future black players. If anything, his demeanor would dictate the future of the black man in what had been a white's only game. That demeanor had been nearly perfect, and yet as of his fifth season in a Brooklyn uniform only four teams (the Dodgers, Giants, Indians, and most recently the Braves) had black players on their major league rosters. A frustrated Robinson might have known that his job was secure (even if he had little respect for the new man who now paid his salary), but he also knew that job availability, much less job security, for black players was bleak at best. So what good had keeping quiet done him? Though Jackie could not answer this question, he continued to comport himself carefully.

Robinson had to be careful about something else as well. Having eased past thirty, his weight was a constant concern. Off-season or in-season, dieting now became a regular part of his daily routine. Given his tendency to put on unwanted pounds, Robinson was less and less able to take those trademark gambles on the base paths. Here irony intrudes again. While kept on Rickey's short leash, he had been a much more adventuresome base runner than he was after his liberation day had arrived. In his first three seasons as a Dodger, Jackie Robinson stole just over 29 bases a season (on better than 41 attempts). During the whole of the 1950 campaign he attempted a meager 18 thefts and was safe only 12 times. Furthermore, National League scouts were in general agreement that his range in the field was on the decline. This was especially the case when it came to flagging down ground balls headed for centerfield. Going to his right had long been a detectable Robinson weakness. Now it was on the verge of becoming a glaring one.

The year 1950 was an unhappy one for Robinson for any number of reasons. Not only were his skills seemingly on the decline, but so was his team. Perhaps not so suprisingly, Jackie began to reveal his frustrations on the baseball diamond. Though his outbursts were not frequent, they did occur—and accumulate. As they did, each incident validated the charge that Jackie Robinson was an incurable hothead. The result was a dangerously self-fulfilling prophecy in the minds of National League umpires. Any hint of Robinson's assertiveness was deemed to be excessive. Therefore, umpires moved quickly to clamp down on this repeat offender. This only added to the Robinson frustration level, which only led to more outbursts, which only heightened the anger and frustration. And around it went.

Robinson was not alone in thinking that umpires were out to get him: Clyde Sukeforth thought the same thing. Still a Dodger scout, Sukeforth was convinced that the men in blue were deliberately "picking on Robinson" all during the 1950 season. "No umpire would pay any attention" to Jackie Robinson, he contended, if he had been "somebody else."

At year's end Eddie Stanky, not Jackie Robinson, was at second base on the United Press All-Star team. Stanky may have been called "The Brat," but he was perceived to be far less the troublemaker than Robinson. This was doubtless a factor in his selection over Robinson for the team. In every major offensive category Jackie Robinson was clearly superior: batting average (.328 to .300), hits (170 to 158), RBIs (82 to 51). But these statistics mattered very little. Robinson's reputation had preceded him.

Jackie Robinson had much to prove come 1951. He wanted to demonstrate that 1950 was an exception rather than the start of some sort of downward trend. He wanted to reclaim his all-star status. And he desperately wanted to restore the Dodgers to the National League pinnacle and capture that ever-elusive first World Series crown in franchise history.

Instead of victory in 1951, the Brooklyn Dodgers suffered not just another defeat, but perhaps the most agonizing defeat in the history of American sport. For much of the season everything had gone the Dodgers' way. They jumped into first place early and stayed there, gradually building a heavily cushioned lead in the process. As late as August 11 they enjoyed a thirteen-game lead over the second place New York Giants, who were a whopping sixteen games behind in the loss column.

From that point, on the margin began to shrink . . . and shrink . . . and shrink. Even as it did, Giant manager Leo Durocher could not quite believe that his team could catch the Dodgers. He began to think differently after the Giants ran off a sixteen-game win streak. With ten games left to play in the regular season, the Dodgers maintained a still comfortable four-and-a-half game lead. Five games later the two teams were in a dead heat following a 4-3 Dodger loss to the Boston Braves. This was a particularly galling defeat, because the winning run scored on a controversial call at the plate. With one out and a runner on third, a Brave batter hit a sharp grounder to second. Robinson fielded it cleanly and fired to Campanella in an attempt to nail the runner breaking from third. Home plate umpire Frank Dascoli (who a year earlier had accused Robinson of hurling ethnic slurs at him) called the runner safe. Campanella leaped to his feet in protest only to have Dascoli just as quickly eject him from the game. Robinson was enraged, but he held his tongue. After the game a calmer Robinson told reporters that Dascoli's decision on the play was "simply a matter of judgment." Not so his decision to give Campy the thumb. That Dascoli had "no right" to do. "In a race like this, the umpires should expect tempers to be a little frayed." So frayed were they that Robinson's inner compass went momentarily haywire. At least that was the report of a policeman who claimed to have seen a cursing Robinson kicking away at the umpires' dressing room door. His denials aside, the league fined him $100. (After the fact, Dodger pitcher Preacher Roe admitted that the door in question had been damaged by his foot, not Robinson's.)

As the 1951 season neared its end, more than Dodger tempers were fraying. The once huge Dodger lead had been whittled away to less than nothing. In fact, at exactly 3:55 P.M. on the last day of the regular season the Dodgers found themselves one game *behind* the Giants. At that moment the Dodgers were losing to the Phillies 8-5 as the Shibe Park scoreboard posted a Giant win over the Braves. The Dodgers, however, went on to tie the Phils 8-8, thus sending the game into extra innings. In the top of the twelfth, Robinson preserved the tie (and the season) by doing what he was not supposed to be able to do. He dove not just to his right, but to the right of second base to spear a line drive with two out and the bases loaded. Columnist Red Smith wrote that it was a case of the "unconquerable doing the impossible." What placed the play somewhere beyond the realm of the possible was the distance that Jackie had gone to his right to make it. "For an instant," concluded Smith, "his body is suspended in midair, then somehow the outstretched glove intercepts the ball inches off the ground." In the next instant Robinson was on the ground. And for the next few, agonizing seconds that's exactly where he remained, out cold.

Two innings later a revived Robinson hit a long home run off Phillies' ace Robin Roberts to put the Dodgers in the lead to stay. After fourteen tense innings the stage was finally set for a three-game Dodger-Giant playoff. The first two games ended in a victory each for the visiting team. What would be absolutely the last game of the 1951 National League season was finally at hand. Each team had its most reliable pitcher ready to go. Seven innings later, Sal Maglie of the Giants and Don Newcombe of the Dodgers were locked in a 1-1 duel. In the top of the eighth the Dodgers broke through for three runs. Six more outs and the pennant that they had once been coasting toward would finally be theirs.

In the bottom of the ninth the Giants sandwiched three hits around an out to cut the score to 4-2. At this point Dodger manager Charlie Dressen made a decision that Dodger fans would debate—and mourn—for years. He removed an exhausted Newcombe and brought in twenty-five-year-old Ralph Branca to face Giant outfielder Bobby Thomson. Two pitches later Thomson launched what would come to be called the second "shot heard round the world." Suddenly, stunningly, the Giants had a 5-4 victory and their first pennant in fourteen years. There has probably never been a more famous, more discussed, more storied, and (by Dodger fans) more lamented season-ending home run in all of major league history.

Jackie Robinson and all of his Dodger teammates were understandably devastated. But Robinson still had the presence of mind to follow Thomson on his trek around the bases, just to make certain that he had touched each one of them. He also had the class and composure to join Dressen, O'Malley, and Campanella in visiting the Giant clubhouse to offer their congratulations. Finally, he defended manager Dressen's decision to lift Newcombe. Later that same day he informed a Brooklyn radio audience that twice during the game Newcombe had gone to Dressen to tell him that he had nothing left. Each time Dressen ordered him back to the mound. Not until those three Giant hits in the ninth inning was he finally convinced to make a change. Charlie Dressen, Robinson assured his listeners, should not be blamed for the Dodgers' defeat. More than that, he was confident that he spoke for the entire team. "We think he's a wonderful manager and just as great a fellow."

Its unhappy ending notwithstanding, the 1951 season had been a wonderful one for Jackie Robinson. He hiked his batting average to .338, equaled his career-high of 19 home runs, and drove in a more than respectable 88 runs. He also committed only seven errors, en route to establishing a new fielding mark for NL second basemen. All this was more than enough to return Robinson to his accustomed place on the post-season All-Star squad. But it was not enough to earn him a second MVP. In the balloting by sportswriters he finished sixth, well behind winner Roy Campanella. Robinson was far from miffed: "He [Campanella] deserves any honor he can get."

If 1951 was not an MVP year for Jackie Robinson, it was a year that marked the debut of the black player who would soon replace Jackie Robinson in the hearts and minds—and imaginations—of baseball fans everywhere. Called up from the Minneapolis Millers of the American Association in early May, twenty-one-year-old centerfielder Willie Mays got off to a terrible start with the Giants. But before the season was over it was clear to everyone that he was on his way to becoming the great black player of *his* era, not to mention one of the greatest players of all time.

With Mays in the majors, there were now fourteen black players in the big leagues. Progress was being made, albeit not very swiftly. And with Mays patrolling centerfield against the Yankees another milestone had been reached: Giant outfielders Willie Mays, Monte Irvin, and Henry Thompson comprised the first all-black outfield in World Series history.

With the approach of the 1952 season, Robinson reached another personal landmark by signing a $42,000 contract. His fifth consecutive raise once again made him the highest paid Dodger player. But the season itself was bittersweet. In early May Jackie found himself enmeshed in yet another controversy with umpire Frank Dascoli. Having been informed that certain Dodger players were showering Dascoli with slurs, National League President Warren Giles delivered a formal letter of reprimand to Charlie Dressen. In it, Giles singled out Robinson as "a greater offender than others." Jack confronted Giles directly, only to be ignored completely. The league president did discuss the matter with Walter O'Malley, who issued a statement expressing satisfaction that Robinson had not "addressed anyone in uncomplimentary terms." But the absence of any sort of an apology from Giles meant that Robinson's reputation had suffered yet another blow. It would not be the last.

A mid-August game between the Dodgers and the Cubs produced a shouting match between Robinson and Cubs manager Phil Cavaretta. Subsequent reports that Jack and a Dodger coach had to be restrained from punching Cavaretta proved false. But once again Robinson's denials could neither dispel the impression that he was a loose cannon nor prevent his detractors from pummeling him in print and from the bleachers. In fact, for the first time in his career Jackie Robinson began to hear occasional boos when he took the field away from Ebbets Field.

Smatterings of boos turned into sustained cascades of the same following an early September incident in a game against the Braves. Campanella was actually at the center of this controversy, which involved an umpire's awarding first base to a Braves batter who subsequently scored the winning run. The Dodger catcher vehemently insisted that the batter had not, as the umpire claimed, been hit by the pitch, but had foul tipped the ball into himself instead. Robinson joined the argument. When the recently installed commissioner of baseball, Ford Frick, reviewed the umpire's report he fined *both* Campanella and Robinson. Incredulous, Jackie refused to pay his $75 share of the assessment, threatening instead to "take my spikes off and never play another game." Whether the ensuing boos or his own sober second thoughts changed his mind, Robinson ponied up—and laced up—only to have the season end just as it had in 1947 and 1949, courtesy of another World Series defeat administered by the Yankees.

For the third time in his six seasons Jackie played a critical role in getting the Dodgers into the World Series. And for the third time in those half dozen seasons he turned in a less than scintillating World Series performance. In a losing effort in the fourth game Robinson was called out on strikes not once, but three times. A chance for amends arrived in the seventh inning of the seventh game with the Dodgers trailing 4-2. But there would be no lucky seven for Jackie Robinson. At bat with the bases loaded and two out, Robinson hit a pop-up just beyond the pitcher's mound. For an instant the Yankees infielders froze. Then New York second baseman Billy Martin raced in just in time to snare the ball, snuff the rally, and preserve yet another Yankee triumph over the Brooklyn Dodgers (and Jackie Robinson).

For the first time in his career, there was talk of a Robinson retirement following the 1952 season. But it was just that, talk. There was little chance that Jackie would quit without a World Series ring. There was also little chance that he would quit while he was still a .300 hitter (though Jackie's average had fallen thirty points, to .308, in 1952).

Controversy of a different sort hovered around Robinson during spring training, 1953. For the first time since his rookie season he seemed to be a player without a position. Dressen wanted to break in a new second baseman and move Robinson to third. But there were problems with both moves. The rookie second sacker, Jim "Junior" Gilliam, was black. His proposed addition edged the Dodgers another step closer to fielding a predominantly black starting lineup. Dodger fans had accepted the addition of Roy Campanella and Don Newcombe. But would they accept a constant influx of black players? Complicating all of this was that the incumbent third baseman, Billy Cox, was not at all happy at the prospect of sharing playing time with anyone. A superb fielder, Cox was clearly on the downside of what had always been a mediocre hitting career. To make matters worse, Dressen had failed to explain his plan to Cox before the team arrived in camp, and Cox possessed racial views that were something other than enlightened. (On that score, it was somewhat ironic that Cox had been acquired from the Pirates as a part of the trade that rid the Dodgers of Dixie Walker.)

Despite the storm signals, Dressen went ahead with his shuffling. After all, what he sought to do seemed to make good sense for the team. It made even better sense when Gilliam sparkled at second base during spring training. When the regular season opened Gilliam was stationed at second, Robinson was at third, and Cox was on the bench. During the course of the year, Gilliam remained on second, Cox got into 100 games at third, and Robinson played every infield postion, as well as left field. In all, Jackie appeared in 136 games, but for the first time in his seven-year career he did not reach 500 at-bats.

Although Robinson played hard no matter where Dressen asked him to play and worked hard to curb his temper on the field, the season was not without moments when it seemed as though Jackie Robinson was spinning out of control. In a July game against the St. Louis Cardinals an argument between Robinson and Cardinal catcher Del Rice threatened to escalate to blows—but didn't. Jackie later insisted that he knew all along that there would be no fight. "Rice kept his mask on the whole time. He wasn't going to fight with a mask on." Nonetheless, the possibility of a fight only served to provide more grist for the rumor mill that Jackie Robinson was an uncontrollable hothead. The stark fact that there was no fight— and the fact that Robinson never once in his ten years in the majors threw a punch—did little to quiet his critics.

Jack's play on the field that year did serve to answer doubters among Dodger fans and front-office personnel. He rebounded to bat .329 and drive in 95 runs. The latter number would be his highest RBI total next to his 1949 MVP year, when he reached 124. The team surpassed even its loftiest expectations by winning more games than any Dodger team in history (105) and clinching the NL pennant at the amazingly early date of September 12.

None of the above mattered when it was time for the Fall Classic and another round with the still-invincible Yankees. Jack had his best World Series ever, batting .320, scoring three runs, and driving home a pair. But he was not really a factor in either Dodger victory as the team lost again to the Yanks in a relatively lackluster six-game series.

The nearly annual Dodger failure aside, 1953 saw more off-the-field progress toward the full desegregation of America's game. At the start of the '53 season only St. Louis persisted with racial restrictions on player accommodations and fan seating. Whenever the Dodgers were in St. Louis the white players checked into the posh (and air-conditioned) Chase Hotel. The black players were confined to an all-black hotel where sleeping was more problematical, given the stuffy rooms and the street noise. This changed in 1953. Chase management finally decided to accept every Dodger player with this proviso: the black players had to agree not to be seen in any public areas of the hotel, including the restaurant. Every black Dodger, except Robinson, refused to accept this condition. Robinson not only stayed in the Chase in 1953, but he kept returning there until the hotel management finally dropped its remaining restriction in 1955. Half a loaf (and the air-conditioning) was better than the alternative—even at the risk of angering his black teammates by accepting the Chase's demeaning demand for public invisibility.

The biggest news of the 1953–54 off-season concerned changes in the highly visible Dodger managerial chair and in the less visible broadcast booth. Because the Dodgers had won two consecutive pennants, Charlie Dressen thought that he deserved a two-year contract. But because the Dodgers had yet to win a World Series, Walter O'Malley refused to break a long Dodger tradition of one-year contracts for its managers. When Dressen balked at honoring that tradition, he was dismissed. Later that same month of October, the Dodgers announced that Red Barber was leaving to join the *Yankee* broadcast team. There was even talk of a trade involving Jackie Robinson. And this time Robinson hinted that he would not object, provided it was to another New York team.

In retrospect, a trade at this point might have been a good thing—for both Robinson and the Dodgers, because 1954 was a year marred by frustration and failure for both the team and its star player. It all began with Robinson contending with Dressen's replacement, Montreal Royals manager Walter Alston (who was operating on the first of what would be twenty-two consecutive one-year contracts). Because Robinson had genuinely admired Dressen's skills at handling both ball games and ballplayers, any replacement would likely have drawn some Robinson criticism. But Walter Alston was not just any replacement. He was the polar opposite of Charlie Dressen, especially in the eyes of Jackie Robinson. Where Dressen had been quick to anticipate his next managerial move, Alston seemed unimaginative, even plodding. Where Dressen had been open and friendly, Alston seemed aloof and rather dull. Where Dressen had been willing to challenge the despised O'Malley, Alston seemed not just loyal to a fault, but loyal to a man whom Robinson deemed despicable.

Robinson began spring training by deliberately testing his new manager. He was routinely late for morning workouts. He also made a practice of whispering to teammates while Alston was speaking to the entire squad. The rookie manager tried to ignore the slights. But before the conclusion of spring training he decided that he had to confront his insurgent veteran. After their private discussion Robinson's behavior did seem to improve. But damage had been done.

By 1954 a lot of damage had also been done to Jackie Robinson the ballplayer. Given the extent of that damage, Robinson picked a poor time for a contest of wills with a new boss. Jack was now thirty-five years old. If his excessive weight had long been a problem, by 1954 it had become a permanent reality. So were his aching knees and heavy legs. For the first time in his major league career he would not reach double figures in stolen bases. (He would have only seven.) And for the first time in his career he would not reach even 400 official at-bats. (He would have but 386.)

At the season's start, Jackie set lofty goals for himself and his team. He wanted another Dodger pennant, followed at long last by a Dodger World Series victory. As for himself, he told the press that he hoped to win his second batting title and his second MVP award. Robinson would achieve none of his goals. The Dodgers won a respectable 92 games but finished a disappointing five games behind the pennant-winning Giants. And Jackie, after a rousing start, barely struggled to a .300 season. (He would finish at .311.) In sum, the 1954 season was the Dodgers worst since 1948 and the most disappointing, most painful, and most contentious of Jackie Robinson's entire Dodger career. Robinson's glory years, his most productive years, were his great Dodger years between 1949 and 1953. Now those years were forever behind him.

What was not behind him was more controversy. In an early June game against the now Milwaukee Braves umpire Lee Ballanfant mistakenly awarded Braves shortstop Johnny Logan a walk after three called balls. When Robinson next came to bat he asked for a similar "gift." A brief argument took place, followed by a swift Robinson ejection. As Jack neared the visitors' dugout, he flipped his bat. His alleged target was the bat rack. But he didn't come close. The bat, wet from a steady rain, slipped from his hands and landed in the box seats. No one was injured, but fans in Milwaukee and across the country, especially white fans, were outraged. Boos rained on Robinson wherever he went. *Sport* magazine labeled Jackie the "most savagely booed . . . ruthlessly libeled player in the game." And nothing could change those boos into cheers, not even umpire Ballanfant's official report, which concluded that Robinson had not deliberately thrown his bat into the stands.

Two months after that incident, a Dodgers-Braves game turned into a beanball contest. A series of close calls ended when Braves pitcher Gene Conley hit Robinson. This resulted in a typical baseball "fight" (meaning much shouting and shoving, some wrestling, and little by way of actual blows). The feature attraction was a battle of sorts between Robinson and Braves third baseman Eddie Matthews. The Braves announcer, Earle Gillespie, did his best to provide his radio listeners with an account of the "action." In the process, he helped inflame Braves fans by calling Robinson an "agitator." Gillespie later apologized privately to Robinson. The remark, after all, was fraught with overtones of Communist subversion at a time when the Cold War was very hot indeed. Jackie accepted the apology, but he must have wondered when—if ever—all the controversy would end, and whether his team would ever end a season by winning the World Series.

The Seventh Inning

Nearly seventy years old when he was so unceremoniously forced out by Walter O'Malley, Branch Rickey could easily have settled into the comfortable role of baseball's preeminent "elder statesman." Or he could have opted for complete retirement from the game. He had earned at least that much, having already accomplished more than any two baseball executives during his years with the Browns, Cardinals, and Dodgers. But neither possibility held any appeal for Rickey, who had never expressed much interest in anything comfortable or settling. Besides, the boredom of such a life would probably have killed him. Long ago, a young Branch Rickey had wondered whether or not he should make a career out of baseball. By 1950 baseball had long since become more than just a career, and more than just a part of his life; it *was* his life. So, when Pirate owner John Galbreath called with a proposal, Branch Rickey was more than willing to listen.

In 1950, the Pittsburgh Pirates were in free fall. Not since 1927 had the team won the National League pennant. Its 1950 edition had just staggered home dead last, $33^{1}/_{2}$ games behind the "Whiz Kids" of cross-state Philadelphia. In between, the Pirates' best recent finish had been a very distant second in 1944, when the dislocations and the demands of World War II had reduced all of baseball to a state of confusion bordering on chaos. Following the war the team had tried to win fans, if not ballgames, by relying on sluggers such as Hank Greenberg and Ralph Kiner. Otherwise, there was no plan for the future. The team seemed destined to go on losing, both on the field and at the gate. Branch Rickey was brought to Pittsburgh to change all that—or die trying.

Armed with a five-year contract, Rickey set about putting together an organization. His first decision was to hire his son to serve as his right-hand man. To the surprise of many, Branch, Jr., had initially chosen to remain with O'Malley's Dodgers. Unbeknown to his father, the younger Rickey had also received offers from the Giants and the Tigers. He rejected both—and in the end decided to spurn O'Malley as well—in order to work for his father again. The choice really was an easy one, given his loyalty to his father and Branch Sr.'s threat to "quit baseball" if his only son refused to accompany him to Pittsburgh.

With son "Twig" at his side, this Branch took root in Pittsburgh. This time his office was located in Forbes Field. There would be no fish tank, but up went the framed motto explaining the differences between bigots, fools, and slaves. Scattered around it were photos of the leading members of Branch Rickey's personal hall of fame: George Sisler, Rogers Hornsby, Leo Durocher, Jackie Robinson, and the ever-present Lincoln and Churchill.

Once established in his new office, Rickey quickly realized that he had "nothing at all . . . to hold onto" and little by way of solid players to build around: the farm system was devoid of prospects, the pitching staff was without a reliable stopper, the regulars were all too irregular when it came to hitting and fielding. The only bona fide star on the team was Ralph Kiner, who had led the National League in home runs every year between 1946 and 1950 and who would outdo himself in 1951 by hitting 42. Essentially a one-dimensional performer, the Pirate slugger was the ultimate individual player in the ultimate team game. Hitting home runs with some regularity qualified him for occasional all-star status. With that status came certain "special privileges" that landed him permanently in Mr. Rickey's doghouse. If the sole Pirate star was not yet a full-blown prima donna, Rickey feared that he was well on his way to becoming one. Better to get rid of him before he did serious damage to what was left of team morale and before he had a demand to match each of his home runs. And even better to do it while there was still some demand for his limited services.

Earlier the Pirates had brought in the left field fence to accommodate Hank Greenberg (hence "Greenberg Gardens"). Kiner wanted it shortened even more. He also requested an air-conditioned clubhouse. Rickey was mortified. Air-conditioning was "impractical and expensive," not to mention "objectionable to the health of the players." Robinson had never put in a request that came close to matching that one. In fact, none of the Dodger greats had. And the Cardinals? Thinking all the way back to his days in St. Louis, Rickey couldn't have imagined the softest member of the hard-bitten "Gas House Gang" succumbing to such a temptation.

In sum, Kiner had to go. To speed this process along, Rickey composed a bit of free verse for owner Galbreath's contemplation:

Babe Ruth could run. Our man cannot.
Ruth could throw. Our man cannot.
Ruth could steal a base. Our man cannot.
Ruth was a good fielder. Our man is not.
Ruth could hit with power to all fields. Our man cannot.
Ruth never requested a diminutive field to fit him. Our man does.

Despite his disparagement of Kiner the ballplayer, Rickey found much to like about Kiner the man. He even appreciated the occasional heroics supplied by Kiner, the long-ball specialist. But with no prospect of a Pirate pennant anywhere close at hand, Ralph Kiner was a luxury that this team could not afford. The problem was that Kiner was a Galbreath favorite.

If anything, the free verse could also be read as praise for Ruth rather than simply as criticism of Kiner. Rickey always had a weakness for ballplayers with weaknesses—especially if they happened to be great ballplayers. Ruth was certainly one of those. So what if he was what Rickey called "erotopathic" or if he "lived his entire life close to the rocks of intellectual indifference." In Rickey's estimation, the worst thing Ruth ever did was to make the stolen base an "antiquated feature of the game." The best thing he did, of course, was hit home runs. But he also did many other things very, very well—and he certainly did them better than Ralph Kiner. For that matter, even as a home run hitter Ralph Kiner was not in Babe Ruth's league.*

Had Ralph Kiner been another Babe Ruth, Branch Rickey surely would have found a way to keep him in a Pirate uniform. Because Kiner wasn't close to being a Ruth, Rickey decided it was time to put his patented rule of thumb to work—and sooner rather than later. No one could know for sure, but it already might have been a year too late to trade the Pirate slugger.

Not until the end of the 1952 season was Rickey able to convince Galbreath to deal Kiner to the Cubs. The move was not terribly popular. Kiner's 37 round trippers had led the National League again in 1952. As a result, Rickey was vilified in Pittsburgh and hung in effigy at least once. Season ticket holders threatened to boycott the team until he was gone. But Rickey was unmoved. He knew that the cash he had received for Kiner was crucial to the team's development. After all, he had already poured in $200,000 of his own money in an effort to shore up the rapidly evaporating Pirate financial reserve. Player reserves were also desperately needed. An infusion of money might make it possible for Rickey to sign prospects. No other part of his original design remained, even as the Pirates remained mired in the National League cellar.

Now heading into his eighth decade, Branch Rickey had run out of innovations, except for introducing helmets for his players to wear at bat and in the field. As of the 1950s, all major league teams had farm systems. And almost all of them also had a lot more money to spend on player development. This was certainly true of the wealthy Yankees and Red Sox, but at least they were in the American league. The greater concern was that it was also maddeningly true for Walter O'Malley's Dodgers. The man who

---

*In retirement in 1961, Rickey took time to do a little math. That was the year that Roger Maris broke Babe Ruth's single season home run record of sixty. Rickey was not terribly impressed. In 1927 American League batters hit a total of 439 home runs. In 1961 that figure was 1,534. On the basis of his 1927 share of home runs, Rickey projected that Ruth would have amassed 209 round trippers in 1961.

had reined in the "extravagant" Rickey was now doling out the kind of money that he had refused to part with when his nemesis was running the team.

Not only were his Pirates losing money, but Branch Rickey also seemed to be losing his touch. In spring training, 1952, Rickey thought he had discovered the next Dizzy Dean. The alleged phenom was a nineteen-year-old Class D pitcher named Ron Necciai. After an exhibition game, Rickey took a Pittsburgh baseball writer aside to give him this scoop: "I've seen a lot of baseball in my time. There have only been two young pitchers I was certain were destined for greatness, simply because they had the meanest fastball a batter can face. One of those boys was Dizzy Dean. The other is Ron Necciai." Rickey was not alone in predicting that Necciai was destined for greatness. Clyde Sukeforth thought that the Pirate rookie had the "liveliest fastball" he had ever seen.

Necciai also seemed to be a physical wonder. Born with what he called "long joints," Necciai had elbows that were almost convex. More than that, he was able to release the ball with a motion so soft and fluid that a fellow pitcher described it as being akin to that of a boy making a yo-yo "sleep." The combination seemed to produce a natural curve ball. Before long, Rickey thought it would produce an endless stream of major league victories.

"Long joints" and all, Ron Necciai started the season with the Bristol Twins of the Class D Appalachian League. He didn't stay there long. On May 13, 1952, Necciai made baseball history by striking out all 27 batters he faced! His next start found him slipping slightly, as he pitched a two-hitter and struck out only 24. That double feat earned him an instant promotion to Class B, where continued success led to a mid-season, 1952, decision to rush Necciai directly to the parent Pirates. At Rickey's insistence, Necciai was given every chance to prove to Pittsburgh fans that he *was* the second coming of Dizzy Dean. He wasn't. Necciai finished the year with a dismal 1-6 record and a 7.08 earned run average. He never again pitched in the big leagues.

By the end of the 1952 season Branch Rickey was mightily discouraged. His Pirates had soared all the way to seventh in 1951 only to fall back to eighth, an incredible $54^1/_2$ games behind the pennant-winning Dodgers. The 1953 season was no better. This time the Pirates finished a full 55 games behind the team that he had built but had been forced to leave behind. Again in 1954 and 1955 the Pirates finished dead last. So much for Branch Rickey's vaunted five-year plan for Pittsburgh. During those five campaigns the Pirates avoided last place only once—and that was their 1951 leap to the heavenly heights of seventh place. Clearly it was time for Rickey to go. Rickey's valedictory statement was an exercise in the obvious: "I did not bring Pittsburgh a winner." This failure, he concluded, represented the "biggest disappointment in my baseball life."

What was less obvious at the time was that Branch Rickey had really not lost his touch, that he had actually laid the ground for future Pirate success. In 1960 the Pirates would capture their first pennant in thirty-three years before defeating the Yankees in a memorable seven-game World Series. There were many Pirate heroes in 1960, but among the most heroic was someone whom Rickey had drafted out of the Dodger organization in 1954. Roberto Clemente was the multi-dimensional player that Ralph Kiner was not. During his nineteen years with the Pirates he would amass exactly 3,000 hits (including 240 home runs and 166 triples). But to Branch Rickey he was not just a great baseball player, he embodied poetic justice as well. To steal Clemente for the Pirates was one thing. To steal him *from* the Dodgers was even better. Ironically, in 1954 Roberto Clemente was playing for a minor league team of more than passing acquaintance to Branch Rickey. That team was the Montreal Royals, which eight years earlier had served as the incubator for another Rickey project of more than minor importance.

But at the end of the 1955 season, Branch Rickey was suddenly devoid of projects. Elevated to the honorific title of chairman of the board, he was effectively out of a job—and effectively removed from actively running a major league baseball team for the first time since 1912. As he emptied his Forbes Field office, a local reporter observed the departing Rickey at the desultory task of sorting through the most recent chapter of his life's work. The reporter tried to put the best light on a dark day. "Now you can do nothing, Mr. Rickey," he offered. Mr. Rickey was offended at the very idea of such a prospect.

"Do nothing, young man? You expect me to do nothing? Preposterous. I started out to do nothing for three days once. I never was so tired in all my life."

By all accounts, however, Branch Rickey could now look forward to a lot of tiring days. Who would want a near seventy-five-year-old man fresh off five years of uninterrupted failure? Still, his entire career had constituted quite a run—even including the last five years. Perhaps no one was in a better position to judge that run—and the runner—than Red Smith. To the New York columnist, baseball had seen the last of Rickey's breed. The game had been wonderful for generalists, but it was already on its way to becoming an enterprise of, by, and for specialists, whether front-office types or (by 1973) on-field designated hitters. Never again, wrote Smith, would baseball find one man to play as many roles as Rickey had, including "player, manager, executive, lawyer, preacher, horse-trader, spellbinder, innovator, husband and father and grandfather, farmer, logician, obscurantist, reformer, financier, sociologist, crusader, sharper, father confessor, checker shark, friend, and fighter." Not to mention, defender of the game. It might have been reasonable to conclude that baseball had seen the last of this particular character—or more accurately, the last of this particular type of character.

As of 1955, it might have been reasonable to conclude that Jackie Robinson's baseball career was over as well. His play in all phases of the game was on the decline. His diabetes was taking hold. His weight was advancing, as was his interest in the world beyond baseball, especially the budding civil rights movement. Still he couldn't give up on the game, on himself, or on his team. At least he didn't want to give up until the Brooklyn Dodgers no longer had to "wait till next year." Which is to say he didn't want to retire until the Dodgers could finally call themselves the world champions of America's game.

The baseball stars seemed to be in proper alignment right from the start of the 1955 season. The Dodgers opened with ten straight wins. Robinson and other Dodger veterans were of course heartened by this fast start. But they had at least two reasons to be cautious as well. After all, promising Dodger springs in 1950 and 1951 had ended in great disappointment. Perhaps because that recent history remained so fresh, these Dodger players were determined not to repeat it. And they didn't. On September 8 the runaway Dodgers clinched the National League pennant by moving a full eighteen games ahead of the second place Milwaukee Braves. No team in league history had ever done better.

Jackie Robinson did not run wild in 1955. In truth, he confirmed his worst fears by having a thoroughly subpar year. He appeared in only 105 games, hit a less than mediocre .256 (which was forty points below his previous low), and drove in a paltry 36 runs. For the first time since 1948 he was not voted to the National League All-Star team. Everything pointed to the obvious conclusion that the end of his wonderful career was at hand.

Given Robinson's numbers, Dodger Manager Walter Alston might have been excused had he chosen to bench his aging star for the start of the fifth Yankee-Dodgers World Series since 1947. But he didn't. Aided by the unsolicited advice of a former Dodger manager, Alston decided that he needed Robinson on the field. Leo Durocher didn't care "what the calendar says." The Dodgers simply weren't "yet ready to win without him." To Durocher, a wounded, paunchy, diabetic Jackie Robinson was still a winner: "Keeping [his] amazing leadership on the shelf would be like pinch-hitting for Ruth in the clutch."

Alston's decision almost paid dividends in the first game. Down 6-4 in the top of the eighth inning, Robinson ignored his aging body and took off from third all on his own. Sliding safely under Yankee catcher Yogi Berra's tag, Jackie stole home for the eighteenth time in his career. But that was the last Dodger run in what turned out to be a 6-5 loss. In retrospect, Robinson conceded that his decision was "not the best baseball strategy," even though two were out. What he wanted to do was give his team "new fire."

That "new fire" was apparently slow to gather force, because the Yankees took the second game as well. Not until the series shifted to Ebbets Field did the fortunes of the Dodgers change. Triggered by more daring Robinson base running in Game Three, the Dodgers went on to sweep all three contests in their own park. Once back in Yankee Stadium, the perennial American League champs took the sixth game handily, 5-1.

Everything came down to the last game (as it had in 1947 and 1952). But more than one thing would be different. This time Jackie Robinson was *not* in the starting lineup. And this time the Dodgers won.

In fact, Robinson never entered what would be the greatest game in Brooklyn Dodger history. In truth, he had had less than a memorable series, hitting only .182 and making two errors afield. The Dodger hitting stars for the series were centerfielder Duke Snider, who hit four home runs and drove in seven, and catcher Roy Campanella, who led the Dodger attack in the third and fourth games. In the seventh game the key Dodgers were a young pitcher named Johnny Podres, who took his second series victory by tossing a five-hit shutout, and a Cuban-born outfielder name Sandy Amoros, who helped preserve a 2-0 victory by making a running catch in left to trigger a critical sixth inning double play. For the first time in team history the Dodgers had won the World Series. And to add to the satisfaction, they had defeated the Yankees to do it.

Although Jackie was not on the field for the final game, he made his presence felt now and again. Early in the series he had used his guile, his daring, and what was left of his legs to give his team a needed lift. Though he stroked only four hits in six games, he was able to manufacture five Dodger runs. Manufacturing something out of the rest of his playing career would prove to be much more difficult.

Jackie Robinson's last year as a major leaguer was 1956. Despite yet another Dodger pennant, it was a mediocre year for Robinson. But more worrisome to Dodger fans was the matter of the team's future in Brooklyn. By the end of the 1956 season it was increasingly clear that Walter O'Malley wanted out. A tantalizing but ultimately unanswerable question surrounds Branch Rickey: if he had been running the Dodgers in 1956, would he have wanted out as well? Evidence points in that direction. Ebbets Field was aging and cramped. Parking facilities were either terrible or non-existent. And the population of the borough was rapidly changing. The Italian and Jewish neighborhoods, which had produced so many loyal fans, were giving way to new immigrant populations. Jackie Robinson's presence on the team notwithstanding, the southern blacks and Puerto Ricans who were then streaming into Brooklyn had no immediate attachment to the team or its colorful history.

As a result, attendance at Dodger games declined steadily between its high point of 1,807,526 in Robinson's rookie year of 1947 to slightly over a million fans in 1955 when they won the World Series. Amazing as it may seem, the 1955 World Champions shared a distinction with the last-place Pittsburgh Pirates of Branch Rickey: they were the only other National League team to report attendance figures lower than the benchmark year of 1941 (which was the last prewar baseball season).

In 1947 a delighted Wendell Smith had penned the following ditty: "Jackie's nimble/ Jackie's quick/ Jackie's making the turnstiles click." Smith may have had a point then, but Dodger attendance did not build on its 1947 record. In fact, Dodger attendance in 1947 was only 11,000 higher than it had been in 1946. A portent of things not to come may have been Robinson's 1947 debut as a Dodger, when only 26,000 fans paid their way into Ebbets Field. This was two-thirds of capacity and 5,000 fans *below* the 1946 home opener.

Robinson or no, fans did not troop into Ebbets Field in record numbers after 1947. For that matter, fans did not exactly flood into major league parks during the Robinson era. Wendell Smith's poetry may have been clever, but it was neither historically accurate nor predictive of the immediate future. Not until 1960 did the National League surpass the total league attendance mark it had set in 1947.

If there was an exception to the general rule of decline, it was provided by the new Milwaukee Braves. In fact, by the mid-1950s this transplanted Boston team was outdrawing the Dodgers by a million fans *per season*. Walter O'Malley could read those numbers (as Branch Rickey might also have read them). More precisely, he had his eyes on points farther west, where he wanted the eyes of television audiences trained on baseball games. As the 1956 season ground on, there was a sense that two eras were about to end. And they did—almost simultaneously. Robinson retired following the 1956 campaign, and a year later his old team moved to Los Angeles.

Surprisingly, Robinson's 1956 production was an improvement over that of 1955. He played in 117 games, pumped his batting average up to .275, drove in seven more runs, and belted out two more homers. Early in the season he also managed to steal home for the nineteenth (and final) time of his career. In all, he made a decent contribution to a Dodger team that edged the Braves to win its sixth pennant in ten years. He even improved on his 1955 World Series performance by garnering six hits and scoring five runs as the Dodgers reverted to form by losing to the Yankees, four games to three. Robinson's overall performance in 1956 actually led him to contemplate the possibility of squeezing yet another year out of his baseball life.

By this point there were a select few Dodger teammates whom Robinson liked and admired. Among them were pitchers Carl Erskine ("the most refined of the bunch") and Clem Labine ("also very intelligent"), shortstop Pee Wee Reese ("a fine team man") and newcomer Joe Black (who in 1952 became the second black pitcher to crack the Dodgers' starting rotation). At the same time, Robinson detested the flagrant, almost routine, womanizing that seemed to be an inevitable part of the travel and the idle hours. Clearly, Jack saw himself as better than all of that. He thought as much when he was single and a Kansas City Monarch, and moreso after he became a married man and a Brooklyn Dodger.

If the distance between Robinson and most of the rest of the Dodger team gradually widened over the years, so did his relationship with catcher Roy Campanella. Tension between them could be detected at least as early as their 1949 barnstorming tour, when Campanella discovered that he was earning less than

Robinson. Relations did seem to improve for a time after that. But by the mid-1950s the two men were thoroughly estranged from one another. The trouble was not traceable to a single incident; rather it was rooted in their different approaches to life. If Robinson was quick to anger, Campanella was anxious to please. Robinson was a battler; Campanella a conciliator. To Roy, a liberated Jackie seemed to go out of his way to seek trouble. To Jackie, an accommodating Roy seemed to go out of his way to avoid it.

The differences did not end there. Robinson was the racial trailblazer, who felt that Campanella should have been more grateful for what he had done. More than that, he was disappointed by the catcher's reluctance to be a fellow pioneer on the racial front. After all, Robinson's campaign was against the ongoing racism that confronted both of them. For his part, Campanella saw himself as a baseball player first, last, and always. If Jackie wanted to be a symbol—or could not avoid being cast as one—Campy wanted no part of it. He wasn't anybody's symbol; he was simply the Dodgers' catcher.

Branch Rickey had been well aware of the differences between these two proud men. He spelled out many of them in a 1952 letter to Dick Young of the New York *Daily News*. As always, Rickey, the scout, was at work. And, as always, there was the matter of Robinson's arm. It was, in Rickey's judgment, "good, not great." Campanella's throwing, on the other hand, was "as good as that of any catcher who has ever lived . . . he is quick in forearm movement, deadly in accuracy, and exceptional in velocity." At the plate, the advantage was Robinson's. He was simply a "corking batsman," not to mention the "most dangerous batsman in the major leagues when the call has two strikes on him."

Rickey refused to make "odious comparisons" between them as men, but he could not help but comment on their differences. Robinson was "very aggressive" and "highly adventuresome." His character and habits were "beyond reproach, and his fidelities [were] well known." On occasion, Robinson "has had great difficulty in restraining his emotional urges," but Rickey remained convinced that he "has enough sense and enough control . . . not to let anything impair his competitive ability."

Campanella's personality was marked by "kindliness" and "affability." He was "natively a square shooter [whose] face could never lie." If Rickey had a criticism to make of a man "with no bad habits," it was that he lived a life of "unmorality" because he never really thought in terms of right and wrong. But Rickey was not quite finished. "Robinson would challenge, but Campanella would placate. Robinson would advance, but Campanella would simply not retreat." The Dodger catcher "would soften to the pressure of emotion," while the second baseman "would harden [and] make it worse."

Rickey's assessment aside, the two men were supremely skilled, highly competitive baseball players. But Robinson's skills and competitiveness could not be divorced from the fact that he was a celebrity as well. Because he was the more famous of the two, Jack came to believe that Roy resented his presumably loftier status. Finally, each was in a curious sense a marginal man. The coal black Robinson was forever marked as an outsider in highly race-conscious white circles, while the light-skinned Campanella (whose ancestry was Italian and African American) had no guaranteed membership in any racial community.

After the 1956 season Robinson and Campanella had one less thing in common. Never again would they be Brooklyn Dodger teammates. In early December Walter O'Malley did the unthinkable by approving the trade of Robinson to the rival New York Giants. In exchange for a certain Hall of Famer, the Dodgers received only a journeyman relief pitcher and $35,000. In truth, Robinson had left O'Malley with few options, since he had made it clear that he would accept a trade only to another New York team. That left the Giants or the equally hated Yankees. Of course, O'Malley could have chosen to do nothing. But with a move to Los Angeles in the offing, did he want to take Robinson west where he would be welcomed as a returning hero?

When a stunned Robinson learned of the deal, he realized that he had more than one decision to make. Earlier in the fall he had signed a $50,000 contract with *Look,* which gave the magazine exclusive rights to a series of articles concerning the inside story of Robinson's retirement from baseball. On the one hand, he wanted to be "fair to the Dodgers," O'Malley's act of treachery notwithstanding. On the other hand, he didn't want to reveal his future, thereby violating his agreement with the editors of *Look.* Therefore, when a Dodger representative called to break the news, Robinson kept silent about his own plans.

In the meantime, the Giants were dangling a $60,000 salary in front of him. That figure, plus many unsolicited letters from fans, prompted more than a few Robinson second thoughts. But in the end he decided to retire rather than report to the Giants. At the most, he had planned on playing just one more year anyway. So why not end his major league career right where it had started? Having broken in with the Dodgers, having had ten mostly great seasons as a Dodger, why not go out as a Dodger—and at a time when he was "even with baseball and baseball was even with [him]."

Besides, Jackie Robinson had always known that there was more to life than baseball. As he told the press in early 1957, "baseball was just a part of my life." But at the same time, it was a part of his life that he was not ready to leave entirely behind him. Branch Rickey had long thought that Robinson would one day make a fine major league manager. He had said as much in his insightful letter to Dick Young. For Robinson's part, it would not have taken much coaxing to head him in this direction. But no one with a job to offer did any such coaxing. (Permitting a black man on the field of play had been difficult enough; permitting a black man to direct others was quite another. Not until 1975 would major league baseball hire a black manager.) Certainly the Dodgers were not interested in Robinson's service, whether on the major or minor league level, or whether as a manager or a coach. "Robinson can't manage himself," Walter O'Malley is supposed to have remarked not long after the two parted company for good.

Jackie confronted all of the possible objections in a July 1956 article in *Sport* magazine titled "Why Can't I Manage in the Majors?" Was it his lack of experience? Would white players resent him or otherwise reject him? Robinson answered each question by pointing to his near decade of experience and acceptance as a big leaguer. But no baseball man with a job to offer was listening—then or later. Following the 1956 season, Jackie Robinson would never again be associated with a major league baseball team. Whether he liked it or not, his baseball life had ended.

Branch Rickey spent much of the late 1950s on the lecture circuit, preaching against the evils of "monolithic Communism" and on behalf of the virtues of the Four Gospels. Wherever he went, he railed against the "perils of complacency," whether the job at hand was an America trying to fend off the Soviet Union or a pennant winner trying to defend its title against all comers. Between his speeches, there was time for both politicking and organizing. Rickey worked with the Eisenhower administration to help eliminate racial discrimination in federal employment. In that capacity, he came to admire Vice President Richard Nixon for his commitment to civil rights. Ever the loyal Republican, Rickey clearly preferred Nixon to the powerful Senate majority leader, Texas Democrat Lyndon Johnson, whom he regarded as "utterly ruthless." And ever-suspicious of southern Democrats, Rickey never flagged in his own commitment to civil rights or his belief that the Republican Party was the best vehicle for achieving full rights for black Americans.

Ever a man of religion, the retired baseball man volunteered some of his time to help give birth to the dream of a young Oklahoma football coach named Don McClanen. His vision was to create an organization devoted to strengthening the moral fiber and religious beliefs of young athletes in high schools and colleges across the country. Certain that Rickey was a kindred spirit, McClanen went to the old man for advice, contacts, and an endorsement. He got all three. And before long all three proved instrumental in the creation of the Fellowship of Christian Athletes.

In 1957 Branch Rickey had occasion to reflect on a death, not a birth. The Brooklyn Dodgers were no more. They had not been his Dodgers for the last seven years, thanks to Walter O'Malley, but they had long been Brooklyn's treasured team.

Branch Rickey's eight "wonderful" years in Brooklyn had given him a "new vision" of America. Despite its size, Brooklyn was a real community, a community of three million people, most of whom were filled with "devotion to its baseball club." Moving the Dodgers to Los Angeles was, to Branch Rickey, a "crime" against that community. A baseball club, he believed, was a "quasi-public institution." But the Brooklyn Dodgers were more than that; they were "public without the quasi."

A few years later Rickey had occasion to stare at a photograph of what a wrecking ball had done to Ebbets Field. What he saw was a "symbol of sadness," not just for himself, but for "hundreds of thousands of people." As it happened, that picture of destruction was taken on the very day that Branch Rickey, Jr., died of complications from heart disease and diabetes. The date was April 11, 1961. At the moment that Branch, Sr., learned of his son's death he was discussing the future of baseball at a Manhattan restaurant. The grieving father left immediately to be with his wife. For the time being, Branch Rickey put baseball aside, but the separation proved to be temporary.

His lunch partner on that April day was a New York lawyer named William Shea. A few years earlier, Shea had begun to push for the creation of a third major league. The advertised idea was to have a New York team anchor the new league, thereby filling the void created by the departure of the Dodgers and the Giants, who, like their cross-town rivals, had left the Empire State for the Golden State. If there was a method behind the madness, it was to force major league owners to grant a National League expansion franchise to New York City. Or so Shea originally plotted.

To advance his scheme, Shea penciled the name Branch Rickey into his starting lineup. But as the two men developed their strategy they came up against National League President Warren Giles, who was on record as asking, "Who needs New York?" They also learned that the new commissioner of baseball, Ford Frick, was opposed to any form of expansion. Given this joint roadblock, Rickey became intrigued with the possibility of actually putting together an entirely new major league. And the more he thought about it, the more convinced he became that it could and should be done.

Here irony intrudes again on the career of Branch Rickey. Perhaps, this time, hypocrisy does as well. The man who had long benefited from baseball's monopolistic practices was now in the position of challenging those very practices and their accompanying powers. The man who often stood accused of being a penny-pinching despot now labeled baseball's owners as "absolute dictators," who opposed anything that smacked of free enterprise. The Browns executive who long ago had been so critical of the Federal League, and the Dodger executive who had once attacked the Mexican League, seemed to be on his way to putting together his own version of that which he had once condemned. Toward that end, Rickey found himself operating out of New York City for the first time since O'Malley had ousted him from the Dodgers nearly a decade earlier. This time his office was not in Brooklyn, but right on Fifth Avenue in the heart of Manhattan. And this time his official title was president of something called the Continental League.

To those who wondered about the feasibility of this venture, Rickey had a single response: "Twenty great cities cannot be ignored." Chief among his select targets, of course, was New York City (which had to be too big for the Yankees alone). But also on his list were cities such as Dallas–Forth Worth, Houston, Atlanta, Minneapolis–St. Paul, Toronto, San Diego, and Seattle. In the name of advancing the interests of their new league and these cities, Rickey and Shea arranged a meeting with Commissioner Frick shortly after the conclusion of the 1959 World Series. On the appointed day the two men strode into Frick's office to ask *the* question: "Are you opposed to the creation of a third major league?"

Frick equivocated. The commissioner then claimed that he had long favored the idea of such a league. But in his very next sentence Ford Frick conceded that he couldn't lend his support to the project, because the owners (who paid his salary) were adamantly opposed to it.

Rickey pressed on: "Why, as commissioner of baseball, do you not embrace it and encourage it and lead it?" This time Frick responded with a silence that was both deafening and embarrassing.

As Rickey rose to leave, he could not resist a parting shot in the form of this piece of advice: "Ford, you must not miss your chance. Ol' man opportunity has long hair in front and is bald in back. When he comes to you, you can snatch him and hold him tight, but when he is past, he could be gone forever."

By 1959 Branch Rickey could continue to take great comfort in knowing that he had not missed his "chance," first in 1945 and then in 1947. And 1959 was an occasion for contemplating what Rickey had begun, for not until then could it be said that all sixteen major league teams had at least one black player in a major league uniform. The last four teams to do so were the Philadelphia Phillies, the Detroit Tigers, the St. Louis Cardinals, and, finally, the Boston Red Sox. With the elevation of infielder "Pumpsie" Green to the Red Sox the cycle was finally, if belatedly, complete. The very team that had given Robinson a bogus tryout in the spring of 1945 had at long last joined the other fifteen major league teams.

No doubt Mr. Rickey would have preferred Green's Christian name (which was Elijah) to "Pumpsie." And no doubt he would have preferred that the distance between Robinson and Green had been a lot shorter than twelve years. But there was still a measure of satisfaction to be taken by the Dodger pioneer on this front.

All along, Rickey had been more optimistic than he had reason to be concerning the twin subjects of baseball and race. After the initial flurry of Dodger and Indian signings of black ballplayers only the rival New York Giants and his other team in St. Louis (the lowly Browns) had dared to follow suit. Rickey had pinned his greatest hopes on major league teams signing black prospects for their minor league farm systems. In fact, he had encouraged other teams (including the Giants) to pursue this avenue (rather than just sign veteran Negro League performers). But only the Browns seemed inclined to follow the Dodgers' example. The year 1947 may have been a breakthrough year, but according to historian Jules Tygiel, the overall integration of the game was at a "virtual standstill" as of the end of the 1947 season.

The next year saw Satchel Paige become not just the first black pitcher in the majors, but the first to pitch in a World Series game. Signed by Bill Veeck to hurl for his Cleveland Indians, Paige made his debut on July 9, 1948. By this point in his long career, Paige may have been forced to rely more on guile than speed, but he still managed to compile a 6-1 record and a 2.48 ERA over seventy-two plus innings. The Indian "rookie" also turned out to be an even better drawing card than the master showman Veeck had expected. More than 200,000 fans poured into Cleveland's cavernous Memorial Stadium over the course of three consecutive Paige starts during the Indians' successful 1948 pennant drive. While Paige made only a brief appearance in the 1948 World Series against the then Boston Braves, the combination of Paige and Larry Doby established a black presence on the field. In fact, following Robinson's participation in the 1947 Series there were black players in every subsequent Fall Classic, save for 1950. Still, the majors continued to move very slowly, and this despite the disbanding of the Negro National League following the 1948 season. As late as 1953 only six of the sixteen major league teams had black players on their rosters.

The next year, however, the next black superstar burst out onto the major league stage. He was also one of the last Negro League players to advance to the majors. After a brief stint in the minor leagues, Hank Aaron (once of the Indianapolis Clowns) was a Milwaukee Brave. His thirteen home runs (and .280 batting average) in 1954 did not necessarily herald the greatness that was to come. Certainly, there was no immediate and overwhelming evidence that he would one day break Babe Ruth's career home run mark. But at the time Aaron had all the evidence he needed to account for his presence in the major leagues at all. In his autobiography, *I Had a Hammer,* Aaron recalled that as a Mobile, Alabama, teenager he informed his father in 1948 that he would be "in the big leagues before Jackie retired. Jackie had that effect on all of us—he gave us our dreams." He also remembered an earlier time in the Aaron household. He and his father were "sitting on the back porch once when an airplane flew over, and I told Daddy I'd like to be a pilot when I grew up. He said, 'Ain't no colored pilots.' I said okay, then, I'll be a ballplayer. He said, 'Ain't no colored ball-players.'" At least not at the major league level.

That changed in 1947. And that change had an impact on a thirteen-year-old boy in Mobile. The next spring young Henry "Hank" Aaron skipped school one day to hear Jackie Robinson speak. The Dodgers had broken spring training camp and were heading north to open the regular season. En route, they played an exhibition game in Mobile. While in the city, Jack agreed to speak to local black youths at a corner drugstore. Henry Aaron was among them. Although he was standing in the back of the crowd, Aaron recalled that he "felt like I was hugging him. . . ." He didn't just see a baseball player standing before the group. Instead he "saw a concerned citizen. He was saying something like, 'Hey, just give yourself a chance. If I can make it, all of you can make it. It may not be in sports, but it can be in something."

That spring day in 1948 far from guaranteed that Hank Aaron would "make it" in sports. But it must have helped. One way or another, it was a day he would never forget.

In 1948 the Dodgers were nearly alone among major league teams in playing exhibition games in the South. By the early 1950s most major league teams were playing such contests in southern cities as they made their way north following the completion of spring training. Furthermore, by this point many major league teams had begun to make an effort to sign young black prospects. Among the signees was Henry Aaron of Mobile. And among the teams most interested in signing such players was the Pittsburgh Pirates of Branch Rickey. In doing so, Rickey was acting in what he thought was the best interests of his struggling Pirates. But he was also out to prove that black critics of the white-run major leagues were wrong. Not that Rickey was suddenly at loggerheads with black America on the subject of baseball desegregation. Far from it. He agreed with those, black and white, who thought that the pace of change was much too slow. But he disagreed with those black baseball writers who feared a return to an all-white game at the major league level. Such pessimistic thoughts were prompted by the gradual collapse of all Negro League baseball. As of 1953, only the Negro American League remained in operation, and it had been reduced to exactly four teams, one of which was Robinson's old Kansas City Monarchs. This situation led a Pittsburgh *Courier* columnist to wonder how major league scouts would find black ballplayers in the future. Rickey was incredulous. Responding in the *Courier,* he argued that the Negro Leagues had come into being primarily because of "necessity and prejudice." With "prejudice" on the way out, could "necessity" be far behind? Forever an optimist, Rickey could imagine what the columnist could not, namely a day when professional baseball had transcended prejudice. The demise of the Negro Leagues was not necessarily to be applauded, but it was inevitable. And it would not mean the end of black players signing with the predominantly white major leagues. At least not if Branch Rickey had anything to say about it.

Of course, black players needed to serve their apprenticeships. But now they could learn their craft in the existing minor leagues, which is to say in the very farm systems that Rickey had pioneered in the 1920s. No longer were the Negro Leagues the primary place for young black prospects to learn the game. In fact, insofar as Rickey was concerned, they were far from the best place for such ballplayers. Better that they learn the system of the parent team. Better that they not be influenced by the carnival atmosphere surrounding Negro Leagues games. Better that they not be a part of the "racket" that had long infected much of black baseball. And to prove his point, he had better sign black ballplayers. Which is what he did while he was running the Pirates—and which he continued to advocate that all teams do after he left that organization.

Ironically, the Pirate team that would win the 1960 World Series was composed of many players who had been signed and scouted by Rickey. But it was an essentially white team. The only black regular was the same Roberto Clemente whom Rickey had spirited away from the Dodgers in the mid-1950s.

By 1960 Rickey was fighting other battles and confronting other ironies. On a separate front in the summer of 1960, Rickey testified at Senate hearings on the question of eliminating baseball's long-standing exemption from antitrust laws. Ever since a Supreme Court ruling in 1922 the two existing major leagues had enjoyed the monopolistic control that Rickey was now fighting. That fight led Rickey to condemn the hypocrisy of major league owners who could behave as though they were operating a "quasi-public trust" one day only to take a "better deal" from another city the next. Moreover, he had little need to remind the senators that that was exactly what was happening. More than a half century of total franchise stability had given way to franchise shifts in both leagues. In 1953 the Boston Braves became the Milwaukee Braves. The next year the St. Louis Browns were transformed into the Baltimore Orioles. And the year after that the Philadelphia Athletics moved to Kansas City. Then came the dual Dodger-Giant trek to California. Next on the major league horizon was Minneapolis–St. Paul, where a ball park had already been built with an eye toward attracting a major league tenant.

Past and potential franchise relocations generated sufficient interest in Congress to hold hearings and cobble together a bill to stymie such shifts in the future. Later in the summer of 1960 this bill failed by a surprisingly slim margin. Defeat aside, Rickey remained hopeful. After all, the bill had been expected to garner only a handful of votes. Perhaps the legislators, in their collective wisdom, would decide that the first tally was close enough to warrant a second vote. Such a vote never took place. But the major league establishment had been put on notice. So concerned were team owners that they moved to grant four new franchises. Rather than risk the potential loss of their antitrust exemption they launched a panicky pre-emptive strike, a strike that instantly killed Rickey's Continental League.

At least William Shea's original goal would be realized. The National League would be back in operation in New York City.

Though disappointed that there would be no third league, Rickey was willing to give his compatriot full credit. Shea "showed intelligence, resourcefulness, courage, indefatigability, and tenacity." Only "daring" was missing from this typical Rickey litany. Still, the responsibility for this limited success was "his and his alone." Gone forever were the New York Giants and Brooklyn Dodgers. About to be born were the New York Mets (as well as the Houston Colt 45s, the California Angels, and the Minnesota Twins, courtesy of yet another franchise shift as the Griffith family moved their Washington Senators to the Twin Cities and a new Washington team was installed in the nation's capital).

In the fall of 1960 Rickey returned to his Pittsburgh home. For the moment he did his best to push baseball into the background. A presidential election was underway. With the Eisenhower years about to be laid to rest, a new generation of leaders was poised to take the reins of government. The member of that generation who most intrigued and appealed to Branch Rickey was not John Kennedy, but Richard Nixon. Rickey, after all, was a Republican of better than sixty years standing. More than that, he was a Lincoln Republican, and he thought that Richard Nixon was one as well. Lincoln had been elected by the "plain people." So had Congressman and later Senator Nixon. President Lincoln had issued the Emancipation Proclamation. Rickey was convinced that as president Nixon would work tirelessly and aggressively to expand civil rights to the descendants of those original slaves. As the 1960 election approached, Rickey had no doubts that Richard Nixon was by far the better candidate. If only he could convince an old friend of his to think the same way.

The trouble was that this old friend was a Democrat. And although he wasn't a terribly active Democrat, Jackie Robinson was someone of stature in the country, someone to whom people would listen. Rickey was convinced of this; so was the Republican presidential candidate. Richard Nixon, meet Jackie Robinson. For Branch Rickey, this was the dream ticket. He could think of no two Americans better able or better poised to advance a cause that had long been dear to him.

Did all this private dreaming and politicking mean that Branch Rickey had finally put his baseball life behind him? It was hard to know. But this much is known. When asked by a young reporter to relate his greatest thrill in the game, this about-to-be-octogenarian had a response at the ready: "Son, it hasn't happened yet."

The Eighth Inning

Robinson's first post-baseball job was far removed from the often dazzling world of major league parks. Instead of reporting to play at Ebbets Field, he commuted to work in midtown Manhattan. Instead of donning a baseball uniform, he put on a business suit. Instead of hearing cheers or boos, he took orders and gave a few of his own. Instead of being a free agent on the base paths, he was an executive behind a desk.

Robinson's new boss was a self-made millionaire named William Black, who had begun his career in the 1920s by selling shelled nuts in New York City's Times Square. Within two decades he had parlayed his original enterprise into a string of fast-food restaurants called Chock Full O' Nuts, which catered to people with little time and not a lot of money. For his customers, Black's specialty was a sandwich on whole wheat nut bread and a nickel cup of coffee. When it came to his workforce, Black had a reputation for looking beyond race in his hiring practices. This was especially the case during World War II, when he lost hundreds of workers, mostly whites, to the war effort. Many of their replacements were black. Much to William Black's benefit, but not at all to his surprise, those workers quickly demonstrated that they deserved the chance he had given them.

By the time Robinson met Black, the latter had acquired a well-deserved reputation in New York political circles as a liberal, a Democrat, and a strong advocate of civil rights. His hiring of Robinson was perfectly consistent with both his business practices and his political principles. It also represented a stroke of public relations genius for the white founder of Chock Full O'Nuts. Jackie Robinson was not just another vice president. Nor was he to be a token employee, an empty symbol, or simply a familiar face. It was Black's intention—and Robinson's—that Jackie would earn the hefty $50,000 annual salary that he was to be paid. Conventional wisdom also quickly had it that the firm's newest executive would not appreciate being confined to a desk. Black's intention was to confine and liberate his vice president for personnel at the same time. Robinson was also promised plenty of leeway when it came to making decisions pertaining to the company workforce. Having generally had the authority to steal bases at will, Vice President Robinson now thought he had been given the go-ahead to make calls of weightier, if less newsworthy, significance.

If William Black thought he had acquired a full-time businessman, he was wrong. A hint of things to come occurred right in the middle of the confusion surrounding Robinson's retirement from baseball. On December 8, 1956, the NAACP awarded him its prestigious Spingarn medal (named for Joel Spingarn, who was one of the founders of this important civil rights organization). Previous recipients of this award included black intellectual and NAACP founder W. E. B. Du Bois, and NAACP lawyer (and later Supreme Court Justice) Thurgood Marshall. The citation explained why Robinson was joining them: "The entire nation is indebted to him for his pioneer role in breaking the color line in Organized Baseball. . . . He opened the doors of the major leagues for Negro stars whose skills, zest, and stamina have entered the national sport."

Never before had an athlete been so honored by the NAACP. And never before had there been a black athlete more committed than Jackie Robinson to pursuing the cause of civil rights. Not Jack Johnson. Not Jesse Owens. Not Joe Louis.

Just as Jackie Robinson was determined not to be a figurehead for Chock Full O'Nuts, he also was determined not to be just a name on an NAACP letterhead. To him, the Spingarn medal was less a reward for past service than a prod to future deeds. Perhaps Roy Wilkins, who then headed the NAACP, had entertained a similar idea all along. In any event, for the time being Wilkins happily welcomed his newest recruit to the civil rights wars. Within weeks of the award the NAACP executive secretary asked Robinson to take charge of his organization's 1957 Freedom Fund drive. A surprised, but pleased, Robinson accepted the challenge—so long as there was real work to be done, so long as he was expected to do that work, and so long as he was convinced that the NAACP was working "for the good of the country" and not just for "Negro-Americans."

Roy Wilkins concurred, as did William Black. In fact, not only did the Chock Full O'Nuts president give Robinson permission to be away from his desk and about the business of NAACP fundraising, but Black signed a five-figure check to head the Freedom Fund drive in the right direction.

That drive took Robinson in many different directions and to many cities across the country. Invitations to speak poured into his New York office. (Not all were accepted, including an unanswered plea from Montgomery, Alabama, where a young Baptist minister by the name of Martin Luther King, Jr., was putting together his own civil rights organization to be called the Southern Christian Leadership Conference.) As a result, Robinson was on the road more than he might have imagined. Many of his stops found Jackie in cities that he had visited as a Brooklyn Dodger. One of them was Pittsburgh, where Robinson shared the podium with another recent retiree from the baseball wars. Branch Rickey not only stood beside his one-time prospect, but in his brief remarks he astounded his listeners (including Robinson himself) by thundering that blacks should use every means short of violence to achieve their full freedom as American citizens.

If Robinson was not at all prepared for Rickey's fiery rhetoric, he was quite ready to take full advantage of his celebrity status to advance the cause of civil rights. Still, neither he nor Wilkins could have anticipated the incredible success of the 1957 drive. For the first time in the history of the Freedom Fund, the NAACP topped a million dollars. Robinson's reward for this successful effort was his elevation to the NAACP national board of directors in early 1958. For the moment at least it appeared that the association between the NAACP and its favorite celebrity athlete promised to be a long and happy one.

But as the 1950s drew to a close Jackie Robinson found himself moving away from the NAACP and ever closer to two Americans who were not closely associated with the nation's premier civil rights organization. For that matter, they were not at all close to one another, either politically or personally. This unlikely twosome in Jackie Robinson's new life was composed of Martin Luther King, Jr., and Richard M. Nixon.

Jackie Robinson met Martin Luther King for the first time shortly after a series of church bombings rocked Montgomery following the successful conclusion of the King-led bus boycott of 1955–56. The agent for the meeting was a mutual friend named Al Duckett, who would at various times serve as a ghost-writer for both King and Robinson. After inspecting the damage to the churches and meeting with King, Robinson paused to reflect on the youthful minister's "dedication" and "calmness" in the face of tragedy and violence. Then and later, Robinson was also impressed with the powers and command of King as an orator. Then and later, the two men agreed that they were working toward the same goal: namely uniting, not dividing, the races.

Toward that end, Robinson journeyed to Jackson, Mississippi, in February of 1958 to urge his black listeners to keep their protests peaceful. Later that fall he took part in what was billed as a Youth March for Integrated Schools in the nation's capital. A few years later King tapped Robinson to lead a drive to raise money to rebuild black churches. At the same time Jackie assisted in King-led voter registration projects across the South. In May 1963, Robinson appeared with Reverend King in a Birmingham, Alabama, church not long after the hotel where the civil rights leader had been staying was bombed.

During these years, Robinson was growing increasingly disillusioned with white political leaders when the subject turned to civil rights. If he had ample reason to be pleased by what he heard from Martin Luther King, Jackie was displeased by what he did not hear from another figure he had regarded as a moral authority—the president of the United States, Dwight D. Eisenhower. Robinson had supported Eisenhower in 1956 (after voting for Democratic presidential candidate Adlai Stevenson in 1952). When those bombs ripped through Montgomery, Robinson expected outrage from the White House. Instead, he was treated to complete silence. Robinson was stunned. After all, in 1956 he had not just voted for Eisenhower, but had actively worked for the Eisenhower-Nixon ticket. At the very least he had expected that the president would issue a forceful "protest against the bombings in the South." Not only had those bombings been launched against innocent black citizens, but they constituted a black mark against the United States in its Cold War against the Soviet Union. With American honor and prestige on the line, the president had said nothing. Robinson was not only stunned, he was hurt. But despite this affront, he was not yet ready to withdraw his support from the Eisenhower administration.

Part of the reason for Robinson's own reticence was his belief in the essential decency of the president. Part of it was traceable to his own commitment to prosecuting the Cold War and his awareness of the importance of a united American front against the Soviets. But part of it also stemmed from Robinson's relationship with Eisenhower's vice president, Richard Nixon.

Robinson had met Nixon for the first time at the 1952 Republican national convention in Chicago. Though the meeting had not been planned, it did leave an impression on both men. It was not, however, the first time that one of them had impressed the other. In fact, long ago Robinson had etched himself on the mind's eye of Richard Nixon. As the then-Senator (and soon to be Vice President) Nixon recalled the scene, it was the fall of 1940 and Robinson was a UCLA halfback. The opponent was the University of Oregon. Nixon, the unreconstructed fan, went on to reconstruct a particularly unusual play from the game. Robinson immediately recalled the incident and his role in it. The bond was instant and affecting. The athlete was impressed with the politician's memory, not to mention his obvious love of sports. And the politician was impressed with the athlete's presence and deep interest in the world beyond sports. It was a case of a frustrated jock (Nixon), who had been a scrub on his Whittier College football team, meeting a famous professional athlete with a budding interest in politics. (In 1960 Robinson would campaign for the Republican presidential candidate.)

During the remainder of the 1950s Robinson and Nixon kept in occasional contact with one another. As the Congress debated passage of the first civil rights legislation since Reconstruction, the two men exchanged worried letters over the Senate's attempt to water down the bill. Robinson urged Nixon to do what he could to secure passage of strong legislation. The vice president promised his liaison to the black community that he would do what he could "to see that a more effective bill . . . is eventually passed." In the end the Civil Rights Act of 1957 did little more than create a civil rights division within the Justice Department and give the federal government the right to file individual voter-registration suits. From the perspective of the historic civil rights legislation of the 1960s, it was not much. But to both Robinson and Nixon it was at least a start in the right direction and no cause to interrupt their still-casual, but potentially historic, alliance.

In the fall of 1957, events in Little Rock, Arkansas, also served to solidify that alliance. At issue was the court-ordered desegregation of that city's Central High School. When Arkansas Governor Orville Faubus moved to block that order, civil rights organizations pleaded with the Eisenhower administration to dispatch federal troops to enforce it. The president hesitated before acting, but act he did. The National Guard was deployed to the scene to ensure the peaceful integration of the school. For the time being, Jackie Robinson was satisfied.

As the 1960 election approached, Robinson found himself in a curious position. More accurately, he found himself operating in two worlds at once. Within the ever-enlarging world of the civil rights revolution, he was moving closer to King and his Southern Christian Leadership Conference (SCLC) and ever further away from Wilkins and the NAACP. Within the world of mainstream politics, he remained on good terms with Eisenhower's heir apparent, Richard Nixon, and was thoroughly convinced that Nixon was far preferable to his Democratic opponent, Senator John Kennedy of Massachusetts.

At one level, the Robinson-King parallel made perfect sense. Just as there had been a time when a rookie ballplayer had to turned the other cheek when confronted with racism on the diamond, so the young minister had been preaching the redeeming virtues of nonviolence to blacks and whites alike. But a significant difference remained. To Robinson, pacifism was a strategy, an occasionally useful strategy to be sure, but one that had been temporarily inflicted on him by "Mr. Rickey." In sum, it was a means to an end, rather than an end in itself. To King, pacifism was the organizing principle of his life.

If young Jackie Robinson had now and then revealed flashes of anger, there was a part of a middle-aged Robinson who remained quite angry—even if he continued to work with the NAACP, for a millionaire businessman, and within the Republican Party. That anger had always been there—and still lurked just beneath the surface. Robinson generally kept it in check, whether or not he was under orders from Mr. Rickey, but it always threatened to burst forth. He could never be the principled pacifist that King was—and he knew it. But he also knew that he could never be a mere tool of the NAACP. To be sure, the strategy of Roy Wilkins and the NAACP was not that of Martin Luther King and the SCLC. The former relied on litigation, the latter on direct action. Still, Robinson was never fully at home within either camp. He was too militant for Wilkins and the legalistic NAACP and not principled enough for King and the SCLC.

In 1960 Robinson's militancy extended to his support for North Carolina black students who were then holding a series of "sit-ins" in local restaurants notorious for refusing to serve black people. Within a few weeks this grass-roots movement had spread to fifteen cities in five southern states. Eventually its organizers would coalesce into the Student Nonviolent Coordinating Committee (SNCC). For the time being, however, they were thoroughly unorganized and grasping for support from their political elders. Their search grew especially intense as more and more young protesters landed in jail for their refusal to accept the dictates of segregation. In very short order, the committee began to focus on Jackie Robinson. Not Roy Wilkins. Not Martin Luther King. Not Joe Louis. But Jackie Robinson. This was the adventuresome Jackie Robinson, the daring Robinson who broke at will from first to second—or even from third to home. Earlier in all of their lives, Robinson had been a hero to these students because of the risks he had taken on the baseball diamond. Now they were asking him to take a different sort of risk by going to bat for them in the Deep South. It was a risk he dared not reject.

With Roy Wilkins temporarily out of the picture—and not all that willing to enter it—Jackie Robinson orchestrated his own fundraising campaign for these beleaguered students. He called upon celebrity musicians, including Duke Ellington, Ella Fitzgerald, and Sarah Vaughan, to join him on the lawn of his Stamford, Connecticut, home. There was born what Robinson dubbed an "Afternoon of Jazz." What could have been more appropriate than an event such as this? It was an improvised benefit concert featuring the improvised music of America's jazz greats, with all proceeds going to jailed students who had improvised their own protest movement. The only departure from this exercise in innovation was that Robinson's musical "Afternoon" was quickly institutionalized into an annual event—one that soon outgrew the Robinsons' front yard.

The year 1960 saw Jackie Robinson operating well beyond the confines of his Connecticut home on a number of fronts. For example, as the year unfolded he began to feel more and more at home within the liberal wing of the Republican Party. And when the issue was civil rights, this was also Branch Rickey's political home. This did not mean that Robinson's endorsement of Nixon for president had been orchestrated by Rickey. Nor was it instant or automatic. In fact, early in the primary season Robinson had supported the candidacy of Minnesota Democratic Senator Hubert Humphrey. Long an advocate of black civil rights, Humphrey was his choice. But when Humphrey was steamrollered by Senator Kennedy in the Wisconsin and West Virginia primaries, Robinson had to search for a replacement. Kennedy was not a likely alternative. Never a darling of civil rights advocates, Kennedy had added to their distrust of him by voting with the moderates (and not the liberals) on amendments leading up to the final passage of the 1957 Civil Rights Act.

Robinson had paid close enough attention to that legislation to conclude that John Kennedy was not an ally of the civil rights movement. With the onset of the 1960 presidential campaign, he had not budged from that conclusion. In fact, Robinson's objections to Kennedy extended to the ex-ballplayer's refusal to be photographed with the Massachusetts Democrat at a NAACP gathering early that year. Still, he did not go so far as to burn all his bridges to Kennedy and the Democrats following Humphrey's exit from the presidential campaign midway through the 1960 primary season.

For his part, John Kennedy pursued Robinson almost as vigilantly as Branch Rickey and Clyde Sukeforth had fifteen years earlier. If Rickey thought that the loss of Robinson would eventually cost the Dodgers more than a few pennants, Kennedy worried that the loss of Robinson's endorsement might well cost him the presidency. So disturbed was Kennedy by Robinson's coolness towards him that the senator asked black entertainer Harry Belafonte to act as an intermediary between the two. In turn, Belafonte suggested that Kennedy ignore Robinson and court Martin Luther King instead. A perplexed Kennedy could not imagine how King might help him. In the senator's estimation, Robinson was the crucial commodity. Given that appraisal, the Democratic candidate would not surrender the idea of coaxing an endorsement out of the former ballplayer. Toward that end, Kennedy arranged a private meeting between the two. It backfired badly. Robinson emerged from the encounter more distrustful of Kennedy than he had ever been, commenting that for whatever reason the Democratic frontrunner "couldn't or wouldn't look me straight in the eye."

Now both of *Robinson*'s eyes were trained on the November election. Two questions were uppermost in his mind. Given the emergence of the civil rights movement, which candidate was best for black America? And given the significance of the Cold War, which candidate was best for the United States of America? To some extent the two questions merged into one. According to Jackie Robinson, the triumph of the civil rights movement in America would also constitute a victory for America in the Cold War against the Soviet Union.

Not until September did Robinson arrive at his answer. Only then did he publicly announce that he would campaign for Nixon and vote for him come November. He went on to reveal that he intended to work for Nixon as well. This news did not sit well with his two most prominent employers. In 1959 Robinson had begun writing a column for the New York *Post*. (Actually, more often than not, the column was ghost-written by Al Duckett, who in 1963 would have a major hand in helping draft King's famous "I Have a Dream" speech.) More often than not, the material that ran under Robinson's byline was political. But if it was one thing for him to take a stand on a controversial issue, it was quite another for him to be in the employ of a political candidate at the same time. At least the editors of the New York *Post* thought so. Because their judgment mattered most, ex-ballplayer Robinson was summarily asked to join the cluttered ranks of ex-columnists.

William Black was just as displeased as were the *Post* editors. But while Black did not force Robinson to resign from Chock Full O'Nuts, he did demand that his vice president take an unpaid leave of absence. This was a costly choice for a father of young children and a husband whose wife had recently returned to college to study for her master's degree; it was an especially costly choice for a family who lived in an expensive home in the Connecticut suburbs. And there was also the troubling matter of Robinson's health. The diabetes that had been diagnosed a few years earlier, while seemingly under control, always threatened to flare up—especially when Robinson pushed himself too hard. In 1960 Jackie Robinson was only forty-one, but he was a rapidly aging forty-one. He did what he could to exercise—golf having replaced tennis as his current athletic passion—but he could not hide the stubborn surplus weight and would not disguise the gray that had overtaken his head. But even if the decision to campaign for Nixon threatened to take its toll on both his pocketbook and his waistline, it was a decision that Jackie Robinson felt compelled to make.

It was also a decision he would soon regret. In early October, Martin Luther King was arrested in Atlanta, Georgia. On the eve of his anticipated release King was ordered to a remote rural jail by a neighboring judge who ostensibly wanted to try King for an old traffic violation. The very next day the prisoner was summarily transferred to a maximum security prison. When this news reached the world beyond Georgia, Jackie Robinson was far from alone in thinking that no one would ever see the civil rights leader alive again. With King's life quite possibly at stake, pleas went out to both the Kennedy and Nixon camps to intervene. Much to Robinson's chagrin, the former responded and the latter did not. John Kennedy personally phoned King's pregnant wife, Coretta Scott King, to assure her that he would do what he could to guarantee her husband's safety. Acting on a second front, Kennedy's brother Robert contacted the judge who had ordered King's jailing and secured the reversal of his original decree. King was released, thanks to the Kennedys, but no thanks to Richard Nixon.

Jackie Robinson was among a handful of Nixon advisers who had worked hard to try to convince their man to lend his support to the jailed King. At one point he sought to reach Nixon directly by phone, only to be rebuffed by a Nixon aide. In retrospect, each candidate's response was thoroughly political. Hoping to score needed points with black voters, Kennedy rallied to King's side. Looking to make inroads among southern white voters, Nixon chose to remain silent. To be fair to Nixon, he also did not want to be caught "grandstanding" on the matter. And given his past support for civil rights legislation, the Republican candidate saw no need to grandstand. Surely Robinson and other black leaders would remember his recent history on the subject of civil rights. Therefore, Nixon was confident that there would be no fall-out over his silence concerning King's plight.

Crushed by Nixon's failure to act, Robinson considered resigning from his campaign. He even entertained the idea of going public with a formal denunciation of Nixon. In the end, he did neither.

Ultimately, the cost to Robinson for his own failure to act was considerable. His reputation suffered greatly at the hands of liberals in general and black civil rights activists in particular. But he was so committed to the larger goal of a black presence within the Republican Party that he held his post and his tongue. Richard Nixon may not have been deserving of his support, but he was only one man and this was only one election. Both the Republican Party and the civil rights cause were bigger than either its current presidential nominee or his most disappointed supporter. Besides, there was always Mr. Rickey to answer to, and Branch Rickey was a solid Nixon man.

Whenever Robinson agreed with Rickey it was not simply out of a sense of deference to the older man. Each man was fiercely independent, albeit quite capable of arriving at similar conclusions. Such was surely the case in 1960 when two very independent-minded men, one a black Humphrey supporter turned moderate Republican, the other a long-time conservative Republican with very liberal views on civil rights, stayed with Nixon to the end. If there was any difference between the two, it was that Rickey was considerably more disappointed than Robinson by their candidate's narrow defeat at the hands of John Kennedy in November.

In the aftermath of the 1960 election, Robinson's sense of independence (and not just from Branch Rickey, but from Richard Nixon, Martin Luther Ling, and Roy Wilkins as well) took him directly into the camp of New York Governor Nelson Rockefeller. In fact, Kennedy's victory over Nixon had barely been recorded when Robinson began making overtures to Rockefeller. Though the two men had met previously, they had not known each other well and had never worked together. Already Robinson and Rockefeller shared three goals for 1964: secure for the New York governor the Republican nomination for president, capture the White House and the Congress for the GOP, and build a substantial black base within their party. In signing on with Nelson Rockefeller, Jackie Robinson was assured of remaining in the political big leagues. Whether or not he would have a Hall of Fame career in this tough game remained to be seen.

As it happened, Jackie Robinson was elected to baseball's Hall of Fame not long after he joined the Rockefeller team, and in his first year of eligibility, no less. Robinson was overwhelmed by the honor. He was also pleasantly surprised. In the first place, ten seasons is seldom sufficient to secure admission to the Hall at any point, let alone immediately. Second, his lifetime batting average of .311 (unsupported by overwhelming home run, runs-batted-in, or stolen base totals) was somewhat low by Hall of Fame standards. But 124 (of 160) voters among the baseball writers thought differently. That total was barely enough, because 75 percent of those casting ballots had to give a candidate their vote. The final result was also surprising to Robinson, because many of those 124 voters were the very writers he had sparred against, attacked, or snubbed. The fact that they could put aside their past differences with Jackie Robinson by electing him to the Hall of Fame had to be gratifying as well. Thanks to them, he would have one more glorious baseball day.

The Hall of Fame ceremony took place on a storm-filled, cloud-strewn July 23, 1962. But there is little evidence that Robinson even noticed the weather. This was his day, a day he chose to enjoy and share with his mother, his wife, Branch Rickey, and a few thousand other Brooklyn Dodger fans. He also shared the platform with fellow inductees Cleveland Indian pitcher Bob Feller and Cincinnati Reds outfielder Edd Roush. If Robinson detected any coldness on Feller's part, he also chose to ignore it. In point of fact the two men had never been close, and the responsibility for the distance between them was largely Feller's. The feud that he had ignited at the time of Robinson's initial signing had not abated. Among other drawbacks, Robinson was then a questionable rookie with "football shoulders [who] couldn't hit an inside pitch to save his neck." Sixteen years later Jackie was an ex-player anxious to bite the hand of the game that had once fed him so very well, at least according to an ungracious Bob Feller.

On the day of his enshrinement Robinson refused to be baited. According to Robinson biographer David Falkner, the Indian pitcher had asked that he not have to share *his* day with a lesser mortal by the name of Jackie Robinson. The former Dodger surely knew of the former Indian's disdain for him. But if Robinson knew anything at all about Feller's petition, he kept that information to himself. The same holds true for Robinson's ongoing objections to baseball's failure to hire black coaches, managers, and front-office personnel. July 23, 1962, was not a day to settle scores, gain revenge, or lobby for reform; it was simply a day to revel in the glory of playing days past. Politics would—and did—intrude soon enough.

And in the world of politics Jackie Robinson was by this point a highly visible and very willing participant in two very different ventures. As the civil rights struggle and the 1964 presidential campaign simultaneously heated up, Robinson found himself deeply involved in both. On the one hand, he found himself increasingly drawn to King's strategy and vision for a peaceful and fully integrated America. On the other hand, he was a member of the inner circle of the "Rockefeller for President" drive. More political insider than movement man, Robinson nonetheless tried to keep a place at both tables.

Meanwhile, maintaining his place at the head of his own family's table was becoming increasingly difficult. In fact, there were times when it was downright taxing, embarrassing, even anguishing. Balancing his family life and his public lives had never been easy for Jackie Robinson. In some respects it was easier for him to master the balancing act of pleasing King and Rockefeller (or King and Wilkins) than it was to keep peace within his household. In the first place, he simply was not there all that much. More important, he had a son, Jackie, Jr., whose increasing resentment of his name and his father's fame triggered frequent outbursts of rebellion at home and in school. Finally, there came a time when Jackie Robinson, Sr., had to cede the major breadwinner's responsibility to his wife, Rachel.

In part, the assassination of President John F. Kennedy triggered that turn of events. Every American who was at least seven years old at the time can remember exactly where he or she was on November 22, 1963. Jackie Robinson not only remembered where he was, he had reason to regret his whereabouts at the moment bullets struck the president as his motorcade passed the

Texas Book Depository in Dallas. Thanks to reporters out for a local angle on the story, New Yorkers soon learned where Jack had been. One of those New Yorkers was his boss, William Black. The president of Chock Full O'Nuts was surprised to read that his most famous vice president had been at a local race track on that fateful day. Jackie Robinson had not been known to spend a lot of time at the track. Unfortunately, that was where he happened to be on November 22, 1963. When Black learned that Robinson had not been on the job, he promptly fired him. No doubt William Black had been looking for an excuse to do just that for some time. That Robinson used company time for politics was bad enough. That much of that time was devoted to a Republican made it worse. Gambling on horses was apparently the last straw.

Suddenly Rachel Robinson's paycheck was not just a nice addition to the family income, it was the family income. When Rachel completed her master's degree in psychiatric nursing, her husband was outwardly pleased. When she returned to the workforce, he was officially supportive. But when she became the sole breadwinner for the family, he could not hide his "annoyance and resentment." But what choice did he have? The bills had to be paid, and his celebrity alone was not paying them.

Instead of carving out a new career in the world of business, Robinson ventured further into the world(s) of politics. There was always time for King and Rockefeller, and even time for golf, even if there seldom seemed to be enough time for refurbishing the family coffers or rebuilding his relationship with his troubled son.

During 1964 Robinson had to make another decision about how to spend his time, much more of which now went to Rockefeller than to King. Robinson had not come to question the importance of King and his movement, but he had concluded that electing Nelson Rockefeller to the presidency was the immediate priority. Never entirely comfortable with Nixon, Robinson was instantly and thoroughly at ease with Rockefeller. In truth, he had never encountered a white politician quite like the New York governor. Where Nixon was stiff and remote, Rockefeller was breezy and open. Where Nixon had been calculating and transparently political, Rockefeller seemed sincere, a man capable of transcending politics. More important, his credentials on the critical issue of race were impeccable. Robinson was hooked. But once again he would be disappointed.

This time the source of that disappointment was less his preferred candidate than his adopted party. During the political season of 1964 Rockefeller would be overwhelmed by the right wing of his own party. His main rival for the Republican presidential nomination was not Richard Nixon (who declined to run in 1964) but Arizona Senator Barry Goldwater. Both Rockefeller and Robinson found the conservative senator's civil rights views appalling. Nonetheless, Goldwater stormed through a primary election season, which culminated with his decisive victory in California. That win clinched his nomination, leaving the Republican convention in San Francisco's celebrated Cow Palace to be the scene of a Goldwater coronation ceremony. It turned out, however, to be much more than that.

Robinson attended that convention as a loyal Rockefellerite. He left it with an even greater sense of dedication to his defeated candidate. In between, Rockefeller was not just voted down by his fellow Republicans, he was shouted down as well. Robinson was stunned. As he remembered it, the 1964 Republican convention was "one of the most unforgettable and frightening experiences" of his life. The "hatred" that he observed on the convention floor was "unique . . . because it was hatred directed against a white man." More than that, it was hatred guaranteed to ensure that his party would become "completely a white man's party." All of this left Robinson dismayed and angry, so angry in fact that he almost got into a fist fight with a Goldwater delegate on the convention floor. And this time Branch Rickey—and even Martin Luther King— might well have egged him on.

Robinson left the Cow Palace mystified and unemployed. How could the party of Lincoln become the party of Goldwater? This last question was especially mystifying to Jackie Robinson, who had occasion to spend a few private hours with Goldwater during the course of the campaign. And following that meeting, Robinson was still mystified, because he left it actually liking the Arizona senator. On a personal level, Robinson discovered that Goldwater was anything but a racist. Nonetheless, the two men agreed to disagree on the need for comprehensive, federally defined and enforced civil rights legislation.

That year marked the high (and low) point of Jackie Robinson's career as a professional Republican. It also came close to the high (and low) water mark of the entire civil rights movement. In June, Robinson was devastated by the news of the murder of three civil rights workers in Mississippi. In July, he was enthused by the passage of the landmark Civil Rights Act of 1964. There was more to come in 1965, when President Johnson (for whom Robinson eventually worked and voted in the fall of 1964) signed the Voting Rights Act into law. From a legislative standpoint, the thrust of the civil rights agenda was now a part of federal law. Jackie Robinson, among countless others, had every right to think that such legislation was long overdue. But he also had every reason to be both grateful and hopeful.

Though Robinson had not played a direct role in the passage of this legislation, his story adds an important dimension to the larger story of his nation during these divisive years. And this *was* his nation. There were those who saw Robinson as a divisive, even a divisively un-American figure. He was not. In fact, Jackie Robinson at his angriest never doubted that he was an American. More than that, he always saw himself as a unifier, whether as a member of a baseball team or a political team, or simply in his everyday roles as a husband, father, and citizen.

There were black leaders who were far more divisive than he. One of them was Malcolm X. If any charge of "Uncle Tomism" ever rankled Jackie Robinson, it was the one from the lips of Malcolm X. The two men tangled frequently during the mid-1960s. The issue might be the role of Jewish businessmen in black Harlem. Or it might be Robinson's past support from Branch Rickey, or Robinson's current support for white Republican politicians. Whatever the issue, Malcolm was invariably there to challenge Jackie, to provoke him, to get under his skin by accusing him of having shed the same for the sake of his white benefactors.

Robinson's first brush with Malcolm X occurred in the context of the latter's attack on the black American diplomat Dr. Ralph

Bunche. The year was 1963, and Bunche was then serving as a delegate to the United Nations. To Malcolm X, Bunche was just another "Uncle Tom," a so-called moderate black more intent on serving the "white man devil" than in promoting the rights and interests of his own people. This brand of rhetoric outraged Robinson.

But Malcolm X was unfazed by Robinson's unfeigned outrage. Instead of retreating, he responded by branding Robinson himself as an "Uncle Tom." Jackie was not about to retreat. Having recently begun his *Post* column, he used it to turn the tables on Malcolm X, accusing *him* of being more interested in making speeches than in advancing the cause of his fellow black Americans. This time Malcolm's preferred mode of expression was a heated letter to Jackie. He began by reminding Robinson that he became a great baseball player only "after your white boss lifted you to the major leagues." He went on to accuse Robinson of letting succeeding white bosses "use" him [to] destroy Paul Robeson." Then, after taking a swipe at Robinson's once close association with Richard Nixon, Malcolm X concluded by charging Robinson with "stay[ing] as far away from the Negro community as you can get, and never tak[ing] an interest in anything in the Negro community until the white man himself takes an interest in it. You, yourself, would never shake my hand until you saw some of your white friends shaking it."

Robinson could not let this barrage go unanswered. In his reply, he accused Malcolm X of "mouth[ing] a big and bitter battle ... but it is noticeable that your militancy is mainly expressed in Harlem where it is safe." According to Robinson, that militancy had no appeal among the black masses. Certainly, it had no appeal to him: "Personally, I reject your racist views. I reject your dream of a separate state." Robinson went on to deny doing anything to "please 'white bosses' or 'black agitators' unless they are the things which please me."

That letter ended their brief correspondence, but it did not end the differences between the two men. No reconciliation was attempted. And after Malcolm X's 1965 assassination, none was possible. Malcolm's death shocked Robinson (who was playing golf in Miami at the time), but it brought forth no forgive-and-forget eulogy from his most famous black antagonist. Nor would Jackie Robinson be among the 30,000 mourners who filed past the slain Malcolm X's coffin.

Fairly or unfairly, Robinson placed black nationalists and conservative Republicans in the same extremist camp. In his view, all were racists, though he certainly did not equate Goldwaterism with Ku Klux Klanism. Nonetheless, Robinson saw conservative Republicans and black nationalists as potentially (if not equally) dangerous because each group embraced a separatist agenda. From Robinson's standpoint, there was an all too "striking parallel" between Goldwaterites, who seemed to want a Republican Party of "lily-whiteist conservatives," and Black Muslims who preached black separatism.

On the latter front, Robinson was equally disturbed by both the rhetoric and demeanor of a Malcolm X disciple, heavyweight boxer Muhammad Ali (formerly Cassius Clay). There was a time when Robinson thought that "Clay" (he could never bring himself to use the boxer's adopted Muslim name) would be both good for boxing and a positive role model for black youth. As of the mid-1960s Robinson had changed his mind. By then he had decided that "Clay's" conversion to the Muslim faith had led him to espouse separatist views harmful to both blacks and whites, as well as to the country at large. He also regretted his earlier endorsement of Ali, saying only that he had "never in my life suspected that [Ali] would ever hold [such] extremist views."

Robinson defended the right of both Malcolm X and Muhammad Ali to be Black Muslims, but he refused to defend the Muslim philosophy of racial separatism. At the same time, Jack had to concede that Ali was hugely popular among blacks and whites alike. Ali, after all, was a supremely gifted athlete and a thoroughly confident man, one with a highly engaging personality to boot. But Muhammad Ali also proved to be a most contentious figure—and not just in the eyes of Jackie Robinson.

Ali's popularity grated on Robinson, but at least he could understand the source of much of it. What Jackie could not understand was the appeal of Ali's tutor, the man he pointedly called the "fair-haired boy of the white press." That must have been it, he finally decided. Malcolm X was a media creation; and he was that because he was contentious. Each fed on the other. Because he was contentious, he was controversial; and because he was controversial, he was news.

In truth, the appeal of both Malcolm X and Muhammad Ali went deeper than that. Jackie Robinson might not have liked it, but young black men found much to admire in both Malcolm and Ali. There had been a time, and not too many years earlier at that, when Jackie Robinson himself had revolutionized the image of the black male in America. Where the model had once been the poorly educated and publicly humble Joe Louis, so he would be replaced by the better educated, highly articulate, and carefully assertive Jackie Robinson. And just as he had supplanted Louis, now another generation of black role models was shouldering Robinson aside. If Jackie Robinson was a step removed from Joe Louis, then Muhammad Ali was light years removed from both of them.

And by this time, less than a decade removed from his baseball days, Jackie Robinson no longer looked the part of the dashing base runner or the slashing hitter. With the diabetes continuing to take its toll, Jack was being forced to come to terms with both his own mortality and his increasing obsolescence. What made matters even more difficult was that he had to deal with his own impending irrelevance on a number of fronts. Whether within his own family (and especially to his elder son), within his political party (especially among conservative Republicans), or within the black community (especially among radical separatists), Jackie Robinson was no longer the "cog in the machine" he had once been on and off the diamond. These were troubling days for a pioneer and a Hall of Famer, for a celebrity and a legend. But even more troubling days lay not far ahead.

The Ninth Inning

Not long after the collapse of the
plans for the Continental League, Branch and Jane Rickey packed
their belongings and returned to the suburbs of St. Louis, where
they would be close to a daughter and two grandchildren. There
Jane would renew old acquaintances and resume a long dormant
interest in sketching. And there her husband would be left to his
own devices—and interests—which at first meant nothing more
than pondering his fate and that of the game that by all accounts
had left him behind.

A St. Louis sports columnist was not so sure: "Less than two
months away from his eighty-second birthday, Mr. Rickey is still a
lion. The hair is still brown. . . . The eyes are piercing. A cane with
which he needs to move about is carefully hidden. [But] the ever-
present cigar is still there, and his mind leaps from subject to subject with lightning speed."

One of those subjects was the state of the St. Louis Cardinal
baseball team. Now owned by beer baron August Busch, the Cardinals had not won a National League pennant since 1946. At that
point there were still a number of Cardinal players who had either been Rickey-procured or Rickey-prepared, or both. Perhaps,
thought Busch, there was a little bit of magic left in the old man
who could claim partial responsibility for the last Cardinal pennant. Hence the decision of the current Cardinal owner to ask the
old Cardinal magician to serve as a consultant to the team. Rickey
accepted immediately.

It hadn't occurred to Rickey that there would be any reason to
distrust Busch or to worry about what other Cardinal front-office

personnel might think of his presence among them. Since he was there to give counsel, Rickey decided that he would go ahead and give it. His first significant piece of advice was vintage Rickey. Following the 1962 season he suggested that it might be time for a certain Cardinal player to retire. The problem was that this wasn't just any Cardinal player; this was "Mr. Cardinal," Stan Musial! Rickey wasn't suggesting that the Cards trade Musial, who had won seven batting titles during a Cardinal career that stretched all the way back to 1941. But he did think it was time for the forty-two-year-old Musial to retire. The problem was that this particular forty-two-year-old had just hit a robust .330 for the 1962 season.

Another Branch Rickey might have tried to make the case that this was the perfect time to deal Musial. After all, he had long taken great pride in knowing just when to jettison a player, even a future Hall of Fame player. Just ask Dizzy Dean. But this Branch Rickey was just a consultant. Besides, he was well aware that Stan Musial was not just another Cardinal. More to the point, he was not even just another Hall of Famer. "Stan the Man" Musial was a St. Louis institution of better than two decades standing. Still, Rickey thought there was nothing wrong in passing along a broad hint that a timely and honorable Musial retirement might be in order.

Near the end of his own Cardinal career Rickey had had a large hand in transforming a young Stan Musial from a failed Class D pitcher into an accomplished major league hitter. Now Rickey's still sharp eyes concentrated on other facets of what was left of Musial's game. "Stan doesn't have the arm [any more]. And he was no longer able to run the bases "the way others could." Although accurate, Rickey's harsh scouting report did not sit well with either Musial or Cardinal General Manager Bing Devine. When Rickey's memo was shown to Musial, the Cardinal star felt insulted and demeaned. Devine voiced his own strong objections to the idea. Before long the press learned of the dispute. Once again, the old Branch Rickey was right where a younger Branch Rickey had been many times before: smack in the middle of a public scrap. This brought August Busch into the middle of it as well. Forced to take a position, he sided with Devine and Musial: "Since when do you ask a .330 hitter to retire?" As it turned out, the right moment for Musial to step down was precisely when Branch Rickey suggested he should. Musial dropped to .255 in 1963 and retired one year too late, not to mention one year before the Cardinals captured their first pennant (and first World Series championship) in eighteen years.

But no matter. The damage had already been done, both to Musial's reputation and to Rickey's relationship with his new bosses. Rickey continued to "consult" with those bosses, but during the winter of 1963–64 Devine moved to take full control of the Cardinal operation. In a direct slap at Rickey, Devine ordered that he personally had to approve any expenditure over $15,000.

This decision prevented Rickey from signing many ballplayers, but it did not prevent him from scouting most of them. One of his tasks was to evaluate current Cardinal players with an eye toward personnel changes before the start of the 1964 season. When it came to the immediate future Busch, Rickey, and Devine were in full agreement that the Cardinals were close to returning to the top. And here Rickey was instrumental in making sure that the nucleus of that team was kept together. Though Stan Musial was no longer part of that nucleus, another outfielder was. His name was Curt Flood, and insofar as Rickey was concerned, Flood was nothing short of "perfection" (save for a tendency to "run with the ball" after catching it and a failure to grasp the "value of bases on balls").

Rickey had played no role in acquiring Flood, who came to the Cards via a 1958 trade with Cincinnati. But he did have a small role in the decision to obtain outfielder Lou Brock from the Chicago Cubs early in the 1964 season. Brock not only helped the Cardinals win the National League pennant in '64, he went on to have a long and productive career in St. Louis. Among Rickey's voluminous scouting reports complied during the 1963 season is this estimate of Brock: ". . . highly desirable on any major league club. He can do everything and should hit .300." "Everything" eventually included breaking Ty Cobb's stolen base record, earning Lou

Brock a place in baseball's Hall of Fame. The player whom the Cardinals dealt to the Cubs for Brock was a twenty-eight-year-old pitcher named Ernie Broglio, who had won twenty-one games for the Cards in 1960. Rickey did not let that achievement cloud his judgment when he rejoined the Cardinals in 1963. Rickey was not overly impressed with this record. At the end of a lengthy and negative evaluation of Broglio following a spring training game, he penned these harsh words: "Broglio has been pitching too long to have so many obvious faults. He *must* be dumb." Despite a Rickey-spotted tendency to shake off the catcher too often and an inability to "hold any good runner on first," Broglio did manage to win eighteen games for the Cardinals in 1963, but the perfect time to trade him had indeed arrived. He would go 7-19 over the course of three seasons with the Cubs and be out of the game at the age of thirty-one.

Whether or not any of Rickey's words helped secure the acquisition of Brock is impossible to say. But what can be stated with complete certainty is that Branch Rickey played a significant, albeit indirect, role in the Cardinal success of 1964 and beyond. Flood and Brock, as well as pitcher Bob Gibson (who was a product of the Cardinal farm system) and first baseman Bill White (who joined the Cardinals via a trade with the Giants in 1959), were not just great ballplayers, they were great black ballplayers, who, thanks initially to Branch Rickey—and to Jackie Robinson— would have a chance to flourish nearly two decades after the successful completion of the Robinson "experiment." In fact, more than a little poetic justice was at work when the Cardinals took the 1964 World Series from the Yankees. Not only were many of the key Cardinal players black, but the Yanks were finally paying the price for their own refusal to sign black players. Not until 1955 did the Yankees have a black player (catcher Elston Howard); as late as 1964 the Yanks had exactly two front-line black players (Howard and outfielder Hector Lopez).

But Branch Rickey would not have a direct role in steering the Cardinals to a World Series victory in 1964. After getting off to a slow start, the Cards had improved little by midseason. In July a frustrated Busch concluded that changes would have to be made. He began right near the top by firing Devine. He then contemplated replacing Devine with Rickey. After all, Rickey's Cardinal clubs had won nine pennants between 1926 and 1946. Why not one more? But at eighty-three even Branch Rickey knew that there was "no way" he could do the job.

In fact, Rickey pleaded with Busch to keep Devine. Despite his past differences with Devine, Rickey's instant scouting report to Busch referred to his immediate superior as a "great general manager." Busch, however, was not persuaded. Devine had to go. His successor was Bob Howsam, whom everyone close to the team saw as Rickey's man. To some extent, he was. After all, the two men had known one another for nearly twenty years, and Howsam had been a close friend of Branch, Jr.

But once on the job in St. Louis, Bob Howsam was not about to rely on words of wisdom from the senior Rickey. Come mid-August the Cards had climbed to within nine games out of first place. Despite this improvement, Rickey was prepared to write off the season and begin experimenting with younger players who might be ready to help the team in 1965. A Rickey memo to that effect was delivered to Howsam. In short order, what came to be dubbed the "Memo of Surrender" was leaked to the press. Even though his recommendations were far from outlandish, it was the beginning of the end of Branch Rickey's second (and much briefer) Cardinal tour of duty. Had Rickey had his way in 1964, pitcher Steve Carlton would have been brought up as a part of that August youth movement. As it happened, Carlton would not have his breakthrough season with the Cardinals until 1967, but once again Rickey's judgment had been on the mark. Steve Carlton would go on to have a Hall of Fame career, and the Cards were very lucky to win in 1964. Had the Phils not completely collapsed in September, there would have been no Cardinal pennant and Rickey's youth movement would have been the sensible alternative.

Following the 1964 season, Branch Rickey's insights, hunches, collected wisdom, and scouting reports would no longer be available to the St. Louis Cardinals. Owner August Busch, had seen to that. To Busch, Rickey was admittedly a "baseball genius." But having returned to the "scene of his greatest glories," Rickey "forgot that he was just a 'senior consultant.'" As such, he had "tried to run everything." Because of such, he had to go. And this time there was no young sportswriter on hand to query him about his "greatest thrill" in the game. It was just as well, because this time he might have had a different response.

Rickey had spent some of his Cardinal consulting time sifting through the memories of his six decades in the game. The result was an autobiography innocuously entitled *The American Diamond*, which appeared about the same time that he disappeared from the Cardinal chain of command. The highlight of the book was Rickey's list of baseball greats. Ever the scout, he could not resist pithy comments on players he had signed or simply observed. Campanella was a "perfect receiver." George Sisler was "modest almost to the point of shyness [but] his justifiable ego made him a great player." Eddie Collins embodied "every man's definition of a gentleman, from Socrates to Churchill. I could not sleep comfortably if I left him off my team." Rogers Hornsby was simply the "greatest right-handed batter of all time."

Rickey's all-time outfield consisted of Cobb, Ruth, and "Shoeless Joe" Jackson. "If God ever permitted birth to a natural hitter it was Jackson [who] suffered a lifetime of penance for his ignorant acquiescence in the Black Sox scandal of 1919." Just below them he placed Tris Speaker, Joe DiMaggio, Ted Williams (whom he rated with Ruth when it came to the "flexibility of his wrists"), and Willie Mays. Among his top pitchers were Christy Mathewson (who "had everything, was everything, and did everything"), Rube Waddell (despite "that ridiculous windup"), Cy Young ("the wildest youngster who ever came to fame as a great pitcher"), Walter Johnson (whose fastball was so overpowering that "he didn't need anything else"), the "imperturbable" Grover Cleveland Alexander (whose "only enemy was himself"), and Dizzy Dean ("hardly a jump below a demon on the mound").

But no matter the player or position, greatness in Mr. Rickey's book demanded the "courage that instinctive play requires. . . . I'd rather have a man embrace the rational hazard of chance than a whole ball field of cautious good ballplayers." Greatness stems from "faith" in one's ability, and "you get faith by action, by doing, by trying something out." At the end of his baseball life, Branch Rickey was still preaching what he had preached all along: the virtues that accompany a sense of "adventure" and "daring." In truth, however, the old man's autobiography was far from as adventuresome as it might have been. In total, it was a book that was as dull as its author's career had been lively. Reviewing it for *Book Week,* baseball writer (and one time Dodger beat man) Roger Kahn mercilessly labeled it "trivial and pretentious."

Whatever the demerits of his own attempts to recapture his life, Branch Rickey's baseball days had been neither trivial nor pretentious. In fact, there was nothing about the game that he found trivial, and there was little about his demeanor (save, on occasion, his vocabulary) that could ever be deemed pretentious. To the end he was first a baseball man. That end came shortly after he attended his final World Series, the 1965 contest between the Minnesota Twins (which under another name might have been a Continental League entry) and the Los Angeles Dodgers (which in an earlier life had been a Rickey property).

For Branch Rickey, there would be no more baseball to watch following that seven-game Series. But there was always one more speech to give. On a bleak mid-November Saturday, Rickey left a St. Louis hospital bed to be driven to Columbia, Missouri, where he was scheduled to watch a college football game before delivering a speech that same evening at the Daniel Boone Hotel. The theme of his remarks was courage, more specifically the crucial distinction between mere physical courage and its more elevated cousin, moral courage. He began with an ordinary story of an old Cardinal player who had suffered a painful injury. Just as he was about to advance to the higher realm of "spiritual courage" he involuntarily lurched back into his seat. "I don't believe I can continue," he muttered as he slipped to the floor and out of consciousness. Those were Branch Rickey's final words. He died on December 9, 1965, not quite two weeks shy of his eighty-fourth birthday and not far removed from the world of sport that had been his life.

At his funeral many instant epitaphs were uttered by Branch Rickey's friends and family who had gathered to say goodbye. The best of the lot came from a third-string Dodger catcher, who in 1946 had ambitions of becoming a first-string Dodger boycotter. "He made me a better man," whispered Bobby Bragan to no one in particular.

Near Bragan sat Jackie Robinson, who had flown to St. Louis to bid his own farewell to the man who long ago had given him a chance to show the baseball world that he was better than a good ballplayer. Jackie Robinson didn't need Branch Rickey to make him a better man. Mallie Robinson had long ago seen to that. But he did need someone to have faith in him, someone to take a risk for him, and, on occasion, someone to remind him that he *was* a better man. There were, in sum, occasions when he needed someone to be the father that he had never had. Weakened by diabetes and heart disease, and challenged by the splintering within the civil rights movement and the GOP, Jackie had more than one excuse to bow out of the trip to St. Louis. But he *knew* that he had to be there.

If only all of Jackie Robinson's decisions could have been this easy; then the life that remained for this ex-ballplayer might have been a good deal longer and happier. But life had never been easy for the man who would entitle his autobiography *I Never Had It Made*. It hadn't been easy before Branch Rickey scouted and signed him. It wasn't that easy while he was a Brooklyn Dodger. And it didn't get perceptibly easier after he left baseball. If anything, life got progressively more difficult, given his ever-worsening health, his repeated political disappointments, his ongoing family problems, and his mounting financial woes.

Robinson's financial difficulties extended well beyond his household. So did his financial goals. Despite Jackie's early support for the founders of SNCC, he was never a fan of SNCC leader Stokely Carmichael and his demand for "black power" in the streets.

To Jackie Robinson, the only brand of black power that made any sense was financial power—all the better if coupled with political power. "The buck and the ballot" were the keys to black success in America.

To be sure, there were cries of "black power" emanating from the mouths of many black radicals of the 1960s. But to Jackie Robinson such calls were at best irrelevant and at worst dangerous to the lives of black Americans. They were also embarrassing. Robinson cringed at the notion that blacks should learn street-smartness from the likes of Malcolm X and Stokely Carmichael. Instead, he wanted them to learn the ropes of the business world. To Robinson, it was nothing short of "pathetic" that black Americans knew so little about that far more crucial, far more rewarding world.

Robinson's attempt to change all of that centered on his role in creating the Freedom National Bank in Harlem. With Robinson himself serving as chairman of the board, this bank represented an investment in Harlem and a step beyond the black ghetto at the same time. Through it, he hoped, blacks would soon come to control their own financial destiny and have a positive impact on the economic development of the entire community as well.

Robinson's position as chairman was unsalaried (at a time when he was in great financial need). Nonetheless, it did represent an important commitment of time and energy on his part. He was determined that the bank would succeed. Once again, nothing was easy.

Internal conflict and insufficient capital beset the bank almost from the beginning of Jackie Robinson's involvement with it. Even before it opened its doors, the Freedom National Bank was rumored to be in deep financial trouble. Hearing those rumors, Robinson began to question his hand-picked president, Dunbar McLauren. A bank promoter and a self-promoter all in one, McLauren had apparently been spending money that the bank did not yet have. When Robinson learned of this he led a successful effort to oust McLauren before the bank officially opened for business. His replacement was William Hudgins, who was both a personal friend of Robinson's and a black man with considerable banking experience (which was rare at the time). With Hudgins at the helm, the Freedom National Bank finally opened for business in December of 1964.

But McLauren was not through. With the aid of black nationalists (and their usual charges of white usurpers invading Harlem), McLauren fought a guerrilla war against Hudgins and Robinson. That war eventually failed, but not without taking its toll on the health of both the Freedom National Bank and Jackie Robinson, who in mid-1965 suffered a serious heart attack.

Both the institution and the man rebounded, though neither was operating at anything close to peak efficiency as 1965 drew to a close. Still, by the first quarter of 1966 the bank did report a small profit. Gradually, major corporations, including General Motors, Ford, and Chrysler, established accounts with Freedom National Bank. These deposits revived charges of white domination by McLauren and his allies but they also brought Jackie Robinson great satisfaction. More important, such infusions of capital helped make his Freedom National Bank the largest black-owned bank in the country by the end of the decade.

The year 1966 also saw Jackie Robinson return to politics. Early that year Governor Rockefeller appointed him to the salaried post of "special assistant." In fact, Rockefeller was in the process of putting together an entire staff of special assistants from the black community as he began to gear up for his 1968 run at the White House. Robinson, in short, was far from the only "special assistant" to the governor, but he was a highly visible one, both within the Rockefeller camp and to the larger worlds, white and black, beyond it.

This appointment, however, was not just symbolic. Instead, it was to involve real work for good money. Operating out of the governor's New York City office, Robinson took very seriously his renewed efforts on behalf of Nelson Rockefeller. He also took repeated hits from black nationalists for serving as the governor's "house Negro." Jackie was undeterred. He was set on contributing to a Rockefeller victory in 1968 and determined that nothing would interfere with that goal.

Unfortunately, Nelson Rockefeller's greatest enemy was Nelson Rockefeller himself. His divorce and remarriage proved very costly politically. So did an on-again, off-again campaign. What had begun as a national crusade to save the Republican Party from Goldwaterism ended up a national joke that could not save the GOP for "Rocky." In the end, the abortive Rockefeller candidacy did little more than prepare the way for the political rebirth of the man Jackie Robinson and many others had left for dead: Richard Nixon.

While Jackie was once again betting on the wrong politician, Rachel was establishing her own career as a psychiatric nurse and Yale professor. Their daughter Sharon was also moving on with her own life, as she headed off to college (and eventually on to a search for her African roots). Second son David was still at home and still in tow. His older brother, Jackie, Jr., however, continued to be an agonizing source of heartache for his parents. After dropping out of school and running away from home, the namesake of Jackie Robinson volunteered for the U.S. Army in mid-1964. A year later he was sent to Vietnam. This was not a recipe for straightening out a confused, tormented young man. When he was discharged in June of 1967, the younger Robinson had suffered battle wounds and acquired a serious drug habit, which quickly worsened on the streets of New York City and Stamford, Connecticut. On March 4, 1968, Jackie Robinson, Jr., hit what Jackie Robinson, Sr., must have hoped was the bottom. He was arrested on a street corner in Stamford at 2:15 in the morning. At the time of his arrest he was carrying several bags of heroin, a stash of marijuana, and a .22-caliber pistol.

This was a wake-up call for more than one Robinson. Whether that alarm had rung in time could not yet be known. Clearly, his father hoped so. After conceding to the press that he probably had had "more of an effect on other people's kids than . . . on my own," the senior Robinson set out to remedy that imbalance. Fortunately for both of them, father and son finally made time for one another. Of course, Jackie, Jr., had to make time for a drug rehabilitation program as well. Similar attempts had been made in the past, but each had failed. Now both father and son were determined to achieve a different result. And this time they succeeded.

After two years in a program run by Daytop, Inc., Jackie Robinson, Jr., emerged not only clean, but anxious to help others who had fallen into drugs. He had just begun that new life—only weeks earlier having completed training to become a Daytop counselor—when in the early morning hours of June 16, 1971, he was killed instantly in a single-car crash along a Connecticut parkway. At the time of the accident he was involved in helping his father organize the annual Afternoon of Jazz, with all proceeds earmarked for Daytop.

At the exact time of the accident, Jackie, Jr., may have been traveling alone. But at that time in his life, he and his father were finally traveling together. In one terrible moment their new journey was over.

By the spring of 1971, Jackie Robinson, Sr., was a prematurely old man. His son's tragic death left him even older. Though barely fifty-two, his hair was white, his gait was unsteady, and he was almost completely blind. Still, his last years with his son had opened his eyes in a new way.

One month to the day after Jackie, Jr.'s, original arrest, Martin Luther King, Jr., had been assassinated in Memphis, Tennessee. In the years immediately before King's death, he and Jackie, Sr., had grown somewhat distant. Though each maintained a façade of friendship and each was officially supportive of the other, serious differences between them had emerged. The straight-laced Robinson was troubled by rumors surrounding King's sex life. While he never confronted King about the stories, it appears that Robinson did give them at least a measure of credence.

King and Robinson were also divided by the Vietnam War and Dr. King's mounting disillusionment with it. As the American military build-up escalated in 1965 and 1966, the civil rights leader was under greater and greater pressure to speak out against the

American presence in Vietnam. Fearful of damaging the civil rights movement, King resisted succumbing to that pressure for as long as he could. It had been his belief that the American war in Vietnam and the war at home for black civil rights were separate wars, and separate issues. But by early 1967 Dr. King had arrived at a different conclusion. Perhaps the pressure had finally gotten to him. Perhaps the frustrating course of the war and the American failure to subdue the North Vietnamese had changed his mind. Or perhaps he had come to see that the two wars were in fact one war, especially considering that a disproportionate share of the dead American soldiers in Vietnam were black, many of whom had been drafted into service by the U.S. government.

Whatever the reason, King finally joined the growing public outcry against the war. In April of 1967 he visibly linked arms with antiwar protesters by taking part in a major antiwar demonstration in New York City. There he was, marching in the first row with Dr. Benjamin Spock and singer Harry Belafonte. Not far behind him were Stokely Carmichael and other SNCC leaders, many of whom were waving Viet Cong flags.

Jackie Robinson swelled with anguish, then outrage, most of which he directed at King. How could his hero join the enemy's side in the Cold War? Whatever his own motives in the Paul Robeson-HUAC confrontation, Robinson had always been a true believer in the American war against international Communism. Nothing had happened between the late 1940s and the late 1960s to change his mind. Not even the obviously divisive, seemingly endless war in Vietnam had budged him from his hawkish position. As of 1967, Robinson was also speaking as the father of a wounded Vietnam veteran. How could King put himself in the position of at least implicitly castigating young men like his son?

In an attempt to reach King, Robinson penned another of his patented "open letters," correspondence he seemed to reserve for black leaders with whom he disagreed. In this missive he began by asking King a question: "Is it fair for you to place all the burdens of the blame on America and none on the Communist forces we are fighting?" Robinson went on to criticize King for calling on the Johnson administration to halt all American bombing "without knowing whether the enemy will use that pause to prepare for greater destruction of our men in Vietnam. He then posed this question: "Why do you seem to ignore the blood that is on their hands and speak only of the 'guilt' of the United States?" He concluded with an expression of "love for this imperfect country" and a request for a reply from Martin Luther King.

King responded by phoning Robinson. After the two men hashed out their differences, Robinson was willing to concede that King was a man of honor and integrity, even if their differences over the war remained firm. To this extent the personal breach between them had been repaired.

At about the same time, another breach was widening, this one between Robinson and NAACP leader Roy Wilkins. At issue was what Robinson regarded as Wilkins's heavy-handed control of the NAACP. When yet another slate of pro-Wilkins delegates was rubber-stamped by the organization, Robinson pointedly accused his former ally of running a "dictatorship." In his rebuttal, Wilkins suggested that had Robinson "played ball with a hot head instead of a cool brain, [he] would have remained in the minors." As far as Roy Wilkins was concerned, Jackie Robinson could go back to the minor leagues of the civil rights movement. For the time being at least, this breach remained solid—and eerily reminiscent of Robinson's final years as a Brooklyn Dodger, years during which he grew increasingly distant from his once treasured teammates, especially catcher Roy Campanella.

If differences between Robinson and Wilkins, as well as between Robinson and Campanella, remained in place, those between Robinson and King did not. During the final year of King's life Jackie Robinson even began to move ever closer to King's position on the war in Vietnam. Robinson also edged closer to concluding that America's racial problems were deeper and more intractable than he had ever imagined.

Two months after the assassination of Martin Luther King, Jr., on the balcony of a Memphis motel, Democratic presidential candidate Robert Kennedy was gunned down in a Los Angeles hotel.

Jackie Robinson had never been a great fan of either John or Robert Kennedy. They were Democrats, and he was not. They had been born to wealth, and he had not. Finally, and most important in Robinson's mind, they were at best latecomers and at worst opportunists on the subject of civil rights. Nonetheless, Robinson used the second Kennedy assassination to issue a King-like attack on the violence that seemed to be overtaking what was already "one of the most violent 'civilizations' on the map."

Between 1968 and 1971 Jackie Robinson's political journey continued in this new, more radical direction. It was not always a journey taken in the footsteps of Martin Luther King or toward a destination he would have approved. In the summer of 1968 Robinson appeared willing to embrace the Black Panthers in their war with the New York police. Despite the Panthers' well-advertised noncommitment to nonviolence, Robinson was quoted as saying that he "could have become a Panther as a teenager." After all, he concluded, their goal of "self-determination" was the goal of all civil rights organizations. This Jackie Robinson may have been a version of the Jackie Robinson who had been a budding gang leader in the 1930s, but it was a far cry from the Jackie Robinson of the late 1950s—or even of much of the 1960s. Had he changed or had his country?

By the fall of 1968 Robinson was ready to leave the Rockefeller camp, but he was not yet ready to leave the world of mainstream politics. Disgusted with the New York governor, Jackie bolted from the Republicans to campaign for Democratic candidate Hubert Humphrey, for whom he voted in November. Robinson's disgust with Rockefeller in 1968 bordered on loathing by 1971. In the fall of that year a major prison riot erupted in Attica, New York. That Rockefeller refused to go to Attica to assess the situation was bad enough. That he decided to put down the revolt with force was far worse. Because that force produced terrible carnage, the governor's handling of the riot was, to Robinson, inexcusable. That many of the dead inmates were black was proof to Robinson that the racial gulf was growing and that Nelson Rockefeller was not the man to bridge it.

To add to Robinson's woes, diabetes, heart disease, and hypertension all continued to have him in their deadly grip. Not even occasional forays into the friendlier world of sports could revive him for any length of time. But he did have his moments. The head of the newly organized major league baseball players union, Marvin Miller, approached Robinson about testifying on behalf of Branch Rickey's "Mr. Perfection," Curt Flood, who was then challenging baseball's reserve system. Robinson readily agreed to help: "Anything that is one-sided is wrong in America." (Flood eventually lost his case to become a free agent so that he could sign with a team of his choosing; a few years later an arbitrator threw out the "one-sided" system, thereby creating the current spectacle of massive player movement and even more massive player salaries.)

At the end of 1971 Robinson was the guest of honor at a celebration marking the 25th anniversary of the publication of *Sport* magazine. On the dais with him were such greats as golfing legend Arnold Palmer, tennis star Rod Laver, future Hall of Famers Bill Russell of the Boston Celtics, Gale Sayers of the Chicago Bears, and Johnny Unitas of the Baltimore Colts. But Jackie Robinson was the main attraction, for he had been selected as "The Man of 25 Years of Sports." Among all of his compatriots and rivals, *Sport* magazine recognized him as the most important athlete of the quarter-century following World War II.

Robinson was close to tears more than once during his brief acceptance speech. Though weak and barely able to do so, he stood to pay tribute to three people: his mother, Mallie Robinson, his wife, Rachel Isum Robinson, and his surrogate father, Wesley Branch Rickey. Because of their standing in his life, he stood to accept *Sport's* award.

In April of 1972 Robinson again found himself among an assemblage of great athletes from the recent past. This time the occasion was the funeral of a Dodger teammate, first baseman Gil Hodges, who, though not quite forty-eight, had died suddenly of a heart attack. A frail and obviously failing Robinson made it to the funeral, but only with great effort. "I always thought," he said "I'd be the first to go." This was the sum of his commentary.

Two months later Jack accepted an invitation from new Dodger president Peter O'Malley to participate in Old Timers' festivities at Dodger Stadium in Los Angeles. The moment had finally come, thought the son of Walter O'Malley, to bind up old wounds. Robinson's initial inclination was to say "no." After all, he had never attended a Dodger Old Timers' game. This time he agreed—but only because of his "good feeling" for Dodger teammate, pitcher Don Newcombe. So on June 4, 1972, Jackie Robinson put on a Dodger uniform for the last time. The Brooklyn Dodger who had once accepted the cheers of the faithful in Ebbets Field now stood in Dodger Stadium to let the applause of Los Angeles fans lap over him. As it was, three Dodger numbers were retired on that historic day: number 32, worn by pitcher Sandy Koufax, who a year earlier had become the youngest hurler ever to be inducted into the Hall of Fame; number 39, that of Roy Campanella, Robinson's longtime teammate and sometime antagonist and a 1969 Hall of Famer; and number 42, that of the man who broke major league baseball's color line.

In an interview given to the Los Angeles *Times,* Robinson could hide neither his pride nor his bitterness. Yes, he was "pleased" to have "played a part" in the desegregation of baseball, "but I'm not subservient to it." Separately, Newcombe, who was then an employee of the Dodgers, offered his guess that Robinson "regretted" his "estrangement" from the game. Robinson himself was not so sure: "I don't feel that baseball owes me a thing and I don't owe baseball a thing. I'm glad I haven't had to go to baseball on my knees." But he did want one more thing from those who controlled the major league game: a black manager. He pointed to three current Dodger players as likely candidates: shortstop Maury Wills, second baseman Jim Gilliam, and outfielder Frank Robinson. But he had no more mentioned their names than he expressed his doubts that the game would see a black manager in his lifetime.

A few months later Robinson summoned enough strength to return to a major league ball park one last time. The occasion was Game Two of the 1972 World Series between the Cincinnati Reds and the Oakland A's. The place was Cincinnati's Riverfront Stadium. The date was October 15, and Jackie Robinson was on hand to throw out the first pitch. He was also there to accept a plaque marking the twenty-fifth anniversary of his National League debut. His acceptance speech was almost as terse as his statement at Hodges's funeral: "I'm extremely proud and pleased. But I'll be more pleased when I can look over at third base and see a black man as manager."

Jackie Robinson did not live to see that day. Two more years would pass before an African American, the very same Frank Robinson (no relation) whom Jackie had mentioned, would be signed to pilot the 1975 Cleveland Indians. By then Jackie Robinson had passed into history. He died on October 24, 1972, at the age of fifty-three.

As the Robinson family prepared for Jackie's funeral, tributes streamed in. So did the mourners. The Reverend Jesse Jackson was on hand to deliver the eulogy. It was vintage Jackson. To him, Robinson had overcome a huge "stumbling block" in 1947. In doing so, he served as a "stepping stone" for others of his race. Many of those who had benefited from Robinson's efforts were there as well. Hank Aaron was among them. To him, Jackie Robinson was simply the "Dr. King of baseball." Also in attendance were Nelson Rockefeller, Roy Wilkins, Joe Louis, and Larry Doby. Among old Dodger teammates were Don Newcombe, Roy Campanella, Joe Black, Junior Gilliam, Ralph Branca, and, of course, Pee Wee Reese. Baseball magnates Bill Veeck and Peter O'Malley were also on hand. Missing from their embarrassingly thin ranks was Branch Rickey. But his absence was entirely appropriate. After all, fathers should always die before their sons.

Bibliography

More than any other team sport, base-
ball stands revealed to us by the written word. Is it the nature of the
game itself? Is it the angst that surrounds it? Is it the precision of
the game? Is it that innumerable baseball fans have turned out to be
writers? And, for that matter, does love of the game turn people into
writers? Or is it that writers inevitably turn to baseball for material?
Whatever the reason, writing about baseball has had a long history
in this country. In fact, its history is almost as old as the American
version of the game itself. What comes under the heading of baseball scholarship is of more recent vintage, but the marriage between
the game and academe is now approaching the half-century mark.
What follows is a compilation, mixed with brief commentary, on
the historiography of baseball as it relates to the subjects of this
book. Included are scholarly and nonscholarly books that were either helpful in the writing of this dual biography and/or deserve
mention for serious students of the game and its history.

General Studies

Two multivolume histories of baseball stand as the starting point
for the general student. The first such set is Harold Seymour's
Baseball: The Early Years (1960), which concentrates on the nineteenth century, *Baseball: The Golden Age* (1971), which takes the
story approximately to 1930, and *Baseball: The People's Game* (1990),
which dwells on the game as played and organized away from the
major league diamond. David Q. Voight has also written a three-

volume history under the general title *American Baseball* (1970–1983) which takes the story from the origins of the American game to the 1980s. Voight's first volume is *From Gentleman's Sport to the Commissioner System;* the second is *From the Commissioners to Continental Expansion;* and the third volume is titled *From Postwar Expansion to the Electronic Age.* James Charlton has edited *The Baseball Chronology: The Complete History of the Most Important Events in the Game of Baseball* (1991). Other important source books include Myron Smith's *Baseball: A Comprehensive Bibliography* (1986); Mike Shatzin, ed., *The Ballplayers: Baseball's Ultimate Biographical Reference* (1990); and John Thorn and Pete Palmer's *Total Baseball: The Ultimate Encyclopedia of Baseball* (1989).

Thorn and Palmer have also produced *The Hidden Game of Baseball* (1985). Thorn alone has edited *The Armchair Book of Baseball* (1985) and *The Armchair Book of Baseball II* (1987) and written *The Game for All America.* (1988). Other single volume entries include Gene Brown's *The Complete Book of Baseball* (1979); Charles C. Alexander's *Our Game* (1991), which takes the story from the "New York Game" to the "Embattled Eighties," Benjamin G. Rader's *Baseball: A History of America's Game* (1992), and Geoffrey Ward and Ken Burn's heavily illustrated companion to the Ken Burns PBS baseball documentary, *Baseball: An Illustrated History* (1994). Other pictorial histories of particular note include David Q. Voight's *Baseball: An Illustrated History* (1987), Lawrence S. Ritter and Donald Honig, *The Image of Their Greatness* (1979), and Daniel Okrent and Harris Levine, eds., *The Ultimate Baseball Book* (1984).

Less scholarly, but nonetheless interesting contributions of a general nature include Tom Meany's *Baseball's Greatest Teams* (1949); Lee Allen's *100 Years of Baseball* (1950); Fred Lieb's *The Baseball Story* (1950); Douglas Wallop's *Baseball: An Informal History* (1969); Robert Smith's *Baseball* (1970); Fred Lieb's *The Story of the World Series* (1965); Jim Enright, ed., *Trade Him: 100 Years of Baseball's Greatest Deals* (1976); Joel Zoss's *Greatest Moments in Baseball* (1987); Joel Zoss and John Bowman's *Diamonds in the Rough: The Untold History of Baseball* (1989); Joseph Durso's *Baseball and the American Dream* (1986); John Helyar's *Lords of the*

Realm (1994). More recently, Leonard Koppett has blended scholarship with his sports writing skills to give us his version of *Major League Baseball* (1998). More specialized contributions of a general nature include Lee Allen's *The National League Story* (1961) and his *The American League Story* (1962); Glenn Dickey's *The History of American League Baseball Since 1901* (1980) and his *The History of National League Baseball Since 1876* (1982); John Durant's *Baseball's Miracle Teams* (1975); John Thorn and John B. Holway, *The Pitcher* (1987); Donald Honig's *The Power Hitters* (1989); Jim Kaplan's *The Fielders* (1989); Kevin Kerrane's *The Hurlers* (1989); Harvey Frommer's *Baseball's Greatest Managers* (1985); Robert Obojski's *All-Star Baseball Since 1933* (1981); Joseph L. Reichler and Ben Olan, eds., *Baseball's Unforgettable Games* (1961); John Thorn's *Baseball's Ten Greatest Games* (1982); Gene Schoor's *The History of the World Series: 85 Years of America's Greatest Sports Tradition* (1990).

Recent Scholarly Monographs of a General Nature

What follows is an alphabetical (by author), briefly annotated (if necessary) compilation of the best of baseball scholarship, as well as journalistic histories of a general nature, paying special attention to books that impinge in any significant way on the lives and baseball careers of Rickey and Robinson, which jointly covered a multitude of years, if not exactly a multitude of sins.

Dave Anderson, *Pennant Races,* (1994).

Eliot Asinof, *Eight Men Out: The Black Sox and the 1919 World Series* (reprint, 1987). Still the best single account of the greatest scandal in the history of the game.

Red Barber, *1947—When All Hell Broke Loose in Baseball* (1982).

Talmadge Boston, *1939: Baseball's Pivotal Year* (1994).

Robert Creamer, *Baseball in '41* (1991). The state of the game on the eve of World War II and the year of the DiMaggio streak and the last .400 hitter (Ted Williams).

Richard C. Crepeau, *Baseball: America's Diamond Mind* (1981).

An examination of the game between the world wars, as well as a commentary on the dual (and often parallel) evolution of American society and America's game.

William Curran, *Big Sticks: The Batting Revolution of the Twenties* (1990)

Bill Gilbert, *They Also Served: Baseball and the Home Front, 1941–1945* (1992)

Richard Goldstein, *Spartan Seasons: How Baseball Survived World War II* (1980)

Warren Goldstein, *Playing for Keeps* (1989). A history of the early days of the professional game.

Dan Gutman, *Baseball Babylon: From the Black Sox to Pete Rose, the Real Stories Behind the Scandals that Rocked the Game* (1992).

David Halberstam, *October 1964* (1994). The Yankee-Cardinal World Series and a rumination of the role of race in the making of the Cardinals and the unmaking of the Yankees.

Jerome Holtzman, *The Commissioners* (1998). An examination of the personalities and roles of baseball commissioners from Kenesaw Mountain Landis through Bart Giamatti.

Noel Hynd, *Giants of the Polo Grounds: The Glorious Times of Baseball's New York Giants* (1988). A history of the National League team that dominated the Dodgers and constituted the New York entry in the National League until the arrival of Branch Rickey and Jackie Robinson.

Roger Kahn, *The Era: 1947–1957, When the Yankees, the Giants, and the Dodgers Ruled the World* (1993).

David Kaiser, *Epic Season: The 1948 American League Pennant Race* (1998).

Brent Kelley, *Baseball's Biggest Blunder: The Bonus Rule of 1953–1957* (1997). The history of the decision and consequences of a rule which Rickey solidly opposed, namely the paying of large bonuses to untested rookies who then had to be kept on major league rosters for two years.

Kevin Kerrane, *Dollar Sign on the Muscle: The World of Baseball Scouting* (1984).

Peter Levine, A.G. *Spalding and the Rise of Baseball: The Promise of American Sport* (1985). A biography of the one the most significant founding fathers of modern major league baseball.

——, *Ellis Island to Ebbets Field: Sport and the American Jewish Experience* (1992). A wide-ranging history of the role of the Jewish athlete in the twentieth century, and one which dwells at some length on baseball in general and Dodger efforts to recruit Jewish athletes in particular.

Lee Lowenfish and Tony Lupien, *The Imperfect Diamond: Baseball's Reserve Clause and the Men Who Fought to Change It* (1980). A thorough history of the imposition of the infamous reserve system which takes the story to its demise in the 1970s.

Arthur Mann, *Baseball Confidential* (1951). The state of the game as seen by a veteran sportswriter and Rickey confidante.

William Marshall, *Baseball's Pivotal Era, 1945–1951* (1999). A year–by–year account of the major league game during the commissionership of A. B. ("Happy") Chandler.

William B. Mead, *Even the Browns: The Zany True Story of Baseball in the Early Forties* (1978).

——, *Two Spectacular Seasons: 1930, the Year the Hitters Ran Wild; 1968, the Year the Pitchers Took Over* (1990).

—— and Harold Rosenthal, *The Ten Worst Years of Baseball* (1982). This is an expansion of Mead's book on baseball during World War II.

Tom Meany and Tommy Holmes, *Baseball's Best: The All-Time Major League Baseball Team* (1964).

J. Ron Oakley, *Baseball's Last Golden Age, 1946–1960: The National Pastime in a Time of Glory and Change* (1994).

Harold Parrott, *The Lords of Baseball* (1976). A memoir of a one-time Dodger official which ranges across the baseball landscape before focusing negatively on Walter O'Malley and positively on Branch Rickey.

Martin Quigley, *The Crooked Pitch: An Account of the Curveball in American History* (1984)

Benjamin R. Rader, *In Its Own Image: How Television Has Trans-*

formed *Sports* (1984). A history of the medium that Branch Rickey mistakenly anticipated would result in a drastc reduction of attendance at major league games.

Steven Riess, *City Games: The Evolution of American Urban Society and the Rise of Sports* (1989).

——, *Touching Base: Professional Baseball and American Culture in the Progressive Era* (1980).

Ray Robinson, *The Home Run Heard 'Round the World: The Dramatic Story of the Giants-Dodgers 1951 Pennant Race* (1991).

C. Paul Rogers and Robin Roberts, *The Whiz Kids and the 1950 Pennant* (1996).

John M. Rosenburg, *They Gave Us Baseball: The Twelve Extraordinary Men Who Shaped the Major Leagues* (1989).

Harvey Rosenfeld, *The Great Chase: The Dodgers-Giants Pennant Race of 1951* (1992).

Harold Rosenthal, *The Ten Best Years of Baseball* (1985).

Russell Schneider, *The Boys of the Summer of '48* (1998).

Gerald W. Scully, *The Business of Major League Baseball* (1989).

Michael Seidel, *Streak: Joe DiMaggio and the Summer of '41* (1988).

Wilfred Sheed, *Baseball and Lesser Sports* (1991).

Curt Smith, *Voices of the Game* (1987). A history and brief biographies of baseball's great play-by-play men, including the incomparable Red Barber, who was the Dodger announcer during the 1947 season.

Mike Sowell, *The Pitch That Killed* (1989). A dual biography of Carl Mays whose pitch struck and killed Ray Chapman, resulting in the only player death on a major league diamond.

Bobby Thomson with Lee Heiman and Bill Gutman, *"The Giants Win the Pennant! The Giants Win the Pennant!"* (1991).

Frederick Turner, *When the Boys Came Back: Baseball and 1946* (1996).

John Vlasich, *A Legend for the Legendary: The Origin of the Baseball Hall of Fame* (1990).

G. Edward White, *Creating the National Pastime: Baseball Transforms Itself, 1903–1953* (1996). A law professor's look at both the creative role of the owners in making major league baseball a middle class game and their less than creative role in retarding everything from the presence of lights in baseball parks to the presence of blacks on major league rosters.

Biographies and Autobiographies

The following is simply an alphabetical listing of the major biographies and autobiograhies of baseball figures, who either were important contemporaries of Rickey and Robinson or were directly involved in issues and/or events that constituted a part of the larger Rickey-Robinson story.

Hank Aaron and Lonnie Wheeler, *I Had a Hammer: The Hank Aaron Story* (1991).

Charles C. Alexander, *John McGraw* (1988).

——, *Rogers Hornsby* (1995).

Maury Allen, *Where Have You Gone, Joe DiMaggio? The Story of America's Last Hero* (1975).

Red Barber with Robert Creamer, *Rhubarb in the Catbird's Seat* (1968).

Rex Barney and Norman Macht, *Rex Barney's Thank Youuuu* (1993).

Edward Barrow and James Kahn, *My 50 Years in Baseball* (1951).

Ira Berkow, ed., *Hank Greenberg: The Story of My Life* (1989).

Yogi Berra with Tom Horton, *Yogi Berra: It Ain't Over . . .* (1989).

Bob Broeg, *Stan Musial: "The Man's" Own Story as Told to Bob Broeg* (1964).

Roy Campanella, *It's Good To Be Alive* (1959).

Albert B. Chandler with Vance Trimble, *Heroes, Plain Folks, and Skunks: The Life and Times of Happy Chandler* (1989).

Ty Cobb with Al Stump, *My Life in Baseball: The True Record* (1961).

Jocko Conlan and Robert Creamer, *Jocko* (1967).

Robert W. Creamer, *Babe: The Legend Comes to Life* (1974).

——, *Stengel: His Life and Times* (1984).

Dennis De Valeria and Jeanne Burke De Valeria, *Honus Wagner: A Biography* (1995).

Leo Durocher, *Nice Guys Finish Last* (1975).

Gerald Eskenazi, *Bill Veeck: A Baseball Legend* (1987).

Bob Feller with Bill Gilbert, *Now Pitching, Bob Feller* (1991).

Ford Frick, *Games, Asterisks, and People: Memoirs of a Lucky Fan* (1973).

Arnold Hano, *Roberto Clemente: Batting King* (1973).

Kirby Higbe and Martin Quigley, *The High Hard One* (1967).

Monte Irvin and James Riley, *Nice Guys Finish First* (1996).

Ralph Kiner and Joe Gergen, *Kiner's Korner* (1987).

Jerry Lansche, *Stan the Man Musial: Born To Be a Ballplayer* (1994).

Willie Mays and Lou Sahadi, *Say Hey: The Autobiography of Willie Mays* (1989).

John McGraw, *My Thirty Years in Baseball* (1995, reprint).

Jack B. Moore, *Joe DiMaggio: Baseball's Yankee Clipper* (1987).

Joseph Thomas Moore, *Pride Against Prejudice: The Biography of Larry Doby* (1988).

Eugene Murdock, *Ban Johnson: Czar of Baseball* (1982).

David Pietrusza, *Judge and Jury: The Life and Times of Judge Kenesaw Mountain Landis* (1998).

Ray Robinson, *Iron Horse: Lou Gehrig in His Time* (1990).

——, *Matty: An American Hero* (1993).

Gene Schoor, *The Pee Wee Reese Story* (1956).

Mike Seidel, *Ted Williams: A Baseball Life* (1991).

Milton Shapiro, *The Dizzy Dean Story* (1963).

George Sisler, *Sisler on Baseball* (1954).

Enos Slaughter and Kevin Reid, *Country Hardball: The Autobiography of Enos "Country" Slaughter* (1991).

Curt Smith, *America's Dizzy Dean* (1978).

J. G. Taylor Spink, *Judge Landis and Twenty-Five Years of Baseball* (1947).

Vince Staten, *Ol' Diz* (1992).

Irving Stein, *The Ginger Kid: The Buck Weaver Story* (1992).

Al Stump, *Cobb: A Biography* (1994).

Bill Veeck with Ed Linn, *The Hustler's Handbook* (1989, reprint).

Bill Veeck, *Veeck—As In Wreck* (1962).

Don Warfield, *The Roaring Redhead: Larry MacPhail—Baseball's Great Innovator* (1987).

Ted Williams with John Underwood, *My Turn At Bat: The Story of My Life* (1988).

Oral Histories

This list of books includes the significant oral histories of baseball players, as well as others associated with the game.

David Craft and Tom Owens, eds., *Redbirds Revisited: Great Memories and Stories from the St Louis Cardinals* (1990).

Dom Forker, ed., *The Men of Autumn: An Oral History of the 1949–1953 World Champion New York Yankees* (1989).

Larry Gerlach, ed., *Men in Blue* (1980).

Donald Honig, ed., *Baseball Between the Lines: Baseball in the 40's and 50's as Told by the Men Who Played It* (1993, reprint).

——, *Baseball When the Grass Was Real: Baseball from the 20's to the 40's as Told by the Men Who Played It* (1993).

Eugene Murdock, ed., *Baseball Between the Wars: Memories of the Game By the Men Who Played It* (1992).

——, *Baseball Players and Their Times: Oral Histories of the Game, 1920–1940* (1991).

Anthony O'Connor, ed., *Baseball for the Love of It: Hall of Famers Tell It Like It Was* (1982).

Danny Peary, ed., *We Played the Game: 65 Players Remember Baseball's Greatest Era, 1947–1964* (1994).

Lawrence S. Ritter, ed., *The Glory of Their Times: The Story of the Early Days of Baseball Told by the Men Who Played It* (1985, reprint).

Cynthia Wilber, ed., *For the Love of the Game: Baseball Memories from the Men Who Were There* (1992).

Rickey and Robinson

Included in this category are books about and/or by Branch Rickey and Jackie Robinson, as well as books dealing with their baseball teammates and organizations, most prominently the Brooklyn Dodgers and the St. Louis Cardinals.

Maury Allen, *Jackie Robinson: A Life Remembered* (1987).

Marino Amoruso, *Gil Hodges: The Quiet Man* (1991).

Joe Black, *Ain't Nobody Better Than You* (1983).

Roy Campanella, *It's Good to be Alive* (1959).

Stanley Cohen, *Dodgers! The First 100 Years* (1990).

Joseph Dorinson and Joram Warmund, eds., *Jackie Robinson: Race, Sports, and the American Dream* (1998).

John Durant, *The Dodgers* (1945).

Leo Durocher, *The Dodgers and Me, The Inside Story* (1948).

Gerald Eskenazi, *The Lip: A Biography of Leo Durocher* (1993).

David Falkner, *Great Time Coming: The Life of Jackie Robinson from Baseball to Birmingham* (1995).

Ed Fitzgerald, ed., *The Story of the Brooklyn Dodgers (1949).*

Richard Goldstein, *Superstars and Screwballs: 100 Years of Brooklyn Baseball* (1991).

Peter Golenbock, *Bums: An Oral History of the Brooklyn Dodgers* (1986).

Doris Kearns Goodwin, *Wait Till Next Year* (1997).

Frank Graham, *The Brooklyn Dodgers* (1945).

Robert E. Hood, *The Gashouse Gang* (1976).

Roger Kahn, *The Boys of Summer* (1970).

Fred Lieb, *The St Louis Cardinals, The Story of a Great Baseball Club* (1944).

Arthur Mann, *Branch Rickey: American in Action* (1957).

——, *The Jackie Robinson Story* (1950).

John J. Monteleone, ed., *Branch Rickey's Little Blue Book* (1995).

Murray Polner, *Branch Rickey: A Biography* (1983).

Carl Prince, *Brooklyn's Dodgers: The Bums, the Borough, and the Best of Baseball, 1947–1957* (1996).

Bob Rains, *The St Louis Cardinals: The Official 100th Anniversary History* (1992).

Arnold Rampersad, *Jackie Robinson: A Biography* (1997).

Branch Rickey with Robert Rieger, *The American Diamond* (1965).

Dan Riley, ed., *The Dodgers Reader* (1992).

Jackie Robinson, *Baseball Has Done It* (1964).

Jackie Robinson with Al Duckett, *I Never Had It Made* (1972, reprint).

Jackie Robinson with Wendell Smith, *Jackie Robinson: My Own Story* (1948).

Rachel Robinson and Lee Daniels, *Jackie Robinson: An Intimate Portrait* (1996).

Carl T. Rowan, *Wait Till Next Year* (1960).

Duke Snider with Bill Gilbert, *The Duke of Flatbush* (1988).

J. Roy Stockton, *The Gas House Gang and a Couple of Other Guys* (1945).

Neil Sullivan, *The Dodgers Move West* (1987).

Jules Tygiel, *The Jackie Robinson Reader* (1997).

Black Baseball, The Negro Leagues, and the Integration of the Game

These books deal primarily with the history of the Negro Leagues, but also included are studies and accounts of black baseball in general, as well as the effort to eliminate Jim Crow baseball.

Bruce Adelson, *Brushing Back Jim Crow* (1999).

James Bankes, *The Pittsburgh Crawfords: The Life and Times of Black Baseball's Most Exciting Team* (1991).

Janet Bruce, *The Kansas City Monarchs: Champions of Black Baseball* (1985).

Bruce Chadwick, *When the Game Was Black and White: The Illustrated History of the Negro Leagues* (1992).

Dick Clark and Larry Lester, eds., *The Negro Leagues Book* (1994).

David Craft, *The Negro Leagues: 40 Years of Black Professional Baseball in Words and Pictures* (1993).

Phil Dixon with Patrick J. Hannigan, *The Negro Baseball Leagues: A Photographic History, 1867–1955* (1992).

Jack Etkin, *Innings Ago: Recollections of Kansas City Ballplayers of Their Days in the Game* (1987)..

Robert Gardner and Dennis Shortelle, *The Forgotten Players: The Story of Black Baseball in America* (1993).

John B. Holway, *Blackball Stars: The Negro League Pioneers* (1988).

———, *Josh and Satch: The Life and Times of Josh Gibson and Satchel Paige* (1991).

———, *Voices from the Great Black Baseball Leagues* (1975).

Buck Leonard with James Riley, *Buck Leonard: The Black Lou Gehrig* (1995).

Effa Manley and Leon H. Hardwick, *Negro Baseball Before Integration* (1976).

Larry Moffi and Jonathan Kronstadt, *Crossing the Line: Black Major Leaguers, 1947–1959* (1994).

James Overmyer, *Effa Manley and the Newark Eagles* (1993).

Leroy Satchel Paige with David Lipman, *Maybe I'll Pitch Forever* (1962).

Robert Peterson, *Only the Ball Was White* (1984).

Jim Reisler, *Black Writers/Black Baseball: An Anthology of Articles from Black Sportswriters Who Covered the Negro Leagues* (1994).

Mark Ribowsky, *The Complete History of the Negro Leagues, 1884–1955* (1995).

———, *Don't Look Back: Satchel Paige in the Shadows of Baseball* (1994).

———, *The Power and the Darkness: A Biography of Josh Gibson* (1996).

James A. Riley, *The Biographical Encyclopedia of the Negro Baseball Leagues, 1885–1949* (1992).

———, *Dandy, Day, and the Devil* (1987).

Donn Rogosin, *Invisible Men: Life in Baseball's Negro Leagues* (1983).

Rob Ruck, *Sandlot Seasons: Sport in Black Pittsburgh* (1987).

Art Rust, Jr., ed., *Get That Nigger Off the Field* (1992).

Jules Tygiel *Baseball's Great Experiment: Jackie Robinson and His Legacy* (1983).

David Zang, *Fleet Walker's Divided Heart: The Life of Baseball's First Black Major Leaguer* (1995).

Index

Rickey & Robinson:
The Preacher, The Player, and America's Game
Developmental editor and copy editor: Andrew J. Davidson
Production Editor: Lucy Herz
Proofreader: Claudia Siler
Cover designer: DePinto Graphic Design
Printer: Versa Press, Inc.